THE KING'S FINEST

THE KING'S FINEST

A Social and Bureaucratic Profile
of Prussia's General Officers,
1871–1914

DANIEL J. HUGHES

PRAEGER

New York
Westport, Connecticut
London

Library of Congress Cataloging-in-Publication Data

Hughes, Daniel J., 1946–
    The king's finest.

    Bibliography: p.
    1. Generals–Germany–Prussia. 2. Prussia
(Kingdom). Armee. 3. Sociology, Military–Germany–
Prussia. I. Title.
UA718.P9H84   1987   355.3′31′0943   87–7012
ISBN 0–275–92320–7 (alk. paper)

Library of Congress Catalog Card Number: 87–7012
ISBN: 0–275–92320–7

First published in 1987

Praeger Publishers, One Madison Avenue, New York, NY 10010
A division of Greenwood Press, Inc.

Printed in the United States of America

(∞)™

The paper used in this book complies with the
Permanent Paper Standard issued by the National
Information Standards Organization (Z39.48–1984).

10 9 8 7 6 5 4 3 2 1

Contents

Tables

Preface

The many debts I have accumulated in the course of preparing this book cannot be repaid, but they can be acknowledged. Professor Lamar J. R. Cecil first suggested this topic and patiently guided its development for several years. Those familiar with his work will recognize his influence in the content if not in the writing style. Professors Gerhard Weinberg and Samual R. Williamson, Jr., of the University of North Carolina, gave generously of their time and talents. The late Professor Frederic B. M. Hollyday of Duke University devoted countless hours to reading the text and suggesting improvements. I benefited greatly from his vast store of knowledge on the Prussian army and deeply regret that he is not here to see the book's publication. Professor Dennis Showalter offered many useful suggestions that substantially sharpened the study's basic focus. I am uniquely indebted to him.

In Germany, Professors Wilhelm Deist and Manfred Messerschmidt took time from their responsibilities to consult extensively with me and made the facilities of the Militärgeschichtliches Forschungsamt (Military History Research Office) available. Dr. Peter-Christian Stahl, then director of the Federal Republic's Military Archives, went out of his way to render valuable assistance, as did many of his fine staff. Herr Friedrich Euler, director of the Institut zur Erforschung historische Führungsschichten (Institute for Research of Historical Leadership Strata) in Bensheim gave me full access to his vast treasure of genealogical information.

Finally, of course, as is the case with most scholars, I must bow to my wife, Linda, whose patience and assistance over several years were essential. To a large extent whatever credits there might be belong to the above persons; the faults are mine.

THE
KING'S FINEST

1

Introduction

On September 29, 1918, an aging Prussian general, who as a young lieutenant had strutted through Paris in the German victory parade of 1871, sadly informed his king that Germany had lost the long struggle against Britain and France. Within a few weeks the entire structure of Imperial Germany collapsed. On November 9 the army's highest officers took the extreme step of urging the emperor to abdicate his throne and to flee the country immediately. As William II boarded the train that would take him into exile in Holland, he may have remembered Bismarck's words spoken two decades earlier: "Your Majesty, as long as you have this officer corps, you can do what you like. Should that ever cease to be the case, everything would be completely changed."[1]

Historians have frequently agreed with the old chancellor that the officer corps and the army were the keys to the empire's stability. Indeed, a widely read, if partisan, treatment of the Bismarckian *Reich* has argued that the chief "innovation" of the collapse of 1918 was the destruction of the old Prussian army.[2] The empire was largely the creation of the Prussian army, whose victories at Königgrätz and in France determined the time and circumstances of German unification. Thus it is hardly surprising that the army was the basis of the entire constitutional structure of Imperial Germany.[3]

The following is a prosopographical study of the men who served as general officers in the Prussian army between 1871 and 1914. Its objective is to measure clearly the social roots of the generalcy and to define the major factors, social and military, in a successful career. It is not meant as a general history of the officer corps during the Imperial era, nor is it a study of the military's ideology or its role as a bulwark of a conservative ruling elite.

I hope, rather more modestly, to define the social content of the generalcy with as much precision as possible. The entire military structure, with its key element the regimental system, was designed to preserve an elusive social homogeneity. What follows, therefore, is also an explanation of how the system, to a remarkable degree, did just that. Finally, the evidence suggests that the most fundamental group characteristic of the army's highest officers was increasing family ties to the state apparatus, both civilian and military, rather than enduring connections with landed interests or increasing ties with industrial circles or business pressure groups.

Such an approach answers some questions, refines traditional answers to others, and raises still more. The entire question of change within the junior ranks of the officer corps and the effect upon the army of the massive influx of bourgeois officers after 1860 are but two of many issues that, touched upon by this study, are beyond its scope. This is a book about generals, about how and why men became generals, and about the way the Prussian army selected, trained, and promoted the preferred types of men to its highest positions.

The destruction of all personnel records of the Prussian army has left historians without an official archival roster of officers of any rank. The author's calculations, based on an examination of the army's annual officer lists, have determined that 2,443 men held the rank of brigadier general or higher between 1871 and 1914.[4] The study excludes the many officers who retired as colonels, and who subsequently received honorary promotions, as well as many German princes and other dignitaries who held titular patents as generals. Most rulers of the various German states have also been omitted because they were not genuine Prussian officers.[5]

Bismarck's empire lacked an imperial army in peacetime, largely because independent states remained within the federal structure. This situation in turn was the result of long-standing mutual mistrust and jealousy among the peoples and rulers of the various German states. The Prussian army formed the core of the imperial forces and acted as the main guarantor of the Prussian state and of the German Empire against internal as well as external enemies. The Prussian-German dualism inherent in the empire's political structure thus extended into its military affairs. It is appropriate, therefore, to begin with a brief overview of the army's place in Prussia and Germany.

The German Empire's forces consisted of independent armies from the four states of Prussia, Bavaria, Saxony, and Württemberg. The king of Prussia, in his capacity of federal commander, appointed the commanding officers of the Saxon and Württemberg armies and had the right to inspect Bavaria's two army corps. Military conventions between Prussia and the smaller states had either incorporated the latter's contingents directly into the Prussian army or had given the king of Prussia special powers to ensure military conformity and efficiency.[6] Numerous technical details within these conventions ensured the dominance of the Prussian system, even down to the number of rows of buttons on uniforms.[7] The monarchical principle remained the basis of the entire system. Officers took oaths of loyalty to their respective rulers and to the supreme commander, not to the German constitution.[8]

Just as no real Germany army existed in peacetime, there was no imperial war minister. Bismarck tolerated no rivals, especially from the army, and defeated even Albrecht von Roon's efforts to achieve parity in Reich (national government) military matters. The Prussian war minister, in his capacity as military plenipotentiary of the *Bundesrat* (federal council), represented the army in its dealings with the *Reichstag* (imperial legislature). Although the state contingents remained independent in theory, the army's total strength had to be approved by the Reichstag in a combined military budget. Throughout the life of the empire, the opposition political parties used this opening to register their complaints against various objectionable aspects of the military system. These parliamentary maneuvers did not reduce the authority of the king over the internal affairs of the army, although the question of the military budget remained a center of controversy.[9]

The central concerns of this study, the Prussian army and its officer corps, were of critical importance in Prussia's history and have been the subjects of numerous investigations.[10] The development of the Prussian state was closely connected with that of the army. In a very real sense, the army was the creator of the Prussian state, both with respect to the expansion of the national boundaries and to the development of Prussia's internal administration. Beginning with the "Great Elector," the needs of the army determined the institutional arrangements of the Hohenzollern lands. Frederick William I built upon the legacy of his predecessors and placed the army on a permanent and sound footing by subordinating all aspects of state policy to military requirements.[11]

It was also during the years 1713 to 1740 that the Hohenzollerns harnassed their recalcitrant nobility to the officer corps. The practice of forcing young noblemen into the army had the political objective of crushing aristocratic opposition to the crown. Equally important in the long run, however, was the nobility's gradual acceptance of the king's military service as an occupation befitting their station in life. The impoverished Junkers of the eastern provinces soon realized that they could profit from the free education offered in the royal cadet schools and that, further, service in the officer corps was beneficial for a variety of reasons. The importance attached to the king's uniform gave these rustic noble officers a social position far beyond what they could have attained on their own. By the time of the accession of Frederick the Great, therefore, the nobility had come to regard the officer corps as its special domain, its "natural profession."[12]

Frederick the Great continued the practice of filling the officer corps almost exclusively from the ranks of the nobility. The casualties of the Seven Years' War forced Frederick to accept bourgeois officers despite his reservations about their reliability. After the conclusion of peace, the king largely succeeded in removing the bourgeois element from his officer corps. Frederick's successor continued his policies so successfully that by 1806 more than 90 percent of the officer corps consisted of nobles.[13] The officer corps thus became part of the ossified social and political structure of the Prussian state. The army became the bulwark of the conservative monarchy and the rallying point for die-hard opponents of political and social reform.

The destruction of the old army and the collapse of the Prussian state under the blows of Napoleon's armies brought some measure of reform even to the officer corps.[14] Many of the high hopes raised by the activities and proposals of the Military Reorganization Commission were to remain unfulfilled or were undone in the years of reaction following the overthrow of the hated Corsican. In 1819 Boyen and Grolman resigned their offices, and the era of reform came to an end. Reactionary elements within the officer corps, including the future king William I, restored the aristocratic character of the army and stamped it with the conservative ideology that dominated Prussia's military leadership throughout the nineteenth century.[15]

The conservative politics and political activities of the officer corps have been the subject of rigorous examinations by historians seeking to define that institution's place in Prussian and German history.[16] Marxist scholars see the officer corps as the ultimate embodiment of an alliance of nobility and bourgeoisie for the suppression of socialist and democratic enemies of the government.[17] Since 1960 the renewed debate among Western historians over Germany's responsibility for World War I has brought the questions of militarism, armaments policies, preventive war, and the entire issue of political manipulation by elites back into the historical limelight. The role of the officer corps has figured prominently in many of the new studies of German internal policies between 1870 and 1914. At the center of the army's role in the resurgence of aggressive nationalism and conservatism before August 1914 are the questions of the social policies and thus of the social composition of the officer corps.[18] Even the best political and strategic treatments of the army have not thoroughly analyzed the social composition of the Prussian officer corps.[19]

At the peak of the army and the officer corps stood the king of Prussia, who was both the supreme commander and the highest ranking officer. A feudal loyalty bound the officer corps to the king, and most officers took their oaths to the monarch quite seriously. One respected historian has quite rightly characterized the army's officers as "paladins of the Hohenzollern throne, loyal followers of the monarch to whom they had sworn personal fealty." The Prussian army and officer corps were indeed "royal" as their titles stated.[20]

The army possessed no single dominant authority or person who stood second in command immediately below the king. Staff and command functions, rather, were divided among several individuals and institutions. All corps commanders possessed the right of direct access to the king on the grounds that he was their only superior officer. This structure was plausible because the army maintained the theory, quite fictional late in the nineteenth century, that the king personally commanded the army.

The war minister, the only individual whose office possessed any potential for exercising unified control over the army, was junior in rank to the corps commanders and after 1883 had responsibility only in purely administrative matters. Personnel affairs, including officer assignments and promotions, were nominally under the war minister through the Section for Personnel Affairs. But since the officer presiding over this section was a personal aide of the king and chief of the Military Cabinet, in reality such functions were largely independent of the war minister.[21] In later years the General Staff, which reached its ultimate prominence under the leadership of Count Helmuth von Moltke, also became entirely independent within its own areas of competence.

This division of authority carried grave risks for the army's unity of command and sense of direction. It also gave wide scope for action to high-ranking officers who chose to meddle in politics and diplomacy.[22] Under William I, who was an active officer in every sense of the term and who was indeed the commander-in-chief of the army between 1861 and 1888, the system worked despite serious internal problems. Under Prussia's last king, however, the lack of a unified command structure, coupled with weak leadership, proved disastrous.

The problems outlined above are important to the social history of the army as well as to its institutional and political history. The roots of the army's personnel policies lay in its unique position in Prussian state and society. It was to the army that the Hohenzollern rulers and their conservative allies turned the crisis of 1848–49. Likewise, it was in the army and its ultraroyal officer corps that conservatives found their ultimate answer to the social democrats. William II's ill-advised proclamations that the soldiers of the guards units might have to shoot their relatives may have been pure royal bombast, but it sprang from a reality inherent in the social and political structure of Prussia: the army was fully as important as a guardian of the established order in internal politics as it was a guarantor of the national frontiers.

The army's struggle to insulate itself from social contamination by unworthy elements and to ensure that democrats, socialists, and other enemies of the state gained no infuence over the officer corps may be briefly summarized by a glance at the history of the Prussian War Ministry in the nineteenth century.

The War Ministry came into being on August 28, 1814, when a royal order dissolved the General War Department (*Allgemeine Kriegsdepartment*) and the Military Administration Department (*Militär-Ökonomiedepartement*). The seven subsections of these institutions came under the newly created War Ministry, whose first head was Hermann von Boyen.[23] Officer selection, assignments, and promotions came under the War Ministry's Section for Personnel Matters, which was headed by an officer from the king's military cabinet. The General Staff at this time was also a subordinate institution under Boyen's jurisdiction with the designation as Section Two of the War Ministry.

The decades before 1848 saw no great upheavals in the army's basic organization. The Constitution of 1850 raised entirely new questions about War Minister Boyen, who found himself caught between the power of the king and his oath to the new constitution.[24] Although Article Forty-six gave the king supreme command over the army, Article Forty-four provided that all acts of government were to be countersigned by the responsible minister and were therefore subject to parliamentary discussion and consideration. The problem was more troublesome for the army because its budget required the approval of the Prussian parliament. On two grounds, therefore, the position of the war minister was a danger to the army's independence from civilian control and from interference by liberal politicians.[25]

The constitutional conflict that began soon after Prince William assumed the regency in October 1858 clearly demonstrated that a war minister with any measure of independence posed a threat to royal control of the army. Albrecht von Roon and Prince William drafted the great reform proposal of 1860 and used a special military commission to circumvent the War Minister Eduard von Bonin, who had strongly opposed changes in the *Landwehr*. Thus the intolerable situation arose in which the war minister sided with the lower house in opposing the reform measures. When Bonin resigned, Roon took over the War Ministry, and the great constitutional struggle began in earnest. Of greatest importance for the future was that the conflict began with circumventing and then replacing the army's highest and only constitutionally responsible officer. From the conservatives' point of view, the war minister's power and his hazy constitutional position combined to make the office the army's weakest link in its chain of defenses against parliamentary interference.

Roon's tenure at the War Ministry saw the first great weakening of that office. During the wars of unification the General Staff achieved complete independence from the War Ministry in all operational matters, thus depriving the Prussian lower house (and later the Reichstag) of any real opportunity to have a voice in strategic planning. In June 1866 a royal cabinet order empowered the chief of the General Staff, Helmuth von Moltke, to communicate his commands directly to army commanders without sending them through the war minister.[26] Bismarck soon found Moltke, not Roon, acting as the army's representative in discussions of strategy and politics.[27] During the war with France, Moltke and the General Staff attempted without success to exclude Roon from the morning briefing sessions and conferences with the king. Their attempts failed, but the war minister had little voice in the planning and operations of the campaign. The General Staff's attitude, as explained later by Moltke, was that the war minister belonged in Berlin supervising the army's administrative matters.[28]

The successful conclusion of the war restored the War Ministry to its theoretical position as the supervisory body over the General Staff. There was no lasting substance to this appearance, however, and in 1882 the new quartermaster general (an operational position, not one of supply), Count Alfred von Waldersee, began to press the issue again. Moltke remained chief of the General Staff as Waldersee, who succeeded the elderly field marshal in 1888, became his chief assistant. In cooperation with the chief of the Military Cabinet, Waldersee succeeded in formalizing the right of the chief of the General Staff to enjoy direct access to the king. This move in effect freed the General Staff from the War Ministry and placed its functions beyond all possibility of meaningful parliamentary control.

The second major area in which the war minister's position as a constitutional minister threatened the army's internal affairs was the question of officer personnel matters. On this issue one must begin in 1856 when Edwin von Manteuffel became chief of the Section for Personnel Matters, then a part of the War Ministry. Manteuffel had for years been a close confidant of King Frederick William IV and of Prince William, and was one of William's personal adjutants. In March 1857 Frederick William IV ordered that in the future all chiefs of the personnel office must be chosen from the ranks of his adjutants or aides-de-camp. This order signified that personnel matters were to be supervised by this officer not primarily in his capacity as a section chief in a constitutional ministry but as a member of the king's personal staff.[29] In May of the same year Manteuffel became chief of the Military Cabinet, a post he held until 1865, when he assumed command of the Prussian troops in Schleswig-Holstein.[30]

The accession of Mantueffel to chief of the Military Cabinet began the extended feud between that body and the War Ministry. At issue was control over personnel matters in the officer corps, from top to bottom. On June 20, 1860, Prince William ordered a communication of the Military Cabinet sent to the army without the war minister's customary countersignature.[31] Manteuffel ruthlessly exploited this and other royal directives in his campaign to deprive the constitutional minister of all jurisdiction over a wide range of matters falling under the king's powers as commander of the army. By 1861, as the later War Minister Karl von Einem remarked, the war minister had nothing more to say to the officer in charge of his own personnel section.[32]

Relations between the War Ministry and the Military Cabinet improved only temporarily when Hermann von Tresckow succeeded Manteuffel in 1865. In April 1872, Emil von Albedyll became chief of the Military Cabinet and the struggle to deprive the war minister of all control over army personnel matters reached the decisive stage. Lieutenant General Georg von Kameke became war minister in November 1873. He was a liberal officer, as Prussian generals went, was a friend of Crown Prince Frederick William, and had earned the contempt of many conservative officers, notably Count Alfred von Waldersee, then a rising star in the General Staff.[33]

The inevitable conflict between Kameke and Albedyll was not long in coming. During one bitter exchange with one of Albedyll's subordinates, Kameke denied that there were any officers actually in the Military Cabinet other than the chief himself, implying that he should be in command of the others because they belonged to the War Ministry. Such a challenge did not go unanswered. Petty quarrels, over such things as who could direct orders to the civilians who worked in the Military Cabinet, became major tests of strength between the two strong-willed men.[34]

Finaly in 1883 William I put an end to the major dispute by removing all personnel matters from the jurisdiction of the War Ministry and assigning them exclusively to the Military Cabinet. The chief of the Military Cabinet thus ceased to be even a nominal subordinate of the war minister. As part of this change, Kameke resigned when William criticized him for not acting forcefully enough in his defense of the army against its critics in the Reichstag.[35]

Kameke's successor, Paul Bronsart von Schellendorff, agreed to preside over the truncated War Ministry, which also lost all remaining vestiges of its former control over the General Staff. Both the chief of the Military Cabinet and the chief of the General Staff thereafter had the formal right of direct access to the king and therefore were responsible to him alone for the performance of their duties. Kameke was ousted in part because he would not put himself in a position of being responsible for this destruction of the War Ministry. His successor had no such qualms although he realized how unpopular these actions would be in the Reichstag and the liberal press.[36]

For the king and the other conservative military leaders, the key issue had been the preservation of the army's ability to conduct its personnel and other internal matters completely free from parliamentary interference. By declaring that all sensitive matters pertained to the king's powers of command (*Kommandogewalt*), Manteuffel and then Albedyll, supported by Bismarck and Waldersee, hoped to exclude them completely from the Reichstag's areas of constitutional responsibility. They succeeded entirely, although with the fateful consequence of fragmenting the army's leadership and unity of command.[37] Personnel matters remained the province of a handful of the king's most trusted advisers.[38] After 1883 the chief of the Military Cabinet reigned supreme in such affairs and was therefore probably the most feared officer in the Prussian army.[39]

All officers, with but a few exceptions among Germany's regnant families, were utterly dependent upon the Military Cabinet, which in turn was responsible only to the king. To the frequent parliamentary interpellations by liberals and socialists in the Reichstag, the war minister could quite honestly reply that personnel matters were outside his competence. The army thus remained beyond public scrutiny and was free to select, assign, promote, and retire its officers as it desired. The social consequences of these policies on the officer corps are the subjects of this study.

Information on the generals is of two basic types: personal and career related. Personal information includes their social class, rank within the nobility when relevant, and various other categories related to occupational and geographic origins. Career information utilized in this study includes, but is not limited to, branch of service, military rank, and years in grade as a general officer. Approximately 50 items of information are thus available for most generals.[40]

The various data sets collected for the generals have been cross-tabulated to form the statistical basis of the study. The Statistical Analysis System (SAS), a prepared program for this type of data analysis, has been used in all computations. Categories of information, for example, social class and high military rank, have been tabulated with each other by chronological arrangement, as explained in the text. In this respect, at least, even the most backward-looking and conservative Prussian generals have been brought into the twentieth century.

The nearly complete destruction of the *Kriegsarchiv* (war archive) in April of 1945 has rendered the collection of information on the generals an arduous task. A note on sources, therefore, seems in order. Biographical information for most generals, including those who received titles after they left the army, has been located in various volumes of the *Gothaisches Genealogisches Taschenbücher*.[41] Some families not listed in the *Gotha* have been found in the more recent *Genealogisches Handbuch des Adels*. Other standard and less well known biographical handbooks have provided useful information not located in the above sources.

Biographical information on bourgeois generals is less easily obtained. Fewer published genealogical guides are available for the very large number of bourgeois families involved. Some may be found in the standard bourgeois genealogical handbook, the so-called *Geschlechterbuch*.[42] The German *Who's Who*, though entirely unsystematic, also contains vital information on a substantial number of officers.[43] The unofficial and incomplete listing of Prussian generals compiled by Kurt von Priesdorff provided information on many bourgeois generals not found in any other source.[44]

Finally, semiofficial published military works have provided useful information on both noble and bourgeois generals. Many regiments assigned one or more of their members to prepare lists of officers for publication with pertinent personal and career information. Many were published under the title of the *Offizier-Stammliste* of the regiment, or some similar title. They are a partial and very useful replacement for the lost personnel files.[45]

It is a curious and inescapable fact of German history that the sources available for research of this type favor the same groups that the army's selection and promotion process favored. Aristocratic families are more frequently listed in the published genealogical information. Noble officers, especially those who served on the General Staff, have left us a larger store of memoirs, letters, and other literary efforts. They are more easily found in the semiofficial sources as well because elite regiments were more likely to have published their histories and lists of officers than were ordinary units, especially of the artillery.

Only a small proportion of Prussia's generals wrote memoirs, and many of those who did were not typical officers, either in their family backgrounds or their careers. A quantitative approach offers a satisfactory way to study the generals as a group while avoiding inaccurate judgments based upon well-known public figures and their memoirs.

2

The Persistence of the Aristocracy

Leopold von Ranke, in a letter written to General Edwin von Manteuffel in 1867, remarked that his son Friedrich, then a young Prussian cavalry officer, had discovered the value of his newly acquired "von" for a military career.[1] Perhaps Friedrich von Ranke did reap some benefits from his father's title, for in 1901 he completed his family's ascent through several generations from the parsonage to the pinnacle of Prussian society with his promotion to the rank of brigadier general of cavalry.[2] As his example suggests, a logical beginning point for an examination of the origins and background of Prussia's general officers is the question of nobility.

Most generals either were aristocrats by birth or had obtained a noble title before promotion to brigadier general. Numerous others had connections with the aristocracy through mothers or wives. Despite recent assertions of a breakthrough by bourgeois elements into the highest levels of the officer corps, social class played a fundamental role in military careers throughout the period 1871–1914.[3] Indeed, as we shall see, nearly all aspects of the structure and personnel procedures of the Prussian army were designed to ensure its social homogeneity quite as much as to promote military efficiency. Given the domestic mission of the army, the dichotomy implied above may be quite false. Although social class by itself was not always a determinant of military success or failure, it remained a fundamental consideration throughout an officer's career. Long after the army could no longer rely completely upon the eastern nobility for its officers, it continued to favor aristocrats and those with proper aristocratic connections. We now turn to the persistence of the generalcy's connections with the nobility.

Table 1
Generals' Social Class: Generals Listed by Decade Promoted to Brigadier General

Class	Before 1871		1871–1881		1882–1892		1893–1903		1904–1914		Total	
	No.	%	No.	%	No.	%	No.	%	No.	%	No.	%
Uradel	81	44.75	142	37.47	159	32.38	216	33.39	187	25.10	785	32.13
Br. A. before birth	56	30.94	97	25.59	112	22.81	148	22.87	172	23.09	585	23.95
Br. A. after birth	7	3.87	15	3.96	14	2.85	18	2.78	19	2.55	73	2.99
Title for genrl.*	16	8.84	33	8.71	43	8.76	22	3.40	28	3.76	142	5.81
Unkn. noble	13	7.18	23	6.07	26	5.30	30	4.64	25	3.36	117	4.79
Noble total	173	95.58	310	81.80	354	72.10	434	67.08	431	57.86	1,702	69.67
Title BG-LG	4	2.21	4	1.06	7	1.43	6	.93	3	.40	24	.98
Title LG-G	0	—	0	—	2	.41	1	.15	0	—	3	.12
Title BMG	0	—	1	.26	2	.41	4	.62	4	.54	11	.45
Title LG	0	—	3	.79	4	.81	3	.46	8	1.07	18	.74
Title Genrl.	0	—	0	—	1	.20	5	.77	2	.27	8	.33
Title ret'd	0	—	16	4.22	15	3.05	15	2.32	5	.67	51	2.09
Bourg.	4	2.21	45	11.87	106	21.59	179	27.67	292	39.19	626	25.62
Total	181	100.00	379	100.00	491	100.00	647	100.00	745	100.00	2,443	100.00

*Title for general before promotion to brigadier general.

Note: BrA. = Briefadel; title before, or after, birth of general. Title BG-LG = title as brigadier general, before promotion to lieutenant general. Title LG-G = title as lieutenant general, before promotion to general. Title BG = title as brigadier general, no further promotion. Title LG = title as lieutenant general, no further promotion. Title Genrl. = title as general. Title ret'd = title after retirement. Bourg. = no title.

As Table 1 indicates, for the empire as a whole, 1,702 (69.76%) of the 2,443 generals were nobles at the time of their promotion to the rank of brigadier general. An additional 64 generals (2.62%) received titles after promotion but before retirement. Only 626 generals (25.62%) remained bourgeois throughout their lives.[4] This proportion fluctuated between 1871 and 1914 and therefore requires a closer examination.

In 1871 Prussia's army began the empire's first decade with an inheritance of 179 generals whose promotions had been granted before 1871 and whose careers continued after the postwar demobilization.[5] These generals, classified separately in Table 1, were of remarkably aristocratic origins. More than nine in ten (95.58%) had been nobles when promoted, and four of the remaining eight received titles before they became lieutenant generals. The purity of aristocratic pedigree established by this select group was not to be duplicated in subsequent years, however, as expansion of the officer corps, and especially of the artillery and technical branches, steadily reduced this legacy of aristocratic predominance.

The nobility's hold on the ranks of Prussia's general officers declined from 81.80 percent of new promotions during the first decade to a still substantial 57.86 percent for the years 1904–14.[6] No definitive calculation of the number of nobles in Prussia or Germany in the nineteenth century currently exists, but the total must have been quite modest. A study completed in 1936 estimated that there were about 45,000 male nobles in the mid-nineteenth century. Even assuming that several times that many aristocrats were alive during the years 1870–1914, they could hardly have constituted more than 5 percent of the population.[7] Certainly the number of nobles among the generals was entirely out of proportion to the nobility's numbers even within the more prosperous levels of the German and Prussian populations.

Precise comparisons with other military groups within the empire are difficult. Hermann Rumschöttel's study of the Bavarian officer corps has established that in 1914 about 15 percent of the active officers were nobles. Because he cites no specific figure for senior officers, either by rank or position, one cannot say with certainty how much more aristocratic the Prussian generalcy really was. Clearly, however, in its social composition the Bavarian army became more homogenous, rather than more diverse, between 1870 and 1914.[8]

Similarly, a preliminary examination of Württemberg's army indicates a greater concern for social homogeneity after the foundation of the empire than had been present in earlier decades.[9] Again, however, direct comparisons are nearly impossible. Given the relatively small size of Württemberg's contingent, moreover, even if precise data were available, they might not be suitable for meaningful comparison.

Of course it was not mere accident that most successful officers were nobles. In the early eighteenth century, Frederick William I had succeeded in bringing the Prussian nobility into the officer corps in large numbers.[10] Gradually the east-Elbian nobility became closely identified with service in the king's army. Prussia's subsequent rulers also exercised considerable influence over military affairs, and William I was no exception. As a young prince, William had served in the army during the Napoleonic wars and as sovereign insisted on retaining a direct role in the selection of those colonels who were to be promoted to brigadier general. The king had personal knowledge of a vast number of officers and was keenly interested in questions of promotions and assignments.[11] In 1884 he proudly boasted to Karl von Einem (later colonel-general and war minister) that until just recently he had personally known all his generals and had supervised all promotions to that select group.[12]

The king's intervention was especially significant because, like Frederick the Great, he firmly believed that most bourgeois families could not impart to their sons the proper "officer's spirit" so essential to his army. William's viewpoint found official endorsement in the Bonin Commission Report of 1858, which held that sons of officers and poor nobles were the best replenishments for the officer corps.[13] Count von Moltke's opinion that many bourgeois men were ill suited to become officers because they were "useless" and because they lacked the way of thinking (*Gesinnung*) "which must be preserved in the army" was representative of the attitudes of many, if not all, senior officers.[14] William I frequently found occasion to impress upon his generals the necessity of recruiting and promoting the right types of young officers.[15]

The advent of William II did not alter the army's basic preferences in promotions although it did bring about major changes in the role of the monarch in military affairs.[16] William followed in his grandfather's pattern by continuing to sign thousands of military patents conferring promotions and bestowing awards.[17] Nevertheless he was hardly a professional officer and lacked his father's and grandfather's interest and extended involvement in the army's daily activities. Because of his attitude, the direct power of the chief of the Military Cabinet over personnel matters reached its peak between 1890 and 1914. The last kaiser reportedly accepted whomever the chief nominated for most posts. The kaiser insisted on the selection of people who were sympathetic to him only in cases of appointments to the guards corps, the royal headquarters, and to the office of chief of the General Staff.[18] The Military Cabinet, therefore, had virtually a free hand to promote to the generalcy whatever officers it desired.

Even had it been so inclined, however, the Military Cabinet could not have continued the aristocratic partiality so prevalent in the years of William I, at least not on the same scale. By 1890 the nobility simply could not provide the number of officers necessary for the expanded army. In his famous "nobility of conviction" (*Adel der Gesinnung*) proclamation, William II recognized that the army would have to draw upon wider circles for its officer recruits. Thereafter, he said, nobles by birth would be joined by nobles of conviction. In fact, this was nothing new; bourgeois elements had always been present in the officer corps.[19]

The continued predominance of noble generals was a reflection of the army's determination to maintain aristocratic quality at the top of the officer corps at a time when bourgeois officers became increasingly prevalent in the lower ranks. In 1860 about 65 percent of all officers were nobles. By 1913 this ratio had fallen to about 30 percent. In absolute numbers, the total of officers increased from about 17,000 in 1875 to about 30,000 just before the war began in 1914.[20] As part of this increase, bourgeois officers steadily advanced upward in the officer ranks and eroded the aristocracy's dominance at all levels.

In spite of this trend, nearly six new promotions to brigadier general in ten during the last decade before the war went to noble officers. This ratio is a remarkable testament to the military aristocracy's powers of regeneration.[21] The nobility itself was hardly a homogenous whole, divided as it was into several tiers based on rank, family prestige, and antiquity of lineage. "Good for the army list (*Rangliste*), but bad for the front" was a popular military saying regarding the presence of many offspring of German royal houses in the Prussian army.[22] Although many princely names graced the guards regiments, especially those of the cavalry, Table 2 demonstrates that royalty did not so bountifully bless the ranks of Prussia's generals.

Only 30 generals (2% of 1,702 nobles) were sons of royal houses or mediatized families. Four others held the rank of prince but were without claim to royalty. Excluded from this consideration are the many princes whose military status was entirely honorary or whose careers were not of a primarily military nature. In the 1870–71 campaign, for example, William I's nephew, the grand duke of Mecklenburg-Schwerin, commanded the 13th Army Corps although he was hardly a typical Prussian officer.[23] In 1889 William II rejected a request by Prince Albert zu Schwarzburg-Rudolstadt for an appointment as a corps commander. Although he had extensive service as an officer and held he rank of major, the prince was not a professional soldier. He failed to receive his corps command and is not included among the 2,443 generals in this study although his name appears in the Ranglisten for a number of years.[24] Inclusion of these types of officers would distort the percentages by giving such diletantes weight equal to that of the professional officers whose lives were devoted to the army. After 1903 the number of princes among the generals was truly miniscule.

More than nine noble generals in ten were of the lower echelons of the aristocracy, barons and knights (von). By far the majority (79.08%) of the

Table 2
Noble Generals Listed By Decade of Promotion to Brigadier General

	Before 1871		1871–1881		1882–1892		1893–1903		1904–1914		Total	
	No.	%	No.	%	No.	%	No.	%	No.	%	No.	%
Royal House	5	2.89	3	.97	2	.57	5	1.15	1	.23	16	.94
Med. prince	2	1.16	2	.64	2	.57	2	.46	1	.23	9	.53
Med. count	1	.58	2	.64	0	—	1	.23	1	.23	5	.29
Prince	1	.58	3	.97	0	—	0	—	0	—	4	.24
Count	11	6.36	14	4.50	15	4.26	23	5.29	21	4.87	84	4.94
Baron	21	12.14	32	10.29	43	12.22	72	16.55	70	16.24	238	13.98
von	132	76.29	255	81.99	290	82.38	332	76.32	337	78.20	1.346	79.08
Total	173	100.00	311	100.00	352	100.00	435	100.00	431	100.00	1,702	100.00

noble generals were simple knights at the time of their promotion to brigadier general—a proportion that fluctuated slightly between 1871 and 1914. Although the great nobles of Germany, members of ruling houses, princes,and other dignitaries (not the least of whom was Bismarck) were fond of wearing their generals' uniforms, in fact, the army was directed by men of much more humble origins and of greater professional involvement.

Any examination of the type of nobility in the officer corps would be incomplete and even misleading if it neglected the most important single ingredient of social standing within the German aristocracy: the date of the family's claim to nobility. The line separating *Uradel* (titles before 1400) for *Briefadel* (all titles awarded after 1400) was a fundamental social distinction. Much in the manner of the nobles of the sword in France, a German Uradel looked down upon his parvenu associates, even if their titles were of a higher rank.[25] This ranking by antiquity did not stop at the Uradel level. Brigadier General Baron Richard von Strombeck exemplified the attitude of many old noble families when he remarked that families without traditions and pride in their past were like Eskimos or residents of South Sea Islands. Furthermore, he argued, families with a good past had "higher duties" than those whose members were born "in the shadow of an insignificant name."[26]

Members of the exclusive club of Germany's Uradel families were exceedingly proud of their ancestors' antiquity and history. Their ancient titles were both the basis of their haughty self-assurance and their most effective weapons against social adversaries, who at times might include the emperor. Very old clans with exceptionally proud and independent traditions, the Dohna family, for example, looked down on the Hohenzollerns and in moments of irritation did not hesitate to remind their audience that in comparison with them the Hohenzollerns were parvenus.[27]

As arrogant as the Dohna clan might at times appear, its attitude on family social standing was hardly unique. The Baron von Guestedt family (title mid-twelfth century), from Prussian Saxony, arrogantly regarded the Hohenzollerns as parvenus and made no secret of its antiquarian superiority.[28] General von Einem, not to be outdone, let it be known that one of his illustrious ancestors, a certain Ritter Heidenrich von Einem, had accompanied Henry the Lion on the Jerusalem campaign of 1172.[29] Although possessing an ancient title was not absolutely essential for a military career, such an advantage enabled the owner to communicate and engage in social contacts on an equal footing with most of Prussia's leading families.[30]

Families whose origins were obscure frequently sought to comfort themselves with the fervent belief that although proof was lacking, they must surely have been very old families.[31] General Maximilian von Mutius, for example, whose family's origins were certain only to the mid-eighteenth century (making this clan relatively youthful and suspect in its claims to social equality), recalled that members of his family were quite confident that they were one of the old landed families and "did not belong to the entirely young" sections of the nobility.[32] Unfortunately, they were never graduated from the Briefadel volumes of the Gotha handbooks into the Uradel sections. An analysis of the dates of the titles of the noble generals will clarify the extent to which Prussia's generals were an elite within an elite.

Nearly half (48.46%) of the officers promoted to brigadier general and beyond during the empire's first decade were of Uradel extraction. The proportion of such families fluctuated but slightly during the subsequent decades, except for a modest upswing in the decade 1893–1903 (53.35%). Although the dearth of precise information on the distribution of titles by date among the entire nobility makes judgments difficult, it is clear that Prussia's best old families continued to send their sons into the army in large numbers and that these officers in turn frequently pursued highly successful careers.

The data in Table 3, however, should not be interpreted to mean that once an Uradel officer reached the rank of brigadier general he was more likely to be promoted to the higher ranks than were his colleagues of less resplendent pedigree. Only 295 (44.03%) of the 670 Uradel generals advanced beyond the rank of brigadier general whereas 110 (45.72%) of the 243 generals with titles originating after 1800 attained higher rank (Table 4). Once an officer reached the rank of brigadier general, his ability or personal connections became increasingly important for promotion. An exception to this rule, however, was the rank of field marshal, which was largely reserved for Uradel officers.[33]

The current state of research, although far from ideal, allows a productive comparison with one other segment of Germany's elite—the foreign office. The nobles holding high-level positions in the Prusso-German diplomatic service, which vied with the office of Landrat and the officer corps for being the most coveted position of service in the Prussian state, held titles moderately less antiquated than did the generals. Envoys appointed by William I held Uradel titles in slightly more than one case in three (35.13%) and possessed titles dating before 1700 in half the cases (49.99%). The corresponding figures for envoys appointed during the reign of William II were 48.18 percent for Uradels and 55.45 percent for titles before 1700.[34] This contrasts with the 67.14 percent of the noble generals whose titles antedated 1700. Clearly the officer corps attracted more than its share of the members of Prussia's and Germany's best families, who may have preferred the army to other types of state service.[35]

Just as the father's family background might provide valuable assets to an aspiring young officer, so could that of his mother. This type of

Table 3
Date of Noble Title: Noble Generals Listed by Decade of Promotion to Brigadier General

Date of Title	Before 1871		1871–1881		1882–1892		1893–1903		1904–1914		Total	
	No.	%	No.	%	No.	%	No.	%	No.	%	No.	%
Uradel	81	50.62	142	48.46	158	48.06	211	52.35	185	45.79	777	48.89
1401–1500	4	2.50	9	3.07	8	2.43	17	4.22	19	4.70	57	3.59
1501–1600	8	5.00	14	4.78	18	5.49	18	4.47	26	6.44	84	5.29
1601–1700	11	6.88	20	6.83	28	8.51	43	10.67	36	8.91	138	8.69
1701–1800	27	16.87	46	15.70	43	13.06	55	13.65	69	17.08	240	15.10
1801–1870	24	15.00	33	11.26	38	11.55	34	8.44	32	7.92	161	10.13
1871–1914	5	3.13	29	9.90	36	10.94	25	6.20	37	9.16	132	8.31
Total	160	100.00	293	100.00	329	100.00	403	100.00	404	100.00	1,589	100.00

*Note:*Information complete on 1,589 (93.36%) of 1,702 generals noble when promoted to brigadier general.

Table 4A
Date of Noble Title by Generals' Highest Military Rank

Date of Title	Brigadier General		Lieutenant General		General		Colonel General		Field Marshal		Total	
	No.	%	No.	%	No.	%	No.	%	No.	%	No.	%
Uradel	375	50.00	197	47.70	85	50.90	5	55.56	8	66.67	670	49.59
1401–1500	31	4.13	13	3.15	7	4.19	0	—	1	8.33	52	3.85
1501–1600	37	4.93	20	4.84	6	3.59	0	—	1	8.33	64	4.74
1601–1700	64	8.53	40	9.69	17	10.18	0	—	0	—	121	8.96
1701–1800	110	14.67	63	15.25	22	13/17	4	44.44	2	16.67	201	14.87
1801–1870	71	9.47	47	11.38	19	11.38	0	—	0	—	137	10.14
1871–1914	62	8.27	33	7.99	11	6.59	0	—	0	—	106	7.85
Total	750	100.00	413	100.00	167	100.00	9	100.00	12	100.00	1,351	100.00

Table 4B
High Military Rank by Date of Noble Title

	Uradel		1401–1500		1601–1800		1801–1870		1871–1914		Total	
	No.	%	No.	%	No.	%	No.	%	No.	%	No.	%
Brig. genrl.	375	55.97	68	58.62	174	54.04	71	51.82	62	58.49	750	55.51
Lt. gen.	197	29.40	33	28.45	103	31.99	47	34.31	33	31.13	413	30.57
General	85	12.69	13	11.21	39	12.11	19	13.87	11	10.38	167	12.36
Col. gen.	5	.75	0	—	4	1.24	0	—	0	—	9	.67
Field marshal	8	1.19	2	1.72	2	.62	0	—	0	—	12	.89
Total	670	100.00	116	100.00	322	100.00	137	100.00	106	100.00	1,351	100.00

Note: Excluded are 351 noble generals who cannot be classified because they died on active duty or were still on active duty in 1914 or for whom information on date of title is incomplete.

Table 5
Mothers' Social Class

Mothers' Class	Noble Generals		Bourgeois; Title after Promotion		Always Bourgeois		Total	
	No.	%	No.	%	No.	%	No.	%
Royalty	14	.93	0	—	0	—	14	.63
Med. pr. & count.*	15	.99	0	—	0	—	15	.68
Countess	75	4.96	0	—	0	—	75	3.38
Baroness	130	8.60	6	1.31	1	.40	137	6.18
von	740	48.94	49	10.72	49	19.68	838	37.78
Noble subtotal	974	64.42	55	12.03	50	20.08	1,079	48.65
Bourg.	533	35.25	399	87.31	197	79.12	1,129	50.90
Foreign	5	.33	3	.66	2	.80	10	.45
Total	1.512	100.00	457	100.00	249	100.00	2,218	100.00

*Med. pr. & count. = mediatized princesses and mediatized countesses.
Note: Information complete on 2,218 (90.79%) of 2,443 generals.

connection was especially important to young officers whose family backgrounds were deficient in other areas. Field Marshal von Steinmetz, for example, though bourgeois at birth had good connections with the Hohenzollerns dating back to his mother's close friendship with the wife of Frederick William IV.[36] Of course not all mothers of young officers had such highly placed and influential connections, but, in the relatively closed society of the officer corps, women could and did intervene in favor of sons and relatives.[37]

The social class of the generals' mothers differed considerably from that of the generals themselves. Of the 1,512 noble generals for whom information is complete, fewer than two in three (64.42%) had noble mothers. More than 500 noble generals had bourgeois mothers whereas 105 (14.87%) of the bourgeois generals had mothers of noble extraction. Easily more than seven generals in ten had at least one noble parent. In the case of an officer who was the son of a bourgeois father, a noble mother could provide useful access to better social circles. On the other hand, many of these bourgeois mothers brought financial assets to their noble husbands, many of whom, especially the officers, had limited resources.

It seems especially interesting that of the two categories of bourgeois generals in Table 5, about one in eight of those who eventually received titles, and one in five of those who did not, had noble mothers. This ratio was many times higher than could have been the case in the entire bourgeois upper-class population and is striking proof that these bourgeois officers came from families of unusual social standing and that they, in many cases, had close ties to the nobility.

3

Geography and Religion

Prussian society was divided not only along class lines as defined by noble and nonnoble names and traditions. Geographic divisions cut through all other considerations at some points. Prussians from the provinces east of the Elbe were frequently more distrustful and suspicious of their fellow Prussians from the western areas than they were of non-Prussians in the east. Certainly the Mecklenburg nobility was closer to Prussian aristocrats from Brandenburg and Pomerania than were the latter to most families from the Rhineland.[1] Given the important differences in the political and social climate between eastern Prussia and the west and south of Germany, it is hardly surprising that an officer's geographic origins could be of some importance to a military career.[2]

As one might expect, the great bulk of Prussia's generals were born in Prussia although the annexations after the successful campaigns that established the empire complicate the picture somewhat.[3] More than half the generals (56.01%) were born in eastern Prussia. This category includes those generals born in the provinces East Prussia, West Prussia, Brandenburg, Silesia, Posen, Pomerania, and Schleswig-Holstein (Table 6). An additional 644 generals (27.27%), including those born in Prussian Saxony, were born in Prussia's western provinces. Thus, more than eight generals in ten came from what was by 1871 Prussian territory.

Both before and after the wars of unification the non-Prussian states of the new German Empire contributed a substantial number of their citizens to the Prussian army.[4] Hesse contributed the largest number of non-Prussians to the ranks of Prussia's generals if one includes both those generals born in the Grand Duchy and Electoral Hesse, which became the Prussian province Hesse-Nassau in 1866. All generals from the latter area

Table 6
Region of Birth: Generals Listed by Decade of Promotion to Brigadier General

Region Born	Before 1871		1871–1881		188–1892		1893–1903		1904–1914		Total	
	No.	%	No.	%	No.	%	No.	%	No.	%	No.	%
Eastern Prussia	115	64.25	214	56.60	268	54.69	312	55.42	392	54.98	1,301	56.01
Western Prussia	41	22.90	110	29.10	129	26.33	159	28.24	205	28.75	644	27.72
Prussian total	156	87.15	324	85.70	397	81.02	471	83.66	597	83.73	1,945	83.73
Mecklenburg	7	3.91	6	1.59	10	2.04	13	2.31	6	.84	42	1.81
Hesse	0	—	7	1.85	21	4.29	20	3.55	18	2.53	66	2.84
Baden	5	2.79	9	2.38	12	2.45	12	2.13	18	2.53	56	2.41
Saxony	3	1.68	2	.53	4	.82	10	1.78	3	.42	22	.94*
Bavaria	0	—	3	.80	0	—	1	.18	0	—	4	.17*
Anhalt	1	.56	2	.53	4	.82	3	.53	3	.42	13	.56
Other German	6	3.35	15	3.97	34	6.93	26	4.62	52	7.29	133	5.73
Foreign	1	.56	10	2.65	8	1.63	7	1.24	16	2.24	42	1/81
Total	179	100.00	378	100.00	490	100.00	563	100.00	713	100.00	2,323	100.00

*Saxony and Bavaria had their own state armies throughout the nineteenth century.
Note: Information complete on 2,323 (95.09%) of 2,443 generals.

were born before 1866 and might logically be included with their fellow Hessians. The total number from both groups was 126—more than 5 percent of all Prussian generals.

The success of the Hessians in overcoming their west-German origins and their ruler's unfortunate decision in 1866 deserves a closer look. About three-fourths of the officer corps of Electoral Hesse joined the Prussian officer corps when their army became part of the Prussian forces.[5] The Grand Duchy's army entered the Prussian army as the 25th Division. This unit, while maintaining a purely nominal independence as a courtesy to the grand duke, was strictly a Prussian unit after 1875. About half the old Hessian officers entered the new amalgamated Prusso-Hessian regiments, whose enlisted men were in large part imported from West Prussia, Posen, and Silesia. About 30 percent to 50 percent of the Hessian officers moved on to other Prussian regiments. Eventually both groups were dispersed throughout the army, as was the Prussian practice, and many went on to enjoy successful careers.

Although Prussian officers were prone to scoff at the Hessian dialect, they apparently erected no insurmountable barriers in the paths of those officers who embraced Prussian discipline and values. Of course not all the Hessians in Table 6 or those classified as born in Hesse-Nassau began their careers in the Hessian army. Throughout the nineteenth century citizens of various German states sought military careers beyond the borders of their own states. If their family circumstances were acceptable to the ruler in whose army they wished to serve, acceptance was quite routine. General Eduard von Fransecky, for example, although a Hessian by birth, considered himself a Prussian because his father had been a Prussian officer during the Napoleonic wars. Given this excellent background, he found easy acceptance into the Prussian officer corps and had a brilliant career.[6]

The case of the Hanoverians who became Prussian generals is even more remarkable. Fully 120 generals were born in Hanover, all before 1866. By all accounts their road to the rank of brigadier general must have been more difficult than that of the Hessians, for a variety of reasons. Hanover's army included 760 officers at the time of that state's annexation by Prussia. The Prussian army accepted 456 of them after King George V finally released his officers from their personal oaths to him. At the time, 400 of these new Prussian officers were in the rank of captain and below.[7] Only one of 15 generals and four of 18 colonels entered Prussian service. Doubtless the chief of the Military Cabinet, Hermann von Tresckow, felt that younger officers would be more pliable and would more easily accept the Prussian system than would their former commanders.[8]

William I had earlier cautioned his regimental commanders to observe closely all the officers coming into the army from "foreign service," not all of whom possessed the qualities required of good Prussian officers.[9] The suspicion underlying the king's concern was present on both sides in the Hanoverian case. Hanoverian aristocratic circles and bourgeois leaders as well resisted incorporation into Prussia.[10] Prussian officers, for their part, remained hostile toward most Hanoverians. In October 1869, Prussian troops destroyed a memorial to Hanoverian soldiers killed in the 1866 war, a rash act that infuriated public opinion and caused a minor crisis in Berlin. The mutual resentment of Hanoverians and Prussians continued into the twentieth century. As late as 1914 young Prussian officers of Hanoverian extraction encountered family resentment of their Prussian uniforms.[11] Even War Minister Karl von Einem always thought that his Hanoverian origins had been detrimental to his career.[12]

Particularism as described above was hardly limited to the Hanoverians. Prussian generals frequently snubbed their noses at the south-German states because they were too strongly under Austrian influence to be entirely trustworthy. Many Prussians, Waldersee among them, feared that liberal political influences were dangerously strong in the southern armies, even among the officers.[13] Ardent Prussian Protestants, moreover, had a special reason for disliking the predominantly Catholic southerners. Only eight generals came from Württemberg and only four from Bavaria. Doubtless most young men from these states anticipated better careers in their own state contingents, even though they were much smaller than Prussia's.

The Prussian army itself, moreover, hardly enjoyed perfect relations with the armies of the other states. In 1871 the Military Cabinet had to recall the first Prussian-appointed commander of Württemberg's Army Corps, General Ferdinand von Stülpnagel, because his arrogant Prussian manners had proven insufferable in Stuttgart.[14] Waldersee subsequently declined that same post because he knew that he would be unacceptable to Württemberg's particularists.[15]

The latent hostility between segments of the populations of the various German states manifested itself in varying forms and circumstances. During the maneuvers of 1898, held jointly between the Saxon and Prussian armies, the Prussian commander had to change his attack formations and tactical maneuvers so as to halt his units at least 20 strides from the Saxons—lest a real battle erupt.[16] Franz von Lenski thought it noteworthy that in 1897 his commander, Count von Haeseler, did not object to his proposed marriage to a woman from Bavaria.[17] It is small wonder that the various officer corps attracted men primarily from their home states.

The problems and particularist sentiments were overcome by capable and determined officers such as August von Goeben and Karl von Einem, both Hanoverians by birth. Both succeeded, and especially Einem, only by embracing and skillfully espousing the most extreme forms of Prussian conservative and monarchical values.[18]

The generals born in Prussia came predominately from five key provinces: Silesia, Prussian Saxony, Pomerania, Brandenburg, and the special zone Berlin-Potsdam, herein considered as a province because of its unique characteristics. Together these areas produced 60.48 percent of the 1,945 generals who were born in Prussia (Table 7).

Although the overall percentage of generals born in eastern provinces fluctuated but slightly during the years 1871–1914, some substantial shifts occurred among the provinces. Generals born in the Berlin-Potsdam area decreased both in numbers and as a percentage of the whole, especially after 1903. The province East Prussia also produced only about half as large a percentage of the generals promoted after 1903 as it had done during the years 1871–81. Like so many figures in this study, however, the decline was relative rather than absolute because more generals promoted during 1904–14 came from East Prussia than had been the case during the empire's first decade. Silesia was the only eastern province showing a substantial gain during the period. A remarkable 19.89 percent of all of Prussia's generals promoted after 1904 had been born in Silesia.

The relatively small number of generals born in the Prussian provinces Westphalia and the Rhineland was the result of strong east-Prussian prejudice against the nobility living in that area as well as anti-Prussian sentiments within the provinces.[19] Many officers born in the provinces were in fact not native sons, but were sons of officers stationed in the area. Even so, only 258 generals (13.25%) were born in the two provinces. Yet the 1910 census revealed that more than 11 million of Prussia's 40 million inhabitants lived in Westphalia and the Rhineland.

The disparity noted above was no accident. On the contrary, it was another indication of the persistence of particularism within Prussia and Germany. In 1885 one officer serving in an artillery unit in the Rhineland attributed the relative shortage of native sons in his unit to a residue of hostility directed against Prussians and the fact that, from the army's point of view, a Rhinelander was in no way an old-Prussian type, although he may have been a good German.[20] Another officer, speaking of the years just before World War I, recalled his doubts that the mass of the officer recruits from the western provinces were drawn from conservative circles whereas eastern officers were definitely politically reliable.[21]

To many high officers, nobles from the Rhineland and Westphalia were simply not on the same footing with real Prussian aristocrats.[22] Arnold Lequis, a Rhinelander writing after World War I, said that his generation (he was born in 1881) remembered the anti-Prussian spirit of its parents but had discarded this attitude and had sought to be officers in the spirit of Frederick II and William I.[23] A few undoubtedly did so, and 163 Rhinelanders became Prussian generals. These were exceptions, however, and most of Lequis's contemporaries were either unwilling to trade their

Table 7

Province of Birth of Generals Born in Prussia: Generals Listed by Decade of Promotion to Brigadier General

	Before 1871		1871–1881		1882–1892		1893–1903		1904–1914		Total	
	No.	%	No.	%	No.	%	No.	%	No.	%	No.	%
East Prussia	30	18.99	33	10.33	30	7.54	25	5.31	34	5.69	152	7.81
West Prussia	3	1.90	11	3.44	12	3.02	19	4.03	37	6.19	82	4.22
Brdbg.	16	10.13	26	8.13	46	11.56	55	11.68	58	9.70	201	10.33
Berlin-Potsdam	30	18.99	50	15.63	54	13.57	62	13.16	39	6.52	235	12.09
Posen	0	—	9	2.81	22	5.53	27	5.73	27	4.52	85	4.37
Pomerania	14	8.87	33	10.31	44	11.06	42	8.92	71	11.87	204	10.49
Silesia	22	13.92	50	15.63	58	14.56	77	16.35	119	19.89	326	16.77
Schles.-Holstein	1	.63	1	.31	2	.50	4	.85	7	1.17	15	.77
Eastern subtotal	116	73.42	213	66.56	268	67.34	311	66.03	392	65.65	1,300	66.85
Pr. Saxony	20	12.66	36	11.24	45	11.31	44	9.34	66	11.04	211	10.85
Hesse-Nassau	3	1.90	8	2.50	8	2.01	17	3.61	24	4.01	60	3.08
Rhineland	6	3.80	22	6.88	35	8.79	48	10.19	52	8.70	163	8.38
Westphalia	7	4.43	22	6.88	16	4.02	22	4.67	28	4.68	95	4.88
Hanover	6	3.50	19	5.94	26	6.53	29	6.16	36	6.02	116	5.96
Western subtotal	42	26.58	107	33.44	130	32.66	160	33.97	206	34.45	644	33.10
Total	158	100.00	320	100.00	398	100.00	471	100.00	598	100.00	1,945	100.00

heritage for the Prussian values dominant in the army or were unacceptable to the officer corps, at least in the highest ranks.

Closely related to the foregoing discussion of the geographic roots of the generals is the question of the source of noble titles of the noble generals. Families whose titles were of Prussian origins constituted a majority of all noble families (Table 8). This type of Prussian predominance was never overwhelming, however, and faded into a minority position for generals promoted after 1892.[24] Some of the 115 Saxon titles should be added to the 830 Prussian patents because most of these families came from Prussian Saxony, which by mid-century had become one of the army's best sources of officers. Although their titles were Saxon (and largely Uradel), their families were firmly steeped in Prussian values and military traditions. The number of these Saxons also declined beginning in 1903. Even if all are considered to have been Prussian by title, they cannot arrest the downward trend for Prussians.

The decline of Prussian aristocrats was one of proportion rather than of real numbers; more Prussian titles were present among the generals promoted during the final decade than in the years 1882–92. Their replacements were distributed evenly among the remaining categories of titles. Mecklenburg titles showed a considerable increase over the life of the empire (3 for 1871–81; 15 for 1904–14), and, if one considers Danish titles along with these, the increase was even more marked.[25]

Other types of foreign titles also merit a special consideration. Most Austrian titles were *Reichsadel* patents dating to different periods of the Holy Roman Empire. Doubtless many of these families had become thoroughly Prussianized by the nineteenth century. Religious factors may have influenced the decisions of nobles from Bavaria, who in any case had their own state army to satisfy their martial ambitions, as did Protestants from Württemberg. Probably few nobles from these states had any inclination to join the Prussian officer corps, and still fewer had bright prospects if they did join.

Religion was an important factor in an officer's background and was an integral part of his career in most cases. The religious factor was also related to the relative paucity of nobles from the Rhineland, Westphalia, and other Catholic areas. Two considerations dominate this issue as it pertains to the officer corps: the extent to which religious beliefs shaped the attitudes and ideology of the generals and the extent to which negative attitudes generally prevented Catholics and others from entering the officer corps or from enjoying successful careers. Religious homogeneity, as it turns out, was a very prominent characteristic of the upper echelons of the officer corps.

Religion was more than a source of spiritual comfort for the officers and men of the Prussian army. It was an integral part of military life.

Table 8
Source of Noble Titles: Generals Listed by Decade of Generals' Promotion to Brigadier General

	Before 1871		1871–1881		1882–1892		1893–1903		1904–1914		Total	
	No.	%	No.	%	No.	%	No.	%	No.	%	No.	%
Prussia	92	57.50	161	56.09	187	58.43	199	49.51	191	47.40	830	52.80
H.R.E.	21	13.13	35	12.19	34	10.62	48	11.94	59	14.64	197	12.53
France	2	1.25	7	2.44	3	.94	7	1.74	16	3.97	35	2.25
Russia	0	—	0	—	0	—	1	.25	0	—	1	.06
Poland	4	2.50	3	1.05	3	.94	4	.99	7	1.74	21	1.34
Denmark	1	.62	0	—	4	1.25	6	1.49	5	1.24	16	1.02
Bohemia	2	1.25	4	1.39	4	1.25	8	1.99	11	2.73	29	1.84
Bavaria	2	1.25	1	.35	4	1.25	1	.25	2	.50	10	.64
Saxony	12	7.50	31	10.80	21	6.56	32	7.96	19	4.71	115	7.31
Württ.	1	.62	1	.35	1	.31	0	—	0	—	3	.19
Baden	1	.62	1	.35	3	.94	2	.50	7	1.74	14	.89
Hesse	2	1.25	9	3.13	3	.94	9	2.24	9	2.23	32	2.04
Meckl.	5	3.13	3	1.05	7	2.18	16	3.98	15	3.72	46	2.92
Anhalt	1	.62	3	1.05	1	.31	2	.50	3	.74	10	.64
Lower Saxon Uradel	0	—	1	.35	10	3.13	11	2.74	9	2.23	31	1.97
Rh. & Westf. Uradel	4	2.50	9	3.13	12	3.75	22	5.47	17	4.22	64	4.07
Thuringia	5	3.13	6	2.09	6	1.88	4	.99	8	1.99	29	1.84
Baltic German	0	—	2	.70	3	.94	6	1.49	1	.25	12	.76
Other German	3	1.88	2	.70	8	2.50	15	3.73	14	3.47	42	2.67
Other foreign	2	1.25	7	2.44	4	1.25	8	1.99	10	2.48	31	1.97
Alsace-Lorraine Uradel	0	—	1	.35	2	.63	1	.25	0	—	4	.25
Total	160	100.00	287	100.00	320	100.00	402	100.00	403	100.00	1,572	100.00

Note: Information complete on 1,572 (92.36%) of 1,702 noble generals.

Compulsory church services, always of the official Evangelical faith, brought officers to military chapels frequently. The army compelled all soldiers, including Catholics and others not subscribing to the official religion, to attend Sunday services at least once a month. On regular schedules entire companies attended church in unison, complete with their officers, who frequently took very seriously their duty of supervising the spiritual welfare of their men.[26] Considerable efforts were made to use military chaplains as agents to infuse loyalty and discipline into the army.[27] Although Catholic soldiers attended Catholic services, they did so in unison and under the supervision of their usually Evangelical officers.

"Church attendance is official duty," answered Count Helmuth von Moltke when someone inquired of him why he always arrived exactly 15 minutes early for chapel services. One should always attend them punctually, according to the venerable old field marshal, just as one would every other duty.[28] In his case personal convictions did not conflict with official responsibilities. This extraordinary officer set the standards for military excellence in the Prussian army and could have done the same for religious piety. Although he had not been a fervent believer in his days as a young officer, he eventually became convinced of the value of religion.[29]

Not all officers, however, found church attendance an uplifting or even a pleasant duty. Erich Ludendorff, for one, an officer without a strong religious upbringing, experienced considerable difficulties in performing his religious duties, especially when the troops were Catholics and their services held in Catholic chapels. Other officers, especially those in Alsace-Lorraine, commented on the necessity of an officer's maintaining a close watch over his soldiers' religious performances regardless of his own convictions.[30] From differing perspectives both examples illustrate the obligatory nature of official religious piety. For most officers probably no serious conflicts existed between religious duties as defined by the army and personal religious beliefs.

Prussia's generals were almost completely Protestant, and, within that broad rubric, were overwhelmingly of the official Evangelical church (Table 9). Nearly nine generals in ten (87.96%) were members of the state church. During the imperial years Catholic generals appeared slightly more often as the decades passed, but they were always a very small part of the whole. No comprehensive figures exist for the religious composition of the officer corps as a whole, and, with the destruction of the personnel records, such information is probably lost forever. One contemporary (1912) estimated that about 16 percent of the officer corps was Catholic.[31] If this figure is accurate, it is evident that only at the lower levels did Catholics serve as officers very frequently and that very few of them advanced to the rank of brigadier general.

This staggering Protestant predominance was highly disproportionate to the religious composition of Prussia and Germany and even exceeded the

Table 9
Religion: Generals Listed by Decade of Promotion to Brigadier General

	Before 1871		1871–1881		1882–1892		1893–1903		1904–1914		Total	
	No.	%	No.	%	No.	%	No.	%	No.	%	No.	%
Evangelical	146	90.12	284	89.87	350	88.61	425	86.39	468	87.14	1,673	87.96
Lutheran	15	9.26	16	5.06	25	6.33	43	8.74	26	4.85	125	6.57
Catholic	1	.72	15	4.75	18	4.55	23	4.67	37	6.89	94	4.94
Other	0	—	1	.32	2	.51	1	.20	6	1.12	10	.53
Total	162	100.00	316	100.00	395	100.00	492	100.00	537	100.00	1,902	100.00

Note: Information complete on 1,902 (77.86%) of 2,443 generals.

33

levels of religious discrimination attained in the bureaucracy and the navy. During the years of Bismarck's empire, never more than 65 percent of Prussia's and 62 percent of Germany's populations were Protestant. It is apparent that Catholics, who made up 34 percent and 37 percent of the Prussian and German populations respectively, were seriously underrepresented among the generals. Research in selected samples of the Prussian Landräte (local government officials) and of the diplomatic service has revealed that Catholics occupied key positions in about 13 percent and 17 percent of the cases. Although precisely comparable data are not available, the evidence broadly indicates that about 14 percent of the naval officer corps was Catholic, at least in the lower ranks.[32]

When the generals' religious affiliations are tabulated by high military rank, the pattern of religious discrimination becomes even more obvious. Table 10 analyzes the 1,605 generals whose religion is known and whose careers terminated in a normal manner. Of this group only one Catholic attained the rank of field marshal and only seven the rank of full general. Only eight (1.64%) of the 187 officers with the rank of general or above were Catholics. These officers who had a difficult time advancing beyond the rank of colonel and, once beyond that hurdle, were very unlikely to advance above the rank of brigadier general.[33]

Geographic factors were in part responsible for this underrepresentation of Catholics. A little more than half the generals were born in the eastern provinces. More than nine of these generals in ten (91.66%) were members of the Evangelical church, and only about one in thirty (3.37%) was a Catholic. Although a substantial number of Catholics lived in the eastern provinces, most were Polish peasants and thus were in no way considered to be officer material. About twice as high a proportion of the generals born in western Prussia was Catholic (7.66%).[34] Nearly 10 percent of the generals born in Hesse were of the Catholic faith, the second highest figure (next to Baden's 13.95%) for any geographic region. If the army had drawn upon the latter areas for more officers, the Catholic content of the generalcy might have increased moderately. Given the army's hostility toward the Catholic church, however, the paucity of Catholic generals was perhaps inevitable.

As in other cases, comparison of the Prussian army with the military forces of the other states can only emphasize the overwhelming narrowness of the Prussian officer corps. The Bavarian army, for example, while drawn from a state with a Catholic dynasty and a Protestant minority of about 20 percent, had an officer corps of which 40 percent to 50 percent were Protestants. Indeed, the leading historian of the Bavarian army has concluded that in Bavaria the question of an officer's religion was "as a rule without significance."[35] Although his own figures seem to dispute so strong a conclusion, clearly religious orthodoxy was not a sine qua non for a typical young Bavarian officer.

Table 10
Religion: Generals Listed by High Military Rank

	Brigadier General		Lieutenant General		General		Colonel General		Field Marshal		Total	
	No.	%	No.	%	No.	%	No.	%	No.	%	No.	%
Evangelical	808	87.74	427	88.03	153	85.48	8	100.00	9	75.00	1,405	87.52
Lutheran	53	5.75	38	7.84	19	10.61	0	—	2	16.67	112	6.98
Catholic	54	5.86	19	3.92	7	3.91	0	—	1	8.33	81	5.05
Other	6	.65	1	.21	0	—	0	—	0	—	7	.44
Total	921	100.00	485	100.00	179	100.00	8	100.00	12	100.00	1,605	100.00

The situation of religious minorities in Württemberg was more complex. No comprehensive study of this issue for Württemberg's army has yet appeared. About 30 percent of that state's population was Catholic. Probably about 14 percent to 17 percent of its officer corps was Catholic although by 1912 about 30 percent of new officers were Catholics. Overall, religious discrimination does not seem to have been a decisive factor in the careers of Catholics serving in Württemberg's army.[36]

Anti-Catholic prejudice permeated the Prussian army from top to bottom. William I disliked Catholics on personal and political grounds. William II, ever prone to extremes, sometimes subjected his audiences to violent anti-Catholic tirades and in moments of severe pique publicly questioned the loyalty of Catholic officers.[37] So great was the pressure on all generals not to deviate too far from religious norms that a general whose religious views were not Evangelical might find his family the target of official retaliation.[38] General Willibald von Arndt, the grandson of Ernst Moritz Arndt, supposedly was denied a corps command because his devoutly Catholic wife had reared their children in her faith.[39]

Many of those generals who were Catholics seem to have been special cases. Brigadier General Eugen von Wulffen, for example, was of a Kurmark Uradel family that had previously owned land in Brandenburg and Silesia. He and his mother were the only Catholics in the family at least as far back as the mid-seventeenth century. His father as well as his great-grandfather and great-great-grandfather had been officers. His two brothers, both officers, and a sister were reared in the Evangelical church. In these circumstances, and as a product of the cadet corps, Wulffen was hardly an outpost of foreign Catholicism within the officer corps. His example and that of Arndt indicate that the cabinet order of Frederick William III that forbade Prussian officers from rearing their children as Catholics was not always enforced. Nevertheless, the spirit of the order dominated the army until 1914.[40]

Although most nineteenth-century officers did not use the language of the "Great Elector" in describing Catholicism as a "vulgar abomination and idolatry," their religious views corresponded closely to those of their Hohenzollern rulers. Most thought that Catholics were too likely to support the Center Party, a notorious enemy of Prussia and the German Empire in military eyes. Furthermore, in the eastern provinces, and especially in Posen, Catholics were associated with Polish culture and resistance to Prussianization.[41] When these factors are added to the genuine religious dislike, the unwillingness of the army to promote Catholic officers and the corresponding resistance of many Catholics to join the officer corps are easily understood.[42]

As the foregoing discussion of the generals' family backgrounds has indicated, many factors could help or hinder a career. Most successful officers were of good families, of the correct religion, and conformed to the army's norms in all important matters. One or more very favorable assets in an officer's background frequently could offset a liability in another area.

There was one liability, however, for which no compensation existed, one stigma for which there was no cure. A practicing Jew who refused to convert to the Evangelical faith had no future in the Prussian officer corps. Perhaps as many as one unbaptized Jew served as an active officer between 1820 and 1848. During the 1870–71 campaign about 60 Jewish men received commissions. They received poor treatment at the hands of their Christian colleagues and soon retired. Few if any other Jews were admitted to take their places. By 1878 probably no Jews were serving in the active officer corps.[43]

Anti-Semitism in the officer corps undoubtedly contained some of the seeds of the radical anti-Semitism that became so prominent after 1918, but before that date, in most cases, it was primarily religious and cultural. Anti-Jewish sentiments could be found in all types of officers, ranging from the rabid anti-Semites such as Waldersee, a supporter of Stoecker, to Albrecht von Stosch, a relatively liberal officer, who felt that Jews were in complete opposition to Christian and Germanic values.[44]

Even superior performance on the battlefield was not a sufficient compensatory factor for being Jewish. General Krafft zu Hohenlohe-Ingelfingen only grudgingly conceded that a Jewish soldier who had won an iron cross at Sedan wore his medal well, despite his Jewish appearance.[45] Most officers found Jews unacceptable on religious grounds and because of their alleged connections with financial speculations and fraud.[46] But the prejudice went much further than such loose associations. Officers frequently regarded Jews with the kind of disdain that could find something wrong with just about any Jew. Count Alfred von Schlieffen, for example, once complained about the "onion-smelling Jews" with whom he was forced to share a train car.[47]

The very few Jews who converted to the Evangelical church and had successful careers were exceptional cases. Reinhold Mossner, one of the few (if there were any others) baptized Jews to reach the ranks of the generals, is a good example.[48] His father was a personal friend of William I and had assisted the prince in his flight to England in 1848. Mossner's father was a wealthy banker who later acquired a fashionable estate (Ulbersdorf) in Silesia. Young Reinhold entered the army in 1866, compiled a distinguished war record, and was ennobled in 1890 while a major. By that time he had married into the Uradel von Wolffersdorf family and was properly Evangelical. From 1892 to 1895 he served as an aide to William II. In 1897 he became a brigadier general and retired in 1910 as general of cavalry and governor of Strassburg. His conversion to Christianity, his wife, his wealth, and above all his special ties to the Hohenzollerns overcame his origins and made his career successful.[49]

These factors also made him an example which few, if any other, Jews could hope to emulate.

Most Jews, even if converted, hardly enjoyed the enthusiastic acceptance of their fellow officers. In the *Bundesarchiv/Militärarchiv*, for example, there rests an officer's personal copy of the Offizier-Stammliste of the 52nd Infantry Regiment.Beside the names of many of the officers are careful annotations: some are good fellows, some are friendly, some are overweight. One officer, Kurt Rösler, is annotated differently than are the rest: "Jude! Hands Off."[50]

It is small wonder, then, that by 1900, Jewish leaders had given up their efforts to gain admission for their fellows into the active officer corps.[51] Thereafter they concentrated their efforts on the reserve officer corps but enjoyed only limited success. The examples of the baptized sons of Gerson von Bleichröder, who were reluctantly accepted as reserve officers, despite the fact that their father's house was off limits to the officers of some of Berlin's regiments, illustrate the marginal position of even the wealthiest and most prominent Jews.[52]

It should be mentioned in conclusion that Prussian Jews who wanted to serve their country as officers fared worse than did their brethren who desired diplomatic careers or who tried to enter the second-largest state army. A very few Jews were allowed to serve as active Bavarian officers, but no new Jews were accepted after 1885. By 1906 all were gone. Usually about 2 percent to 3 percent of Bavaria's reserve officers were Jewish.[53] In the Prusso-German Diplomatic Service, Jews found their ways into higher ranks in about 1 percent of all cases.[54] Such a thing was unheard of and even unthinkable in the Prussian officer corps.[55]

Prussia's generalcy clearly lacked a broad geographic base, a fact that both reflected and caused a narrowing of its social origins. An entirely disproportionate number of generals came from the sparsely populated eastern provinces, the traditional recruiting ground of the officer corps. Throughout the empire the army chose its generals from aristocratic, east-Elbian, and Protestant circles whenever such men were available. That these men dominated the ranks of the army's generals throughout the period was neither accidental nor insignificant.

4

Occupational Background

As the foregoing discussion has suggested, exclusivity was a fundamental tenet of officer selection and promotion in the Prussian officer corps. That institution's success in limiting the intrusion of undesirable elements has prompted some historians to describe the officer corps as a distinct class, a caste separate from the rest of Prussian society.[1] Numerous contemporary observers, most officers included, were of the same persuasion. One general, writing in 1894, proudly proclaimed that the officer corps was a special kind of weapons-bearing order entitled by its service to enjoy unique privileges.[2] In addition to a host of social benefits, officers enjoyed the right to wear side arms and to be judged by their peers in military courts. Once commissioned, even the newest Prussian lieutenant was eligible to attend court, regardless of the circumstances of his birth. Above all, officers felt bound by a unique code of honor that placed them above all other elements of society. Membership in this elite group was a privilege not to be extended to everyone.

A critical question for an individual's eligibility for membership in the officer corps, and even more for promotion to the generalcy, was his family's place in society as determined by its occupational activities. More, perhaps, than any other army in Europe, the Prussian army stubbornly resisted opening its highest ranks to officers whose family occupational backgrounds were unorthodox. As the Prussian general, military theorist, and writer Baron Colmar von der Goltz wrote in his widely read book *The Nation in Arms*, officers must come from the privileged social classes, which "exercise even in ordinary life a natural superiority over the masses."[3] This "natural superiority" is the key to understanding the social composition of the generalcy.

Prussia's army emerged from the Napoleonic wars triumphant over the external enemy but with an officer corps that was disturbingly heterogenous in its social composition and perhaps in its political views. An excessive number of officers of unusual backgrounds had flocked into the army from all over Germany. Some former French officers remained after the wars were over. These unacceptable officers, whose service had been a wartime necessity, were entirely anathema to the arch-conservative foes of those who would modernize and rationalize the army. The reformers, especially Boyen and Scharnhorst, courageously attempted to broaden permanently the social and political base of the officer corps. Like much of the reform program, their efforts on this point came to nothing. Throughout the 1820s the officer corps went through a purification process that restored the predominance of the traditional military families.[4]

Try as it might, however, the army never completely resolved the problem of maintaining the desired quality of the officer corps. At mid-century, Prince William, later King and Emperor William I, noted his concern that the "good elements" were leaving the officer corps and that no suitable replacements would be found.[5] Expansion of the army in the 1860s gave the king an additional reason for concern. Heavy officer casualties in the Franco-Prussian War further complicated the issue. After the successful wars of unification, the Prussian war minister expressed his fears that the army was being forced to rely upn "wider circles" for its officer replacement than had been the case in earlier years.[6] Solutions were not readily available. Just a few years before World War I began, War Minister Karl von Einem complained that sons of old officer families no longer desired to serve as officers and that rich parvenus were taking their places.[7] The central concern in each of these cases was the doubt that young men entering the army had grown up in families capable of instilling in them the proper attitudes toward state and society.

The old-Prussian types of replacements for officers traditionally relied upon and so eagerly sought after in the nineteenth century were sons of officers, landowners, and high bureaucrats.[8] These occupational groups produced officers who were politically reliable, who inherited strong monarchical traditions from their families, and who possessed the particular way of thinking desired by the kings of Prussia. As long as the army had been able to rely upon the nobility for its officer replacements, it had encountered no critical problems in finding men with acceptable social backgrounds. In the second half of the nineteenth century, however, this was no longer the case.

One must examine the occupational origins of the generals against this background. These successful officers represented the Military Cabinet's best efforts to promote preferred types of officers to the army's key command positions. The "alien elements" so feared by the army were substantially less successful in penetrating the generalcy than they were in becoming second lieutenants.[9]

Generals came from landed families in slightly more than one case in four (26.13%; Table 11). When all types of landowning fathers are considered together, there were no large variations between 1871 and 1914, although the percentage of landed fathers peaked in the decade 1882–92. Generals promoted after 1904 were less likely to have been sons of landowners than were their older counterparts in the second and third decades, but these generals showed no meaningful variation from the standards established by the generals promoted between 1871 and 1881.[10]

It is tempting, therefore, to conclude that about one general in four was of the rustic type of landowning family frequently pictured in German literature and historical writing. The complexity of landownership as an occupation defies such a simplistic conclusion. Many, indeed most, of the landed fathers also pursued careers in the army or in some part of Germany's bureaucratic structure. Only about one landed father in three (223 of 590) was engaged in purely agricultural pursuits.

Secondary occupational categories within the larger total of all landed fathers indicate substantial diversity. The proportion of landed fathers who were also officers dropped sharply from the decade 1871–81 (12.74%) to that of 1904–14 (5.04%). Landed fathers who were also civil servants increased from 4.24 percent during the decade 1871–81 to nearly 10 percent during the years 1893–1903, but likewise decreased after 1904.[11] During the same period, by way of contrast, the proportion of landed fathers without other occupations increased from 6.63 percent to 12.32 percent. The combination of these subgroups showed an overall slight decline after 1903. However concerned the army's leaders may have been over the shortage of old-Prussian types among the lower levels of the officer corps, the generals continued to be drawn from sons of landowners to about the same extent throughout the life of Bismarck's empire.[12]

Historians have long assumed as basic, even if statistically untested, a close relationship between the officer corps and Prussia's landowning aristocracy. A widely read biography of William II states that "most officers were drawn from the landowning class and lived on their peasants as well as on their pay."[13] Likewise, a recent study of Bismarck and Bleichröder states that German officers "came overwhelmingly from the old landed aristocracy in Prussia."[14] Frequently these judgments about the role of landed families hinge on the inexact term "Junker." Is it true, as has been argued, that the Prussian army was led by "Junker officers" or that this type of officer dominated the army?[15]

The problem of arriving at an accurate assessment of the relationship of the officer corps to Prussia's Junker class is all the more difficult because of imprecision and variation in the use and meaning of the term.[16] One

Table 11
Fathers' Occupations: Generals Listed by Decade of Promotion to Brigadier General

	Before 1871		1871–1881		1882–1892		1893–1903		1904–1914		Total	
	No.	%	No.	%	No.	%	No.	%	No.	%	No.	%
Landowner	10	5.56	25	6.63	46	10.70	54	10.11	88	12.32	223	9.98
Landowner/officer	26	14.45	41	10.88	47	10.93	34	6.37	33	4.62	181	8.10
Landowner/general	4	2.22	7	1.86	5	1.16	4	.75	3	.42	23	1.03
Landowner/civil ser.	7	3.90	16	4.24	22	5.12	51	9.55	46	6.44	142	6.35
Landowner/royalty	4	2.22	3	.80	4	.93	6	1.12	1	.14	18	.81
Landowner/business	0	—	0	—	0	—	2	.37	1	.14	3	.13
Landowner subtotal	51	28.35	92	24.41	124	28.84	151	28.27	172	24.08	590	26.40
Officer	59	32.79	142	37.66	130	30.24	141	26.40	168	23.54	640	28.65
General	44	24.44	72	19.10	61	14.19	73	13.67	79	11.06	329	14.72
Civil servant	23	12.77	55	24.59	97	22.55	140	26.22	188	26.34	503	22.50
Business	1	.55	8	1.12	9	2.09	12	2.25	57	7.98	87	3.89
Academic	1	.55	2	.54	2	.47	7	1.32	2	.28	14	.63
Lawyer	0	—	0	—	0	—	2	.37	6	.84	8	.36
Church	1	.55	4	1.06	4	.93	4	.75	28	3.92	41	1.83
Doctor	0	—	1	.26	0	—	1	.19	7	.98	9	.40
Foreign diplomat	0	—	0	—	1	.23	1	.19	1	.14	3	.13
Prussian diplomat	0	—	1	.26	2	.46	0	—	0	—	3	.13
Misc.	0	—	0	—	0	—	2	.37	6	.84	8	.36
Total	180	100.00	377	100.00	430	100.00	534	100.00	714	100.00	2,235	100.00

Note: Information complete on 2,235 (91.49%) of 2,443 generals.

scholarly study of a number of landed Junker families assumed that to qualify a family must possess, among other things, a title before 1888, property in the eastern provinces, Protestantism, and no close relationship with western German, Saxon, or the Mecklenburg aristocracies.[17] More recently a German historian has concluded that a Junker is usually understood as any east-Elbian noble but that this popular concept is too broad. That author's own definition appends possession of rural property to the popular definition of the term.[18]

In its application to Prussia's generals, the term by either definition is of questionable validity. As was pointed out earlier, only a bare majority (56.01%) of the generals were born in the eastern provinces, including many nonnoble generals who were in no way Junkers. An even smaller majority (52.80%) of the nobles held Prussian titles. This latter figure includes titles held by Prussian families from the western provinces. These families can hardly be considered Junkers; many were barely Prussian in their outlook and had very little in common with the eastern nobility. If one further stipulates that a Junker officer should be a member of an eastern landed family, as well as being a Prussian noble, the term clearly has little application to the generals. In fact, only about 70 percent of the propertied fathers in Table 11 owned land in the eastern provinces.[19] No more than one general in five, and probably fewer than that, may be properly termed a Junker if the word implies a family landed connection. Count Moltke's statement in the Reichstag that the number of officers who could possibly inherit property from their parents was "exceedingly small" was not far from the truth, at least for the generals.[20]

The army's relationship to the landed aristocracy was more complex than is usually assumed. Doubtless there is a kernal of truth in Ernest Bramsted's description of an officer corps formed of a "closed and elegantly aristocratic group in which especialy the younger sons of landed proprietors found their livelihood and profession."[21] Nevertheless, the statistical evidence now available clearly belies the assumption that these officers were in a position to dominate the army. Certainly they were a small minority among the generals. The availability of employment in the officer corps may have been more important to the families and individuals involved than were they to the army. It cannot be maintained that the officer corps was more dependent upon Junkers from landed families than it was upon any number of other groups. Landed families, on the other hand, frequently relied upon military or bureaucratic service for a portion of their livelihood.

A typical Junker may not have been an officer in the normal sense of the term. Unfortunately, there is no comprehensive study of the occupations pursued by sons of the eastern landlords. Lysbeth Muncy's limited examination found that whereas more than half the Junker men in her sample served as officers, fewer than one-fourth of them were career army men. Most Junkers served only a few years. They regarded the army as a "stop-gap, a congenial occupation with a salary," which they normally abandoned after a short time.[22]

In fact, substantial evidence shows that many Prussian officers recognized the ambivalent position of landed officers, who were usually not professionals and who were not very deeply commited to the army. This was the view, for example, presented in the unpublished memoirs of Ludwig von der Leyen, a guards officer in the early twentieth century.[23] Count Friedrich von der Schulenburg, a guards officer in the 1890s, recorded the same impression of many of his landed fellow officers.[24] Some career officers later spoke contemptuously of their landed colleagues who never had any intention of making the army a career. They were of but little use to the army, commented one officer bitterly.[25]

The highly visible and extravagant styles of living established by military playboys (landed and otherwise) undoubtedly affected the popular image of the officer corps. Cavalry lieutenants and other young officers from the guards regiments were prominent figures in the social life of Berlin. The public image of the officer corps may therefore have been largely shaped by these officers, many of whom were quite unprofessional in their military and career goals. Nevertheless, despite the public prominence of such officers, generals and regimental commanders were the dominant forces in the army, not lieutenants, regardless of the latter group's public displays of arrogance and opulence. However visible such Junker officers may have been, they were not typical of the upper echelons of the army.

Prussia's generals of the Imperial period were primarily drawn from families with traditions of military service. Sons of officers made the best officers, as the army viewed the matter. For the empire as a whole, more than half the generals (52.77%) were sons of officers.[26] These 1,179 fathers included 210 who were also landowners. Sons of generals, it might be said, made the best generals. Unfortunately, the relatively small size of the officer corps before 1860 and the tendency for generals to hold their posts for extended periods restricted the available supply of fathers who had been generals. There were simply not enough of these fathers to go around. Still, a remarkable 352 generals of the Imperial period (15.75%) were sons of men who had previously been generals.[27]

Although generals with such desirable fathers increased slightly between 1871 and 1914, they held a steadily decreasing portion of the generalcy. The same may be said of the sons of officers as a whole. Whereas their numbers increased from 1871 to 1914, their proportion of a more rapidly expanding number of generals declined from 70.04 percent of new promotions in the years 1871–81 to a much smaller 39.78 percent for the period 1904–14. This latter percentage was still the largest occupational subgroup within the generals and was more than half again as large as the corresponding figure for all types of landowners.

The Prussian army made no effort to hide its preference for sons of officers and did not hesitate to give young men from this background special consideration if they chose to pursue military careers.[28] A popular army handbook published in 1886 stated in unequivocal terms that sons of officers were considered better officer material than sons of men engaged in other professions. Sons of officers, moreover, were more likely to gain admission to the cadet corps and received special financial considerations if necessary.[29] The concern traditionally and officially shown by the army's highest officers has been mentioned with regard to officer selection and the preferential treatment accorded nobles. This same striving for homogeneity was the primary reason for the army's preference for sons of officers—a preference that began with the monarch and extended downward throughout the officer corps.

The sons of officers so preferred by the military establishment differed from their landed colleagues in more than merely occupational categories. Most generals who were sons of officers had fathers who possessed no other visible means of support beyond their official salaries. For the entire period, more than four generals in ten (43.37%) fell into this category, which experienced a steady decline from 1871 to 1914. Even in the last prewar decade, however, more than one general in three (34.60%) was of this type.

The issue is important because of the ambivalent nature of the economics of service as a Prussian officer. In many cases a military career was a considerable financial burden and therefore a privilege of the wealthy rather than a career pursued in a modern professional sense. Social obligations and expenses incumbent upon service in elite regiments were beyond the means of officers lacking considerable private incomes. Although a specific amount of private income was not required of officers by army regulations, in fact by late century most junior officers needed some source of additional revenue. Many regiments demanded evidence of substantial personal income as a condition of entry.[30] Uniforms, and frequently horses, were expensive and were to be provided by the officer as best he could. Although some of the officers from landless families received support from landowning relatives other than their parents, it seems likely that most were dependent upon their salaries and whatever their officer/fathers could provide from their usually limited resources.[31]

The position of an officer from a landless family differed significantly from that of a colleague who could rely upon his family's estates should his military career flounder. We have already noted that landless officers were frequently, if not always, more serious in their devotion to the officer corps than were many landed officers. Officers without independent means were bound to their king by far more than their personal oaths and traditions of monarchism. Landless officers and their sons were largely, if not entirely, dependent upon military pay. Although historians have rarely discussed the implications of this aspect of the relationship between the monarch and his officer corps, there can be no doubt of its long-term importance.[32]

An officer's career could be terminated at any point by an unfavorable efficiency report that might question his devotion to duty, his character, or his loyalty to the monarch, as well as his military performance. On questions of early dismissal or retirement, there was no appeal of the decision by the Military Cabinet. The unfortunate officer simply received a note informing him that he was considered unsuitable for further promotion. This was a not-too-subtle hint that he should request a voluntary retirement. Anyone not quick enough to interpret the message soon received orders to place his name on the next list of officers requesting separation.[33] Occasionally an involuntary retirement of an officer who was out of favor caused a sensation in the press, always, however, without any effect upon the case.[34] Normally the retired officer sank into oblivion and middle age to make ends meet as best he could.

As the percentage of landowners and officers declined, and as other types of fathers filled the gaps, the occupational background of the generalcy began to change. Civil servants, including those who owned land, increased in number after 1881 but reached a peak of 35.77 percent of new promotions in the period 1893–1903.[35] Although the absolute number of officers with fathers who were civil servants continued to increase, their proportion of the total fell slightly after 1903, a result entirely of a reduction in the number of fathers who were landowners as well as civil servants.

With regard to the continued dominance of old-Prussian types among the generals' fathers, it should be noted that virtually all of these fathers were civil servants of some distinction. Nearly all held positions in level (*Rangklasse*) IV or above; only an insignificant few were subaltern civil servants.[36] Broadly speaking, civil servants followed the pattern of landowners and officers among the generals' fathers. The proportions of all three old-Prussian types of fathers declined noticeably if not catastrophically in the later decades. This decline, however, was at a markedly slower rate than was generally the case among the officer corps.

By 1914 a few strange names appeared in the generals' sections of the Prussian Ranglisten. Their intrusion into the upper officer ranks capped the long process that had already transformed the lower levels of the officer corps and had at last become evident among the generals. Before 1870 these new types had been largely unacceptable. The son of a doctor, for example, could scarcely have hoped to become a Prussian general before 1870. Likewise, sons of businessmen increased from nearly total absence (.55%) among the generals promoted before 1871 to 57 (7.98%) in the decade 1904–14. Promotions of sons of doctors, lawyers, and clergymen also increased during the latter two decades although their totals remained at very modest levels.

It should not be surprising that even by 1914 there were so few sons of businessmen, doctors, and laywers among the generals. The generals from these backgrounds must have been extraordinarily capable officers, for they achieved their places only by overcoming a decades-long tradition of prejudice. A friend of Edwin von Mantueffel, General Hans von Schack, once described officers from such uncouth backgrounds as nothing more than wealthy peasants, who only in exceptional cases produced material useful for the officer corps. Certainly they produced a small number of generals.[37]

With regard to the fathers' occupations, it should be further noted that a large majority of the fathers were wholly or partially dependent upon government service for their income. Nearly two generals in three (65.86%) had fathers who were officers or civil servants without other visible means of income. These generals were at least two generations, and in many cases even further, removed from the land. Their percentage decreased somewhat between 1871 and 1914 but never fell below 60 percent. Nearly eight generals in ten came from fathers who were either officers or civil servants and landowners who also held these occupations. One can safely conclude that government service was characteristic of the vast majority of the generals' fathers and was far more prevalent than was entirely independent landownership.

The impact of bureaucratic or military professionalism on the nobility is a complex and little-investigated aspect of nineteenth-century German social history. This is despite its obvious relevance in Prussian and German history throughout the latter half of the century. Hans Rosenberg's classic study of the aristocracy before 1815 has shown that bureaucratic families and landowners frequently clashed over political and social questions.[38] The nineteenth-century familial drift away from the land and into government-related professions probably affected the world view of the families involved; however, few historians have directed their attention toward this interesting question.

Nevertheless, the neglect has not been total. At the very least, as one scholar has written, such dependence reinforced the power of the monarch and his government's ability to maintain political and ideological conformity among at least a portion of the nobility.[39] Muncy's study of a selection of prominent Junker families found that government employment eroded the individual's loyalty to his previous social group, "especially if his connection with his group had been weakened by his loss of landed property."[40] The families of most generals were largely dependent upon royal service and goodwill for their income; in the case of the generals themselves, much of their social position was also dependent upon the monarch's continued satisfaction with them.

The gradual decline in the percentage of nobles among the generals and the simultaneous increase of generals of less than perfect backgrounds were interdependent trends reflecting important changes in Prussian society as well as in the army. Before the Napoleonic era a noble, by the mere fact of his nobility, probably possessed an occupational background acceptable to the officer corps. The old patterns persisted long after the legal restrictions on occupational options for nobles were lifted. Even in mid-century, nobles who desired to maintain their social respectability had relatively few choices for employment of their talents and energies.

In contrast to these nobles, bourgeois families had a wide range of available occupations. Most of these, however, were unacceptable for a Prussian officer. Nevertheless, the bourgeois gentlemen who streamed into the army after 1860 significantly broadened the occupational background of the officer corps. They did the same for the generalcy, but to a lesser extent and only in the later years of the empire. In an effort to relate these changes specifically to the generals, social class has been cross-tabulated with the occupations of the generals' fathers.

Table 12 clearly demonstrates the very limited options available to noble families and the problems faced by the army when forced to promote bourgeois officers to brigadier general. Whereas nearly six counts in ten (58.53%) had landowning fathers, fewer than three knights (von) in ten (29.01%) and only about one bourgeois general in ten (11.30%) were so endowed.[41] Only a very few counts and barons pursued careers outside the acceptable old-Prussian occupations, as did very few knights. Bourgeois generals, however, frequently came from other types of families and only very infrequently from landed fathers.

The low incidence of landed fathers among the bourgeois generals is especially interesting in view of what has been termed the "pseudodemocratization" of the landed estates in eastern Prussia. Throughout the nineteenth century, and especially after 1873, an increasing percentage of the estates in Prussia passed from noble into bourgeois hands.[42] Nevertheless, only a very few (65) sons of bourgeois landowners became generals. If young men from these families had chosen to pursue military careers in a serious manner, they would have presented the army with a reasonable compromise between the need to promote bourgeois officers and the desire to draw upon traditionally reliable and acceptable social circles. Erich Ludendorff is probably the most famous son of a bourgeois landowner to have attained high military rank.[43] Relatively few men of Ludendorff's circumstances reached the ranks of the generals. Evidence on the point is very fragmentary, but probably sons of bourgeois landowners chose military careers in relatively few cases.[44] A few may also have received titles and thus appear as noble officers. Their numbers must have been quite small.

Bourgeois families therefore emerged from strikingly different types of families than did their noble colleagues. A very large percentage (40.88%) of the bourgeois generals were sons of civil servants without land—a

Table 12
Fathers' Occupations: Generals Listed by Social Class

Fathers' Occup.	Royalty & Mediatized		Count		Baron		von		Bourgeois		Total	
	No.	%	No.	%	No.	%	No.	%	No.	%	No.	%
Royalty	17	53.12	1	1.22	0	—	0	—	0	—	18	.81
Landowner	0	—	14	17.07	24	10.30	138	10.51	47	8.17	223	9.98
Landowner/officer	0	—	16	19.51	32	13.73	129	9.82	4	.70	181	8.10
Landowner/general	2	6.25	2	2.44	0	—	18	1.37	1	.17	23	1.03
Landowner/civil ser.	0	—	15	18.29	19	8.15	97	7.39	11	1.91	142	6.35
Landowner/business	0	—	0	—	0	—	1	.08	2	.35	3	.13
Officer	10	31.26	11	13.41	67	28.76	426	32.45	126	21.91	640	28.64
General	2	6.25	18	21.96	41	17.60	249	18.96	19	3.30	329	14.72
Civil servant	1	3.12	5	6.10	44	18.88	218	16.60	235	40.88	503	22.51
Business	0	—	0	—	1	.43	18	1.37	68	11.83	87	3.89
Academic	0	—	0	—	1	.43	3	.25	10	1.74	14	.63
Church	0	—	0	—	1	.43	7	.53	33	5.74	41	1.83
Lawyer	0	—	0	—	0	—	2	.15	6	1.04	8	.36
Doctor	0	—	0	—	0	—	0	—	9	1.56	9	.40
Foreign diplomat	0	—	0	—	1	.43	2	.15	0	—	3	.13
Prussian diplomat	0	—	0	—	0	—	3	.25	0	—	3	.13
Misc.	0	—	0	—	2	.86	2	.15	4	.70	8	.36
Total	32	100.00	82	100.00	233	100.00	1,313	100.00	575	100.00	2,235	100.00

Note: Information complete on 2,235 (91.49%) of 2,443 generals.

49

percentage five times as high as that for those who were sons of landowners without other occupations. Bourgeois generals were significantly less likely to have had fathers who were officers but were much more likely to have had fathers from business families. Given the dearth of nobles active in business occupations, it is not surprising that 68 of the 87 fathers in business or industrial occupations were bourgeois. All of these men possessed considerable personal financial resources and could be expected to uphold the conservative social order upon which the army based its strength. A sprinkling of academicians, lawyers, and doctors combined with a more substantial number (33; 5.74%) of clergymen to round out the occupational picture of the bourgeois generals' fathers.

Perhaps the most significant characteristic of the bourgeois fathers in Table 12 is their overall respectability. Although they showed a greater diversity than did the fathers of the noble generals, this group of fathers contained relatively few mavericks. It would probably be erroneous to consider almost any bourgeois father as a true old-Prussian type.[45] Nevertheless, nearly eight bourgeois fathers in ten (77.04%) were engaged in careers usually categorized as old-Prussian. Seen from this perspective, the influx of bourgeois officers caused only marginal changes in the social types among Prussia's generalcy.

Social preference based on a family's occupational background did not begin and end with an officer's father. In marginal cases career success or key promotions and assignments depended upon the paternal grandfather as well as on the father. The cases of Erich Ludendorff and Wilhelm Groener provide striking examples on this point. In 1908 the two officers, both colonels, were under consideration for the important General Staff position of chief of Operations. Their military capabilities seemed about equal and both were well suited for the position. Ludendorff was chosen because he had numerous officers in his family tree. The less fortunate Groener had no ancestors who had been officers. Ludendorff became chief of Operations, while Groener, the son of a paymaster, and not at all of the traditional officer class, became chief of Transport.[46] Ludendorff's case illustrates clearly that a good occupational background in the fathers' generation was enhanced greatly if earlier ancestors had served king and fatherland.

An occupational analysis of the generals' paternal grandfathers has been prepared along the same lines as for their fathers. Caution must be exercised in using Table 13 because of the large percentage of grandfathers whose occupations are unknown. Information is complete on only 1,515 (62.01%) of the 2,443 paternal grandfathers. The remaining 928 unknown grandfathers are heavily concentrated among the bourgeois families. Although the information on the grandfathers is not as definitive as was that for fathers, it is adequate for revision or confirmation of previous findings on family occupational background.

Table 13

Paternal Grandfathers' Occupations: Generals Listed by Decade of Promotion to Brigadier General

	Before 1871		1871–1881		1882–1892		1893–1903		1904–1914		Total	
	No.	%	No.	%	No.	%	No.	%	No.	%	No.	%
Royalty	8	5.63	4	1.56	3	.98	7	1.81	2	.47	24	1.58
Landowner	20	14.08	38	14.84	47	15.31	59	15.24	55	13.00	219	14.46
Landowner/officer	28	19.73	50	19.53	41	13.36	64	16.54	68	16.08	251	16.57
Landowner/general	0	—	2	.78	2	.66	7	1.81	7	1.65	18	1.19
Landowner/civil servant	29	20.43	27	10.55	43	14.01	59	15.25	52	12.29	210	13.86
Officer	21	14.79	58	22.66	79	25.72	83	21.45	102	24.11	343	22.65
General	10	7.04	14	5.47	16	5.21	28	7.24	24	5.67	92	6.07
Civil servant	20	14.08	43	16.80	55	17.92	60	15.50	76	17.97	254	16.77
Business	3	2.11	5	1.95	6	1.95	9	2.33	22	5.20	45	2.97
Academic	1	.70	2	.78	4	1.30	6	1.54	4	.96	17	1.12
Doctor	0	—	1	.39	1	.32	1	.26	0	—	3	.20
Church	2	1.41	10	3.91	7	2.28	4	1.03	9	2.12	32	2.11
Foreign diplomat	0	—	0	—	0	—	0	—	1	.24	1	.06
Prussian diplomat	0	—	0	—	1	.32	0	—	0	—	1	.06
Misc.	0	—	2	.78	2	.66	0	—	1	.24	5	.33
Total	142	100.00	256	100.00	307	100.00	387	100.00	423	100.00	1,515	100.00

Note: Information complete on 1,515 (61.01%) of 2,443 paternal grandfathers.

Paternal grandfathers had direct connections with the land far more frequently than did the generals' fathers. Nearly half the grandfathers (47.60%) were landowners, as compared to about one father in four (26.13%). Fluctuations in the incidence of landed grandfathers were remarkably similar to those of their sons, except among the grandfathers of the generals promoted before 1870. The number of landowning grandfathers decreased between 1871 and 1893, increased during the following decade, and declined again during the years immediately before World War I. Grandfathers, moreover, were more likely to have been landowners without other occupations (14.46%) than were the generals' fathers (9.98%). The number of landowner-only grandfathers increased slightly between 1871 and 1893 but decreased moderately during the final decade. Thus, in both generations the incidence of landownership showed a moderate but fairly constant decline.

Military grandfathers were present to approximately the same extent as were landowning grandfathers. Slightly fewer than half the grandfathers (46.54%) were officers, including 251 (16.57% of the 1,515 known cases) who were landowners as well. Among the families of the generals promoted after 1871, officer/grandfathers constituted a remarkably consistent percentage of the whole, for both grandfathers who were officers only and for those who were landowning officers. The generals' grandfathers, therefore, were officers in a slightly smaller proportion (46.54%) than were their fathers (52.77%).

Civil servants of all types were marginally more numerous among the grandfathers (30.63%) than among the generals' fathers (28.85%). Civil servants without land were also more common among the grandfathers than among the fathers, and the difference here probably has some significance, although its importance should not be overestimated. There was a tendency, present here also, for the families to move away from bureaucratic occupations and into the officer corps, culminating in a grandson who became a general.

With regard to nonagricultural and nonbureaucratic occupations, including the military, the grandfathers were even a more homogenous group than were their sons. The lack of complete information on the bourgeois families distorts the numbers of grandfathers in these occupations greatly. Doubtless many of the bourgeois grandfathers were doctors, lawyers, and businessmen of various types. For those grandfathers whose occupations are known, barely 1 percent were doctors, lawyers, or "miscellaneous." About the same percentage of grandfathers were of the Protestant clergy as was the case for the generals' fathers, a modest 2.11 percent of the total. Academicians were also very seldom to be found among the grandfathers, with fewer than 1 percent of them having been so occupied.

When grandfathers are considered as government professionals in the same manner as were the generals' fathers, the composition of the two generations differs substantially. Fewer than half the known grandfathers (789; 45.49%) were either officers or civil servants without land. Nearly two fathers in three are in this category. When landowners who also held military or bureaucratic posts are added to officers and civil servants, the percentage of grandfathers who were at least partially dependent upon government employment for their economic or social livelihood increases to 77.17 percent, about the same proportion as that for the generals' fathers. From this perspective, only the internal ratios varied. For both generations the generals were of families primarily involved in governmental service, secondarily from landed families and only very marginally from other groups. The trends among both grandfathers and fathers were toward reduced numbers of landowners and increased representation for occupations not previously considered as worthy of a Prussian officer.[47]

Cross-tabulation of the occupations of the generals' fathers and grandfathers produces a profile of the families over three generations. Table 14 presents a summary of occupational mobility in a number of families active in key occupations. The data therein may be cautiously used to arrive at estimates of occupational trends and mobility within the families. The numbers represent the total number of fathers in each category who followed grandfathers whose occupations are listed on the left. For example, 64 fathers who owned land (without other occupations) were themselves sons of men who were in the same occupational category. Only 64 generals, in other words, came from families in which purely landowning grandfathers were followed by fathers who were also landowners without other occupations.

In most cases, once a family became involved in the officer corps it was likely to remain so occupied. Far more grandfather/officers (336) were followed by father/officers than were any other category of grandfathers. A substantial 111 grandfather/civil servants (44.23% of the families with such grandfathers) were followed by father/officers, but only 43 grandfather/officers were followed by father/civil servants. Many families surviving on an officer's income could not have afforded to provide their sons the education necessary for most bureaucratic posts.

A similar trend is in evidence for landowners who were also civil servants. Only 44 generals had fathers who were landowners or landowner/officers and grandfathers who were nonlanded. Yet fully 192 generals had the reverse relationship, that is, grandfather landowners or landowner/officers and landless fathers who were officers. More than four times as many families moved away from the land into full-time military service as did the reverse.

The trend toward military service was even more marked with regard to other occupations. In only four known cases were grandfather/officers followed by fathers who are classified under the headings of business, academic, church, lawyer, or doctor. Three of these four fathers were clerics in the Evangelical church. On the other hand, 30 generals had

Table 14
Family Occupational Mobility: Grandfathers' and Fathers' Occupations, Selected Cases Only

Grandfather	Father		
	Occupation	No.	%
Landowner	Landowner	64	29.63
	Landowner/officer	38	17.59
	Landowner/civil serv.	30	13.89
	Officer	71	32.87
	Civil servant	10	4.63
	Business	2	.93
	Academic	1	.46
	Total	216	100.00
Landowner/officer	Landowner	40	14.39
	Landowner/officer	59	21.15
	Landowner/civil serv.	52	18.64
	Officer	112	40.19
	Civil servant	16	5.73
	Total	279	100.00
Landowner/civil servant	Landowner	28	13.46
	Landown/officer	35	16.82
	Landowner/civil serv.	52	25.00
	Officer	63	30.30
	Civil servant	28	13.46
	Academic	1	.48
	Church	1	.48
	Total	208	100.00
Officer	Landowner	14	3.35
	Landowner/officer	30	6.93
	Landowner/civil serv.	6	1.39
	Officer	336	77.60
	Civil servant	43	9.93
	Business	1	.23
	Church	3	.69
	Total	433	100.00
Civil servant	Landowner	10	3.98
	Landowner/officer	15	5.98
	Landowner/civil serv.	10	3.98
	Officer	111	44.23
	Civil servant	98	39.04
	Business	2	.80

Table 14 (continued)

Grandfather	Father		
	Occupation	No.	%
	Academic	2	.80
	Church	3	1.19
	Total	251	100.00
Business	Landowner	5	11.38
	Landowner/officer	2	4.55
	Landowner/civil serv.	2	4.55
	Officer	14	31.81
	Civil servant	9	20.85
	Business	10	22.73
	Academic	2	4.55
	Total	44	100.00

grandfathers in the latter five categories and fathers who were officers. Clearly the generals from these backgrounds represented families using the army as a method of attaining upward social mobility. Doubtless there were large numbers of lower officers who had military grandfathers and nonmilitary fathers. These officers were very unlikely to attain the rank of brigadier general or higher, even allowing for the large number of unknown cases.

The declining percentage of sons of landowners and the decline in landed connections generally should not blind the historian to the increase in the real number of landed officers over the decades. Probably the relative decline was simply a question of supply and demand. Just as there were not enough nobles to go around, neither were there enough sons of landowners, especially those who were true professionals, to keep pace with the expanded numbers of generals needed by the army.

5

Joining the Army: Finances, Education, and the Career Choice

Several basic factors are important both to a retrospective study of the social content of the generalcy and to a contemporary's decision to become an officer. Education in Prussia was closely linked to social status and income. The latter factors, in turn, were basic determinants both of an individual's eligibility to serve as an officer and of the type of career he would pursue. The decision to attempt a military career, then, included considerations of finances, education, and social status as well as personal interest in the army. These seemingly disparate factors, therefore, must be considered together as essential determinants of the social types most likely to have been successful officers.

A young man joined the army as an officer candidate in one of two ways. Graduates of the cadet corps chose the branch of service they wished to enter and requested a particular regiment. The Military Cabinet then assigned them to individual regiments according to the needs of the army. It was not bound by the expressed preferences of the cadets. Because the best regiments, especially the guards units, always had enough officers, the Military Cabinet normally assigned cadets to regiments chronically short of officer replacements. Only in special cases did the Military Cabinet assign cadets to guards units, usually only if their fathers had been killed while serving in the regiment or if their families were especially influential.[1]

A young man without a cadet's education applied directly to the commander of whatever regiment he wished to join. The commander was then free to accept or reject the application according to his personal evaluation of the applicant. This responsibility of ensuring that only suitable candidates gained admission to his unit was one of the most important duties of every regimental commander.[2] Control over who entered "his" regiment was also the most cherished and jealously guarded of all the prerogatives of a regimental commander. Karl Demeter has rightly termed this selection process the basic pillar of the entire army structure.[3]

If the candidate had relatives who were senior officers or who were in the regiment in question, an appointment in even the desirable regiments came easily. Otherwise, a potential officer had to search until he found a regiment for which he was suited. Count von Schlieffen, for example, originally gained admission into the elite Second Guard Ulan Regiment through the intervention of his father's uncle, Count Wilhelm von Stolberg-Wernigerode, then an officer in the regiment. A female relative who was married to a guards officer opened the door for Martin Chales de Beaulieu, who entered one of the elite regiments in 1876.[4] Although an exact estimate cannot be made, a large number of officers entered the army with the aid of well-placed relatives or close family friends.

Only one regiment was an exception to this procedure. All appointments to the First Foot Guards Regiment required an all-highest cabinet order. This regiment was the most elite of the genuinely military regiments and was the original unit for all Hohenzollern princes. William I customarily wore the uniform of this unit and referred to it as "my regiment."[5] The army was naturally quite concerned over maintaining quality among the officer candidates entering this particular aristocratic preserve.

After an officer gained the approval of the regiment's commander and passed the examination for that rank and for the rank of second lieutenant, his commission was then dependent upon the officers' "election." In this procedure the entire officer corps of the regiment affirmed by voting that the candidate was worthy to enter its midst. If one or more officers cast a negative vote, the candidate could not become an officer in that regiment. Although technically the case was then referred to the commanding general (corps commander) for final disposition, in fact the unfortunate candidate normally had lost all hope of becoming an officer.[6]

Once an officer was admitted to a regiment and had received a commission in that unit, he was likely to remain there at least until he attained the rank of captain, and in many cases until he either made major or had to retire. It was therefore especially important that officers find regiments for which they were suitable, which they could afford, and with whose officer corps they could live in at least minimal harmony.

Anyone considering a career as an officer had to ponder his financial position very carefully. This consideration, writ large for the entire officer corps, thus had a substantial impact on the latter's social composition. The army assumed that all officers would be prepared to meet certain expenses by drawing upon their own resources. Officers routinely incurred some costs that, while regarded as duty-connected and thus unavoidable, did not involve any financial support or extra pay from the paymaster. The special expenses varied with the type of regiment and with time but were broadly applicable to a large segment of the officer corps throughout the nineteenth century.

Officers had to purchase their own uniforms and maintain them in a fashion suited to their station in life. Regimental paymasters automatically deducted part of an officer's monthly salary to help pay for the necessary uniforms. A second lieutenant earning 75 marks a month in the 1880s lost 24 marks each month for this purpose.[7] Many officers, especially in the elite regiments, also purchased uniforms from civilian clothiers. For example, Count von Schlieffen's financial records indicate that in 1866 he spent at least 724 marks on uniforms at private clothing stores in addition to the mandatory deductions. He was at that time an adjutant in the elite First Guard Cavalry Brigade.[8]

Not all officers incurred expenses of this magnitude for their uniforms. Rabenau's last prewar officer's handbook estimated that a young officer needed about 24 marks a month for uniforms, or exactly what the army would deduct in any case.[9] This was, of course, applicable only to line infantry regiments. Cavalry officers and those serving in guards infantry regiments needed more money for uniforms. Such costs varied markedly from regiment to regiment, with the guards cavalry regiments stationed in Berlin and Potsdam being the most expensive. Some officers possessing only modest personal financial resources met their clothing requirements by using old uniforms either passed down or sold by older officers.[10]

Officers whose duties required them to own horses had to pay for them from personal funds. Not all officers, however, needed horses. An infantry officer in the rank of captain and below did not, unless he served as an adjutant.[11] All cavalry officers and most, if not all, officers in the field artillery had to purchase their own horses, which occasionally were ruinously expensive. A pair of the best steeds available might cost as much as 7,000 marks. This, however, was the upper range of the price of horseflesh. General Martin Chales de Beaulieu recorded that in 1881 he bought a good horse for 1,200 marks, of which the army advanced him 825. In 1902 another horse cost him 1,800 marks, "a relatively enormous price." Horse trading in the officer corps was a point upon which many an honorable gentleman came close to compromising his principles by selling his worn-out mounts to unsuspecting buyers at inflated prices in order to avoid financial loss.[12]

By 1914 the army had come to the rescue of officers in the cavalry and field artillery. Lieutenants occupying budgeted positions could obtain horses from their regimental stocks without charge. Each officer in these units also received about 16 marks a month for each horse to help defray costs. When a new horse simply had to be privately purchased, the army offered to advance up to 1,500 marks toward the purchase price.[13]

All officers to some degree faced the expenses involved in entertaining and in maintaining at least the minimal social standards appropriate for their regiments. The nature and amount of these costs varied with the unit. Service in the elegant guards units in the Berlin area entailed considerable outlays for entertainment; in small or remote garrison towns such expenses were much lower. Wealthy officers encountered few problems in paying for the fancy parties, dress uniforms, transportation in expensive carriages, and the other costs associated with good social conduct. Officers of modest means frequently felt obliged to keep pace with their more affluent colleagues and to return invitations, even if they could not easily afford to pay for such entertainment. The unfortunate results were often unavoidable. More than a few officers accumulated large debts in this manner, and occasionally a former officer bitterly denounced the entire system in later memoirs.[14]

In view of the inevitability of these and other expenses, a young man considering a military career had to consider carefully his personal financial resources. Especially in the lower officer grades, the monthly income simply did not suffice for many regiments. Pay remained relatively low in the junior grades throughout the nineteenth century. After the Napoleonic wars, second lieutenants received 51 marks a month in official pay. A first lieutenant received 75 marks a month and a captain, about three hundred. On this pay, as one historian has remarked, even a beer was a luxury.[15] In 1850 a second lieutenant received the same 51 marks a month.[16] Pay increases and conversion from the thaler to the mark changed the pay tables considerably by 1875. A second lieutenant in that year received 900 marks a year; a first lieutenant, 1,080 marks. Junior captains received 3,160 marks a year while senior captains were paid 3,600 marks. A general, by contrast, received 12,000 marks annually.

In addition to basic pay, the army established a complicated system of extra pay for living quarters and for certain assignments. A second lieutenant, for example, received between 216 and 540 marks a year for quarters and 900 to 1,164 marks for other expenses connected with his duty. Officers attached to embassies, military schools, and other positions received extra pay in varying amounts.[17] Normally the extra duty consumed virtually all these supplements. A young lieutenant, therefore, retained but little for himself after meeting all necessary expenses.[18]

Pay remained at this very low level without major changes until 1909. A new salary scale effective that year raised the basic pay for a beginning lieutenant to 125 marks a month. Senior first lieutenants received 200 marks monthly while captains received between 283 and 425 marks a month. Quarters allowances also increased, to amounts varying between 220 and 1,300 marks a month for lieutenants and captains.[19] Although junior officers did not become wealthy through the pay increase, their lot was eased considerably.[20] Lesser but still significant pay raises for captains and majors gave them what one officer described as "sufficient income."[21]

Official salaries were substantially higher than the prevailing wages of most German workers. In 1871 the average German industrial worker earned 500 to 750 marks a year and in 1913 about 1,300 marks. In 1900 about 87 percent of the Prussian taxpayers had incomes between 900 and 3,000 marks, roughly the same range as that for the lower-ranking officers without their private income and some official supplements.[22] Because many workers remained in the lower fringes of the latter income range, it is clear that officers were paid decently by moderate middle-class standards. The question of personal finances revolved around expenditures rather than intolerably low pay.

In addition to the financial demands discussed above, a young man considering a military career had to satisfy the sometimes vague and, fortunately for many, flexible educational requirements of the officer corps. The continuation of its minimal educational requirements were, in fact, a major part of the army's efforts to preserve the social homogenity of the officer corps. For many a youth hoping to become an officer, these same standards made the officer corps more attractive and more accessible than were numerous civilian and bureaucratic occupations. The generals' educational background is therefore both an important aspect of their collective biography and a further measure of the army's concern for social homogeneity. Especially for the generals, the roots of the question extend to the very early years of the nineteenth century.

Efforts of the Napoleonic era reformers to establish a rigid examination system resulted in a regulation of 1808 affirming the principles of knowledge and education as the basis of acceptance into the officer corps. Conservative elements within the army, not the least of which was Frederick William III, consistently frustrated all efforts to enforce this principle. Even after the experiences of 1806, the various divisions continued to sponsor their own schools for sons of active and pensioned officers. Young boys entered the division schools at the age of 14 and studied until ready to enter the army as officer candidates. It is now generally recognized that these schools were devices for giving virtually unschooled young men a mere pretense of education before granting them commissions.[23] Most were still unable to meet minimum educational requirements even after completing their respective courses of study. Because individual regiments controlled the acceptance of applications, except for cadets, the educational principles of the reformers came to nothing on this important point.

In early and mid-century the problem facing the army regarding education was simple to recognize but difficult to resolve. The higher the educational requirements demanded of officer candidates, the more difficult would be the army's task of filling the officer corps with old-Prussian types. Prince William, later King and Emperor William I, headed a commission founded in 1825 that proposed to abolish the lower levels of the obviously inadequate division schools and to demand a higher level of education for all officer candidates. Reliance solely upon education, however, would exclude many desirable social types. The commission therefore proposed that the government fund several hundred positions in *Gymnasia* all over Prussia for sons of poor officers.[24] If this proposal had been fully implemented, such replacements and the annual graduates of the cadet corps might have enabled the officer corps to replenish itself almost entirely from its own families, at least for a while. The government, however, did not provide funds for the positions, and the old system remained intact with no significant changes in the educational requirements. This meant, in effect, that semiliterate officer candidates could still join the army if they could find regiments willing to accept them.

Hermann von Boyen's second term as war minister saw renewed but unsuccessful efforts to demand higher educational attainments of officer candidates. In 1844 a regulation stipulated that young men wishing to become officers must possess the *Primareife* (certificate of eligibility for higher schooling) before they took the first examination for officer candidature. This meant that officers would have had to be eligible to enter the upper two levels of a Gymnasium (classical grammar school). This effort may be seen as a continuation of the reformers' efforts to wed the educated middle classes of Prussia to the throne. It would also have deprived many old-Prussian types of their commissions because, despite their ability to pass moderate examinations, many had no opportunity to attend a Gymnasium. Boyen further wished to favor those who held the *Abitur* (certificate of eligibility for study at a university) and probably even hoped eventually to make it a prerequisite for all officer candidates. All his efforts failed against a tidal wave of conservative opposition. A similar effort to liberalize the composition and education of the cadet corps also failed. Regimental commanders and the officer corps of each regiment retained full control over admission of officer candidates.

The first major step toward compelling all future officers to possess minimal educational skills came in a cabinet order of 1870 specifying that as of April 1, 1872, only those persons who possessed the Primareife could take the officer candidate's examination. Numerous exceptions were still allowed, with the objective of admitting old-Prussian types who attended the many private schools designed especially to prepare young men for the officer candidate examination. In 1899 William II ordered a strict enforcement of the primareife principle and a corresponding reduction in a number of exceptions. Nevertheless, between 1902 and 1912 more than 1,000 young men received dispensations from the educational requirements.[25]

Many of the generals entered the army long before the 1870 regulation demanding the Primareife, and virtually all the remainder became officer candidates before the army began to enforce it. Their educational backgrounds therefore represent what the Military Cabinet wished to promote, based on social considerations, rather than what the army might have had to accept if educational requirements had been enacted earlier and enforced consistently.

Nearly half the generals were graduates of the cadet corps (Table 15). The proportion of generals educated in these harsh military schools varied but little between 1871 and 1914. Considering the relatively small size of the cadet corps before 1870, and the rapid increase in the number of new officers after that year, the high proportion of former cadets among the generals acquires increased significance.[26]

By 1914 there were about 2,640 cadets in all, of whom about 240 entered the army each year. This was about 20 percent of the yearly intake of new officers, which stood at around 1,200 just before World War I.[27] Cadets became generals in proportions at least twice as great as their representation in the entire officer corps. Given the small enrollments in the cadet corps in the early years of the nineteenth century, the number of graduates among the generals is even more impressive.

The importance of the cadet corps in producing future generals and its role in establishing the academic climate of the army merit a closer examination of this fundamental military institution.[28] The reformers of the Napoleonic era had desired to abolish the cadet schools completely, "for the schools were really nurseries of class prejudice while pretending to give the sons of Junkers at least a modicum of education."[29] Likewise in the 1860s German liberals viewed the cadet corps primarily as the seedbed of the nobility in the officer corps and demanded its replacement by liberal educational institutions.[30]

The cadet corps consisted of a number of lower schools, *Voranstalten* (eight in all by 1914), and the main cadet school in Gross-Lichterfelde near Berlin. Students remained at the provincial schools through the *Ober-Tertia* and moved to the main cadet school for the *Sekunda* and *Prima* years.[31] The higher school offered a more intensive program of military instruction.

At the end of the Ober-Sekunda, cadets took the officer candidate examination and either entered the army in that rank or went on to the Prima. After two years and upon completion of the Ober-Prima, some cadets made the abitur and entered the army as officer candidates. The army predated their commissions to improve their positions on the seniority lists. Another group, about 10 percent of the total, became *Selektaner*. These were the elite of the cadet corps and frequently were its best officer material as well. This group spent a final year at the main cadet school in military training. At the conclusion of this final year they entered the army as second lieutenants.

The course of instruction in the cadet corps was roughly equivalent to that of a *Real-Gymnasium* although the academic standards were considerably less demanding than those of most Gymnasia.[32] Teachers in the cadet schools included some civilians of good reputations and

Table 15
Education: Generals Listed by Decade of Promotion to Brigadier General

	Before 1871		1871–1881		1882–1892		1893–1903		1904–1914		Total	
	No.	%	No.	%	No.	%	No.	%	No.	%	No.	%
Cadet corps only	82	45.55	167	44.06	200	44.34	208	43.97	320	47.06	977	45.17
Cadet corps and gymnasium	7	3.89	20	5.28	22	4.88	16	3.38	12	1.76	77	3.56
Gymnasium	29	16.11	103	27.18	59	13.08	69	14.59	73	10.74	333	15.40
University	5	2.78	15	3.96	12	2.66	19	4.02	20	2.94	71	3.28
Private	57	31.67	71	18.73	154	34.15	159	33.62	252	37.06	693	32.04
Realschule	0	—	3	.79	4	.89	2	.42	3	.44	12	.55
Total	180	100.00	379	100.00	451	100.00	473	100.00	680	100.00	2,163	100.00

Note: Information complete on 2,163 (88.54%) of 2,443 total generals.

63

appropriate training and many officers who were war invalids and whose academic credentials were at best questionable.[33] Seen from a purely educational standpoint, there can be no doubt that the cadet schools had numerous serious shortcomings.

One might well ask why parents would send their young sons to such a place as the cadet corps. The low expense of such an education was certainly a factor in many cases. While Gymnasia students paid tuition as well as fees for books, uniforms, rooms and board, and other items, the single fee of the cadet corps covered everything at a substantially lower cost to the parents.[34] Some parents sent their unruly offspring to the cadet corps in the hope that the iron discipline there would improve their study habits before it was too late. In some cases this tactic worked because Prussian military discipline could intimidate even the most boisterous child of 11.[35] Children whose academic talents were minimal sometimes found themselves in the cadet corps because teachers gave special attention to the poorest students if they were of the proper type of background.[36] The cadet corps was clearly without peer as a preparation for an officer's career.[37]

After cadets the second largest educational category among the generals was that of private instruction. This type of education defies precise analysis, especially for the years before 1870. Private instruction ranged from individual tutors of mixed quality to excellent formal schools and included the many shadowy institutes specifically designed to prepare ignorant young men for the officer candidate examination.[38] Some students doubtless received excellent educations in various kinds of private programs. Others were just as certainly quite poorly educated.

A small proportion of the generals carried their education into the Gymnasia of Prussia or even into a German university. Gymnasia students actually made up a smaller proportion of the generals promoted between 1904 and 1914 (who therefore entered the army in the early 1870s to 1880s) than of the generals promoted between 1871 and 1881. This may not be entirely correct, however, because some officers classified as having private educations may in fact have spent some time in Gymnasia. The basic consideration, however, is the very small proportion—certainly fewer than one general in four—with any exposure to the humanistic Gymnasia system.[39]

The army's emphasis on seniority, time in grade, and age at each rank discouraged potential officers from finishing a course of study in a Gymnasium. With few exceptions, most officers were commissioned by the time they were 19 or 20. Those who attended a university for any period of time, therefore, fell behind their contemporaries. Likewise, if a young man remained in a Gymnasium long enough to complete the Ober-Prima and receive the Abitur, he found himself three to four years behind officers of his same age who had entered the army earlier. About 76 percent of the

Gymnasia and Real-Gymnasia graudates of 1871–75, for example, were 19 or older.[40] Because they needed another one and one-half to two years before receiving a commission, their education jeopardized their military careers.

Capable officers were sometimes able to overcome these handicaps, but ultimately official assistance became essential. In 1900 the army began to predate the commissions of men who held the Abitur by up to two years to rectify the inequity.[41] None of the generals of the Imperial period benefited by this, however, because they had all received their commissions much earlier. Because it was so definitely to an individual's advantage to enter the officer corps as soon as possible, the seniority principle reinforced the army's practice of placing low priority on the educational attainments of its officers.

As has been noted, the Prussian army emphasized social standing and class over education. Because it also preferred a certain type of education over others, we might expect a corresponding correlation between educational and occupational background. About two-thirds of all generals whose fathers are classified as officers without other occupations attended the cadet corps. The corresponding percentages for sons of landowner-only fathers was 43.23 percent and that for civil servants a mere 28.18 percent. Sons of businessmen received their education in the cadet corps in fewer than one case in four (24.42%). Because sons of businessmen were overwhelmingly bourgeois, it is not surprising that most of them (58.13%) received some sort of private education. It may be assumed that these men had better educations than many of their noble counterparts with lesser financial resources although in most cases they did not significantly delay their entry into the army in order to advance their educations. That nearly one in four chose the academically inferior education in the cadet corps speaks powerfully for the importance of that institution and the willingness of this section of the bourgeois business community to trade excellence in schooling for early entry into the officer corps.[42]

We may conclude this section on the educational prerequisites for a military career by recalling a remark William I made in 1825. The future king and kaiser in that year approved a report submitted by a study commission headed by General von Witzleben that concluded in the testing of young men for officer material, mere knowledge was not sufficient because it would not measure the more important factors and might exclude the "better elements." The prince's attitude and that of the officer corps remained largely unchanged even up to 1914.[43] The army obviously concerned itself more with a man's social origins and his occupational background than with his education. The very minimal educational standards of the early nineteenth century eventually gave way to moderately higher demands, but these came too late to have had any effect on the generals and were never rigorously enforced. The best commentary on the role of education in a young officer's career is that nearly half the generals were products of the cadet corps.

In considering the educational and financial aspects of a military career, one must remember that the officer corps was attractive to differing types of young men for different reasons. Some had little choice because of their relative poverty; others, because of their exalted social position. Others entered for prestige, especially after 1870. Most generals, of course, joined the army before that final great triumph of Prussian arms.

In 1910 a retired Prussian lieutenant colonel argued that young men joining the officer corps could be divided into two categories. For a substantial number a military career was a foregone conclusion almost from birth. Officers in this group never seriously considered the possibility of pursuing a different path. A second type of officer chose a military career because at the particular time when he was called upon to make a decision, the army offered the best chances for success. Lieutenant Colonel von Trotha went on to remark that while the first type was usually a credit to the officer corps, the latter specimen, of a more diverse background, was frequently lacking in the proper motivation and attitude essential for an officer.[44]

Many of the 1,179 generals whose fathers were officers came from military families in which the officer's career had been the obvious choice. Erich von Manstein, later to become famous for his activities in World War II, was typical of such officers. His great-grandfather, grandfather, and father were officers, as were his four brothers. His mother's father and grandfather were officers. Her brothers likewise wore Prussian uniforms, and her younger sister married Paul von Hindenburg.[45] Brigadier General Oskar John von Freyend was a less famous but equally illustrative example. His father and paternal grandfather were officers. His grandfather married Ernestine von Freyend, an officer's daughter. Two uncles were officers. Of 15 male children born between 1770 and 1900, 13 served as career officers, including the general's brother and one son. The Stülpnagel clan provides yet another interesting example. Joachim von Stülpnagel, a young officer before World War I, had been preceded in the officer corps by his father, grandfather, and great-grandfather. His mother's father and grandfather were generals, in the former case Paul Bronsart von Schellendorff. Three brothers were also career officers.

Young men from these families grew up in surroundings totally dominated by the officer corps; frequently they never considered any other career. Paul von Hindenburg spoke for many of his military colleagues as well as for himself when he remembered that there had been no decision involved in his becoming an officer; it was obvious from his earliest days. General Maximilian von Versen likewise recalled that from his earliest days his desires centered solely on a military career.[46]

Military careers were attractive to many families for the simple reason that the education and military training required of an officer were relatively inexpensive. The cadet corps, the most efficient and perhaps the least expensive road to a commission, was particularly advantageous for military families. The Prussian army made a substantial number of positions available to sons of officers to assist them in following their fathers' footsteps. Numerous generals received state educations at no cost to their impoverished families, including such a distinguished officer and writer as General Count Colmar von der Goltz.[47] Young men whose families qualified for the budgeted positions thus found their route to an officer's commission as easy as the original decision to follow that path.

Military families unable to obtain budgeted positions in the cadet corps could, nevertheless, send their sons at substantially reduced rates. Tuition ranged from a high of 800 marks a year (about 1900) to as little as 80 marks, depending on the father's contribution to royal service.[48] Many cadets who were to become generals found this arrangement ideally suited for their socially acceptable but financially embarrassed families. A well-informed contemporary observer (1898) estimated that the expenses of education in the cadet corps totaled about 6,000 marks, from entry at age 11 until the gaining of the commission, including one to one and one-half years as an officer candidate.[49]

Even if an aspiring candidate did not attend the cadet corps, and most did not, an education sufficient for the army was appreciably cheaper than that required for most, if not all, civilian professions.[50] At no time did the Prussian army demand any university education nor even an Abitur of its officers.[51] Most good bureaucratic posts demanded university or comparable advanced schooling. The expenses of these preparatory years thus ran into the thousands of marks and were beyond the means of many families. Training for a legal career cost about 25,000 marks, that for a church career bout 15,000, and that for the medical profession about 18,000.[52]

Expenses, therefore, although a barrier to service in many regiments, were a key element causing families to send their sons into the officer corps rather than into the bureaucracy or even some private occupations. Count von Schlieffen, while advising his younger brother not to leave the army in 1868, pointed to financial considerations favoring the army over a bureaucratic career. His brother was better off in the army, Schlieffen wrote his mother, because the career was cheaper to prepare for, officers received higher pay than most bureaucrats, received quarters in most cases, and had better promotional possibilities. Schlieffen's family, moreover, could provide no more than 150 marks a month in private income—an amount entirely insufficient for a student at a German university.[53] Such considerations caused some young men to enter the army even though service as an officer was not their first choice. General Hermann von Holleben, for example, would have preferred to become a merchant. Because his family lacked the resources to prepare him for that career, he became an officer instead.[54]

Other financial factors also helped to make the officer corps a more attractive choice than many civilian occupations. An officer began receiving pay at age 18 or at most 20.[55] A legal student beginning in the bureaucracy could expect to receive a salary first about age 28 at the earliest. Clerics in the Evangelical church could expect pay at age 26.[56] The relative rapidity of thus achieving "an independent position in life" was an important advantage an officer held over his civilian counterparts.[57] An officer who received a commission at age 18 or 19 was active in his profession while his civilian contemporaries were still in the upper levels of the Gymnasia.[58] Military pay not only began earlier; it was higher than that for most comparable positions in the bureaucracy. A lieutenant general, for example, was approximately the equivalent to a civilian *Regierungs-Präsident* (district head of government). The maximum salary for the latter post was 16,000 marks in 1914 whereas a lieutenant general could earn as much as 19,250 marks a year.[59]

Officers enjoyed other advantages over their peers in civilian society. The tremendous prestige attached to the officer corps was a major factor in attracting young men into the military profession. Children from officers' families began to experience the deference accorded the uniform while still quite young. General Otto von Below remembered that on his first day at school in a small garrison town he was placed in the first row because as the captain's son he naturally had precedence over the other children.[60] The newest Prussian officer, whether noble or bourgeois, was *Hoffähig* (eligible to attend royal functions), whereas only bureaucrats in Rang-klasse II and up—the rough equivalent of a colonel—enjoyed this privilege as a result of their professional status.[61] This social advantage extended beyond the royal palace and far into society at large, giving an officer access to the best social circles. Officers were considered essential to many social functions, and hostesses vied with each other in attracting the dashing officers from the best regiments. The uniform and the officer's commission were indeed "a passport for the entire life."[62]

Much of the discussion of this and previous chapters raises the issue of the personal or family wealth of the generals. These men, ranging from the highest of the nobility to the respectable if unspectacular bourgeois families, were hardly of uniform financial backgrounds. Many were of substantial wealth whereas others came from impoverished families. In the army they faced both the routine financial demands common to all officers in all regiments and the potentially much greater expenses of the individual regiments. The question, then, is the role of private wealth in the careers of Prussia's most successful officers.

A recent study of German generals and their place in state and society has argued that young officers were absolutely unable to live on their military pay alone and that they remained in the officer corps only because their families could guarantee a monthly private income of varying amounts.[63] This impression has long been a common, although not entirely accurate, view of the officer corps.[64] The argument is not valid for all generals of imperial vintage nor, even more certainly, for the entire officer corps throughout the entire nineteenth century.

The amount of private income (*Zulage*) needed by a young officer varied considerably with time and even more with different units. In the most elite cavalry regiments stationed in Berlin and Potsdam, the monthly Zulage had to be fairly substantial. Prince Heinrich Schönburg-Waldenburg recalled that while he was a member of the Life-Guard Hussars during the early 1880s his parental allowance was 500 marks a month. Officers from his family normally received only 4,000 marks annually, so he was better off than most of his relatives. The lifestyle of these officers and their families may best be judged by the prince's insistence that such an income did not mean that they lived extravagently.[65] The figure of 500 marks a month for the guards cavalry has found confirmation in the memoirs of Baron Paul von Schoenaich, who served as a lieutenant in the Second Guards Dragoon Regiment during the same years.[66] By 1914 some exceptional units demanded the enormous sum of 1,000 marks a month. There were, however, few regiments with such exorbitant requirements.[67]

Because generals had been officers for more than 30 years before their promotion to brigadier general, and because many generals were promoted before 1880, the standards prevalent in 1914 have no necessary relevance to most of the generals. Indeed, nearly half the generals were in the lower officer grades in the 1830s and 1840s. They therefore escaped many of the severe financial problems encountered by later generations of officers. An accurate assessment of the issue for Prussia's generals thus requires a backward glance to the very early years of the nineteenth century.

In the period immediately following the Napoleonic and through the 1840s at least, most officers probably lived, though with difficulty, on their official pay alone. The guards units, infantry as well as cavalry, were exceptions. At a time when officers could live modestly or even in genuine poverty without feeling embarrassed by their meager financial resources, it was possible for sons of poor families to serve in the officer corps. In those cases where officers have recorded the amounts of Zulage they or their fellow officers received, the sums were usually quite small. Karl von Steinmetz, later a field marshal, received no money from his widowed mother and had to appeal to two aunts to assist in the purchase of his first uniforms. General Hermann von Holleben recorded that as a second lieutenant in the 1820s he had to exercise the strictest economy to live on his lieutenant's pay, which was his only income. He succeeded, he said, because as a member of a very poor family he was accustomed to such reduced circumstances. [68] Herman von Chappuis remembered that in the Second Guards Foot Regiment in the 1820s lieutenants had lived very modestly, because their maximum income was only 57 marks a month and the "majority had insignificant income from home."[69] This impression is confirmed by the example of General Count August von Werder, who manged to make ends meet in the First Foot Guards Regiment during the 1820s while receiving only a very small Zulage.[70]

The decades between 1850 and 1870 saw little change in most regiments although a gradual influx of officers from more prosperous backgrounds, especially in the guards units, had become evident. For example, General Lothar von Schweinitz received no money from his family while serving as a lieutenant in the First Foot Guards Regiment in the 1840s. He was forced to live very modestly. Despite depriving himself of many evening meals, he was able to remain in the army only by contracting debts.[71] General Max von Versen, in the very elegant First Guard Dragoon Regiment, survived on a very small and irregular Zulage. The resulting frugality forced upon him was the source of numerous embarrassments in front of his comrades.[72] Officers serving in line infantry regiments could still survive on very little private income, but with increasing difficulty.[73] Officers who were later to lead the army through the constitutional crisis and the wars of unification served in the lower ranks during the early decades of the century. Generals von Moltke, Edwin von Manteuffel, von Voigts-Rhetz, von Stosch, von Roon, and von Waldersee—all could count on very little or no financial assistance from their relatives during their early years.[74]

During the middle decades of the century, regiments began to acquire their own particular financial character to a much greater extent than before. Correspondingly, of course, branches of service did the same. This in effect meant that each branch of service came to be broadly characterized by relatively high or low Zulage demands. The cavalry was the most expensive branch, and within it, the guards cavalry regiments stationed in the capital. Artillery became the second most expensive arm, a result primarily of an influx of wealthy bourgeois officers who could not gain admittance to cavalry regiments and who desired to avoid the infantry. Of the three main branches, infantry was the least expensive, with the exception of the guards regiments, which could be fully as expensive as line cavalry units. Count von Schlieffen cautioned a cousin in 1863 to exercise care in attempting to join a guards cavalry regiment. Because of the expenses of service in the regiment as well as the costs of living among such well-to-do officers, only wealthy people should enter the guards cavalry regiments, he warned.[75] General von Lessel, in the 27th Infantry Regiment during the 1860s, recalled that few of his fellow officers had Zulage of more than 30 marks a month—only about one-fifth of Schlieffen's private income.[76]

Regimental commanders who were determined not to allow luxurious living in their units took extraordinary measures to enforce limits on Zulage. Otto von Hoffmann, who had himself received only nine to fifteen marks a month in the 1830s, became a regimental commander in the early 1860s. He allowed his officers only 30 marks a month in private income and confiscated any amount over that sum, returning it to the officer involved only when he went away from the regiment on leave.[77] This enforced modest standard of living was not exceptional. General von Verdy du Vernois recalled that in 1850 many officers in the 14th Infantry Regiment lived entirely without any support from home.[78] During this same period Lieutenant (later General) Eduard Leibert lived on 174 marks a year in a line infantry regiment stationed in Glogau.

Within a few years after the founding of the German Empire, the ever-increasing luxury in many regiments attracted the attention of the army's high leadership. War Minister von Kameke's memorandum of 1876, entitled "On Luxury in the Army and the Dangers Involved with It," addressed the problem very directly. Kameke complained that a few line infantry regiments were demanding a private income of at least 75 to 90 marks a month while many cavalry regiments had raised their requirements to 180 marks or even more. He went on to cite private income figures collected by the War Ministry for officer candidates during the years 1868 and 1874. For 1868, 376 (60.06%) possessed private incomes of fewer than 60 marks a month. Of a total of 626 officer candidates, 210 (33.55%) had private incomes of 45 marks or less; only 19 (3.04%) exceeded 150 marks a month. By 1874, of 642 officer candidates, only 176 (27.41%) had private incomes of 60 marks or less, while 57 (8.88%) had 150 marks or more.[79] Kameke was further concerned that some guards cavalry regiments expected their officer candidates to have 300 marks a month, while line cavalry regiments were demanding 150 marks in many cases.

Although the former chief of the Military Cabinet, Edwin von Manteuffel, noted his disagreement with Kamake's contention that luxurious living was much more commonplace than it had been in the earlier years, substantial evidence supports the war minister's statement.[80] As a corps commander in the 1870s General Hermann von Tresckow found it necessary to warn his regimental commanders against demanding excessive private incomes of incoming officers. Tresckow argued that excessive Zulage demands would deny commissions to officer candidates whose military potential was excellent but whose families were not wealthy. As a result, he said, too many sons of high finance and large industry would take the places of old-Prussian types. For wealthy people, he continued, the army was merely a sport.[81]

This, too, was the central concern of Kameke's memorandum. Only a few generals, he noted, could afford to send their sons into the cavalry. Officers from the social circles that had in past years provided the army with its best officers were then being replaced by wealthy men from less traditional backgrounds. Field Marshal von Manteuffel, himself from a modest background, noted his emphatic agreement with Kameke's statement that excessive demands of private income would have serious consequences for the army.[82]

Despite efforts of high officers and a warning from William II in 1890, luxurious living came to be an ever more prevalent characteristic of many segments of the officer corps. Symptomatic of this was the steadily increasing necessity for a large private income. Because the army continued to lack a universal regulation governing private income requirements, regiments continued to set their own standards. Max von Mutius, a lieutanant in a guards infantry regiment in Berlin in the 1880s, noted that his Zulage of 100 marks a month was sufficient for his own needs, but that it was relatively low compared to those of his comrades.[83] After 1880, graduates of the cadet corps understood that a Zulage of 150 marks a month was the minimum for any cavalry officer. This figure found confirmation in Vogt's semiofficial army handbook published in 1901 and in Firck's handbook of 1909. Both cited 150 marks as a fair guideline for cavalry officers.[84] In fact, by 1900 some cavalry commanders were informing the fathers of prospective officers that they should give their sons *only* 150 marks a month so that life in their units might remain simple and because many other officers had no such income.[85]

The army's efforts to prevent excessive demands of private income from excluding sons of officers, small landowners, and civil servants are an indication of the consequences of the rising expenses of service as an officer in the final years before 1914. Although lacking an official regulation, the War Ministry attempted to establish some guidelines on the matter. The two handbooks referred to earlier indicated that regimental commanders were under instructions to demand no more than the following amounts: infantry, 45 marks a month; artillery, 70 marks; and cavalry, 150 marks.[86]

These were only guidelines. Regimental commanders could disregard them with impunity and many apparently did so. In the *Garde-Schützen* (guards marksmen) battalion, stationed in Berlin-Lichterfeld, officer candidates had to show proof of a monthly income of 120 marks.[87] Guards infantry regiments in Berlin demanded 80, then 100 marks a month. Given the high prices of the city and the expenses of the regiments, this amount did not allow an extravagant standard of living, insisted one officer.[88] Some artillery regiments demanded 150 marks a month, more than twice the official guidelines.[89] Regiments stationed in the Rhineland were notorious for their wealthy young officers. Regimental commanders were hard pressed to prevent the sons of wealthy manufacturers and merchants from pursuing totally outlandish styles of living.[90]

It would be erroneous, however, to conclude that by 1914 all officers were from wealthy families or that they all had large private incomes. On the contrary most officers were of relatively modest means. Kurt von Bülow, an officer in a line infantry regiment about 1900, had only about 30 marks a month in private income. Many of his officer comrades, he reported, were entirely without Zulage, as was he after the death of his father.[91] Max van den Bergh also recalled that many officers survived with very limited private incomes. This meant dry bread for evening meals and problems in relations with officers who had more money. Still, many poor officers persisted.[92] Erich Ludendorff, another successful officer, later insisted that as a young officer he had very little private income and was basically left to his lieutenant's pay.[93] Erich von Manstein, a guards infantry officer in the period between 1906 and 1914, stated in his memoirs that many officers, even in the Third Foot Guards Regiment, were of no sizable wealth.[94]

Likewise, even in the cavalry not all officers were wealthy although all certainly had some private income. In speaking of the Third Kürassier Regiment, Ernst Köstring noted that his Zulage of slightly more than 300 marks a month made him a veritable Croesus in his regiment. Köstring went on to argue that in most cavalry regiments the officers lived modestly.[95] This was a relative standard, of course, and what was modest by cavalry standards was luxurious in many line infantry regiments. A study prepared for the Military Cabinet in 1908 concluded that a normal private income for infantry varied from a low of 30 marks a month to a high of 150 in the guard corps.[96]

If an officer candidate were of a family defined as "poor" by the upper-class standards of the officer corps, he might still become an officer and make it through the difficult years as a lieutenant by the strictest of economies. Rabenau's handbook printed a sample budget, based on a private income of 60 marks a month, which contained a surplus of 18 marks a month for savings. It went on to state that many officers lacked even this moderate income.[97] In such cases an even more restricted lifestyle was necessary and possible. Krafft's 1914 handbook informed aspiring officer candidates that an infantry officer could make ends meet with a monthly private income of 20 marks if he were prudent.[98]

Finally, it must be noted that throughout the nineteenth century, and up to World War I, determined men accustomed to living in relative poverty became successful officers without any income from their families. This was always difficult and became increasingly so during the later yeas of the empire. The army maintained a special fund to support men from very desirable families who would otherwise have been unable to serve as officers. The nature and size of this fund, the *Königs-Zulage* (king's subsidy), is virtually unknown today.[99] Max von der Leyen, in describing the fund (sometimes called the emperor's subsidy), stated that in the provincial regiments some officers survived on these 20 marks without any other private income.[100] Franz von Lenski stated that the fund was available only to sons of officers and that it was in the amount of 20 marks a month.[101] He was not entirely correct on eligibility; at least one general, Paul Von Heimburg, whose father was not an officer, is known to have used the Königs-Zulage.[102] One officer's wife, in describing her husband's infantry regiment in 1909, remembered that eight young officers were living entirely on the Kaisers-Zulage.[103]

One can only conclude that the anonymous author of *Das alte Heer* was correct when he said that within the officer corps the differences between rich and poor were much greater than those between noble and bourgeois. Opposite the wealthy guards cavalry officers of Berlin and Potsdam and the wealthy regiments in the Rhineland stood the poor infantry officers in the small eastern garrisons.[104] The enormous imbalance in the distribution of wealth within Imperial Germany was evident on a smaller and less tragic scale in the officer corps.

Most officers of the Imperial period, and certainly most generals, came from families accustomed to modest styles of living. Because the generals entered the army no later than 1885, they passed through their most difficult years before the expensive tastes common after 1900 became a critical problem. Young men with sizable private incomes always found an officer's career easier and more comfortable than did those whose families could not provide massive supplements to the army's pay. Especially in the early years of the century, many infantry officers had little such income or none at all. Totally impoverished officers could not hope to serve in the cavalry nor, by mid-century, in the guards infantry regiments. In this respect the army underwent a fundamental transformation between 1850 and 1900.

High financial demands were an additional guarantee that sons of lower-class families would not slip into the officer corps. Unfortunately, these same monetary standards eventually excluded many poor nobles or sons of officers without wealth. The army never fully extricated itself from this dilemma although the increased rates of military pay after 1909 helped. In this question, as in many others, the War Ministry remained powerless to prevent individual regiments and their commanders from establishing their own arbitrary standards. The entry requirements, both educational and financial, clearly achieved their goals of excluding undesirable social elements and in assisting old-Prussian types to enter the officer corps. At the very least, the standards provided the army with a sufficient supply of traditional types to allow the promotional system to maintain the basic homogeneity of the upper levels of the officer corps. The generals were living testimonials both to the merits and the faults of this system and its goals.

6

Getting Ahead:
The Road to the Generalcy

After the regimental commander had given his final assent and the officer corps had elected a young man to the regiment, the candidate at last received his commission and began his career as an officer. Only a small minority of those who received commissions completed the long road from the rank of second lieutenant to brigadier general. Failure to perform duty in a satisfactory manner was possibly the primary reason for early termination of careers, but other factors were also important. Unfavorable efficiency reports ruined many promising careers as did social failings. Excessive gambling and drinking, the accumulation of large debts, and poor judgment in the choice of a wife were frequent pitfalls for young officers.

As we have seen, cavalry was the most expensive and the most socially prestigious of the four basic branches. The *Guarde du Corps* (life guards), a cavalry regiment, was the most elite and the most expensive regiment in the entire army. Other cavalry regiments, especially the Life-Guard Hussars, the First and Second Guard Dragoon Regiments, and the Guard *Kürassiers*, stood clearly above the rest.[1] The cavalry retained its long-standing aristocratic character to a much greater extent than did the other branches. Cavalry officers maintained an elegant lifestyle appropriate to their social position in the army and society.[2]

The infantry prided itself in being the main weapon of the army, the kernel of Prussia's armed might.[3] Infantry was the largest branch, offered the most opportunities for promotion (until shortly before World War I), and was much less expensive than the cavalry or artillery. Considerable friction and jealousy arose between officers of the cavalry and infantry, and neither group hesitated to make its feelings apparent to the other.[4] Court balls were the occasion of great rivalries between the officers of the Garde du Corps and the First Foot Guards Regiment. Fights erupted between men of impeccable honor over the issue of who was to lead the first dance and to whom precedence belonged.[5] Infantry officers eventually became contemptuous of the expensive and militarily questionable cavalry regiments.[6]

Artillery traditionally served as the refuge of those whose social backgrounds were not good enough for the cavalry or the better infantry regiments. Cavalry officers looked down upon their counterparts in the artillery as the "misera plebs" of the officer corps.[7] Artillery officers naturally resented the social presumptions and arrogance of their rivals in the cavalry.[8] The low prestige attached to a career in the artillery was demonstrated by the practice of promoting artillery lieutenant generals to generals of infantry when they attained the rank of full general. Louis von Colomier, for example, became general of infantry upon his retirement in 1872, although he had never served in an infantry unit. Other generals whose branch was artillery became generals of infantry, including many who remained in active service in that capacity.[9] In fact, the artillery was for many years commanded by officers from other branches. General Theophil von Podbielski, who was general inspector of artillery from 1873 until his death in 1880, was a cavalry officer. Although he had a distinguished record in the Franco-Prussian War, his service as general inspector of artillery is most remembered for his ludicrous efforts to force the artillery to adopt all the drill exercises of the cavalry.[10]

Not all notables avoided artillery despite its lowly position. Some, such as Prince Krafft zu Hohenlohe-Ingelfingen, entered the artillery because their families could not afford the cavalry.[11] Count Adolf von Westarp, the brother of the more famous Kuno von Westarp, served in the artillery and became a brigadier general in 1909. Prince Friedrich of Saxe-Meiningen was a career artillery officer and pursued quite a normal career in that branch. The best aspect of service in the artillery was that numerical increases after 1889 created better promotional opportunities in the lower officer ranks than were available in the other two main branches.[12]

Little need be said of the engineers. Although a few generals made their careers in this branch, it was definitely at the bottom of the army in social standing, except for the "Strafftruppe" (penal units) of the trains, which produced no generals, and the supply officer corps, members of which were not really officers.[13]

Cavalry regiments produced a sizable proportion of the generals, although comparisons between the branches are difficult. About one general in ten (13.52%) entered the army in one of the Prussian cavalry regiments (Table 16). It is especially interesting that so few generals began their careers in the elite guard cavalry regiments. The 60 generals whose

Table 16
Original Unit: Generals Listed by Decade of Promotion to Brigadier General

	Before 1871		1871–1881		1882–1892		1893–1903		1904–1914		Total	
	No.	%	No.	%	No.	%	No.	%	No.	%	No.	%
Guard du Corps	5	2.79	2	.53	3	.64	0	—	0	—	10	.46
Guard Cav.	10	5.59	14	3.70	14	2.97	3	.63	9	1.32	50	2.28
Line Cav.	21	11.73	53	14.02	44	9.34	44	9.21	74	10.83	236	10.78
Guard Inf.	43	24.02	60	15.87	60	12.74	99	20.71	78	11.42	340	15.53
Line Inf.	71	39.67	143	37.84	199	42.25	219	45.81	362	53.00	994	45.42
Guard Arty.	4	2.23	12	3.17	8	1.70	8	1.67	9	1.32	41	1.87
Line Arty.	8	4.47	21	5.56	47	9.98	31	6.49	107	15.66	214	9.78
Engineers	7	3.91	24	6.35	22	4.67	14	2.93	26	3.81	93	4.25
Non-Prussian elite	3	1.68	11	2.91	19	4.05	8	1.67	2	.29	43	1.96
Non-Prussian infantry	6	3.35	31	8.20	42	8.92	47	9.83	12	1.76	138	6.30
Non-Prussian Artillery	1	.56	6	1.59	13	2.76	5	1.05	4	.59	29	1.32
Non-Prussian Engineers	0	—	1	.26	0	—	0	—	0	—	1	.05
Total	179	100.00	378	100.00	471	100.00	478	100.00	683	100.00	2,189	100.00
Cavalry subtotal	36	11.75	69	18.25	61	12.98	47	9.84	83	12.15	296	13.52
Infantry subtotal	114	63.69	203	53.71	259	54.99	318	66.52	440	64.62	1,234	60.95
Artillery subtotal	14	6.70	33	8.73	55	10.66	39	8.16	116	16.98	255	11.65

Note: Information complete on 2,189 (89.60%) of 2,443 generals.

77

first regiment was one of the eight or so guard cavalry regiments constituted 2.74 percent of the total number of generals and 25.42 pecent of those who began their careers in the cavalry.

Generals promoted after 1870 were substantially less likely to have been guard cavalry officers than were the hold-over generals promoted before that year. This was even more true of the most elite unit in the army, the Garde du Corps. Only five generals promoted during the imperial years began their careers in this entirely aristocratic regiment, and none who received promotions after 1893 had done so. This was despite the extraordinary social advantages of the regiment and the many opportunities to meet influential persons.[14] The paucity of such officers among the generals reinforces the possibility, examined earlier, that many officers in the best cavalry regiments were not serious career-minded professionals.[15] About one general in ten (10.78%) joined the army in a line cavalry regiment. The ratio for this group showed no significant variation between 1882 and 1914, though it fell slightly from the 14.02 percent for the decade 1871–81.

A variety of factors renders difficult any direct comparisons between the generals' original units. The time factor is one problem. Imperial era generals joined the army between 1830 and 1885. Changes in the number of the various kinds of regiments, in the authorized officer strengths of the regiments, and in the actual number of new lieutenants in each branch or regiment each year make all definitive judgments impossible. In 1900, for example, cavalry regiments were authorized 18 first and second lieutenants. Infantry regiments had an established strength of 52 such officers; artillery had 32.[16] The army usually had about two infantry regiments for each cavalry regiment and about two for each artillery regiment. Because each infantry regiment had about three times as many lieutenants as did cavalry regiments, one might logically expect the ratio of total infantry officers to total cavalry officers to be about six to one. These figures, of course, are approximations and do not consider the actual strength of the regiments or the probably higher rate of turnover among the lower ranks of the cavalry regiments. Seen in this light, nevertheless, line cavalry regiments contributed to the ranks of the generals in a ratio substantially higher than their numbers might suggest.

Most generals began their careers in infantry regiments. The proportion of generals whose first unit was an infantry regiment increased substantially from the first decade of the empire (53.71%) to its last (64.42%). This was entirely the result of a large increase in officers from the line infantry regiments. Guards infantry regiments contributed relatively fewer generals in the period 1904–14 (11.42%) than during the period 1871–81. Generals promoted in the years 1893–1903 were far more likely (20.74%) to have served in a guards infantry regiment during their initial years. These elite officers had joined the army while the Military Cabinet was headed by Edwin von Manteuffel, February 1857 to June 1865; Hermann von Tresckow, June 1865 to March 1872; and Emil von Albedyll, April 1872 to August 1888, all of whom had strong preferences for officers of old-Prussian origins.

Whereas about one general in seven (14.98%) served as an artillery officer, a somewhat smaller percentage (11.65%) began their careers in Prussian artillery regiments. The increasing importance of artillery and the improved promotional opportunities are reflected in the increase in the numbers and proportion of generals who began their careers as artillerymen. Only 6.70 percent of the pre-1871 promotions had first entered artillery regiments; by the final decade the corresponding figure had risen to 16.98 percent. As was the case with other guards units, the guards artillery provided a decreasing share of the generals and especially of artillery generals. For the 1871–81 period, nearly four artillery generals in ten (12 of 33; 38.71%) had begun their careers in the guards artillery, whereas by the decade 1904–14 their proportion had fallen to 16.08 percent (41 of 255). By 1914 there were proportionally far fewer positions available in the guards artillery than had been the case before 1870.

Officers who had begun their careers in non-Prussian regiments made up a substantial proportion of the total number of generals during the first three decades of the empire and quite naturally decreased after 1904.[17] Officers brought into the Prussian army from other contingents by the amalgamation process between 1866 and 1873 had by 1904, for the most part, either reached the rank of brigadier general or had gone into retirement.

The importance of the social desirability of some regiments over others is reflected in patterns of regimental selection among nobles and nonnobles. No bourgeois generals, as defined in Chapter 1, entered the army through the Garde du Corps, whereas ten noble generals found their initial acceptance in this regiment. About one noble general in seven (14.09%) joined a cavalry regiment to obtain his commission. This contrasted sharply with the corresponding figure of 5.15 percent for bourgeois generals. The cavalry remained a very aristocratic branch, especially when considered as a source of generals. Infantry, the second most socially desirable branch, attracted the lion's share of future noble generals (67.50%). Included in this total are the 23.02 percent of noble generals whose first units were one of the guards infantry regiments. Only about half the bourgeois generals began their careers in infantry regiments. Artillery units attracted relatively few nobles who later became generals (4,95%) but contained a substantial number of nonnobles (139; 26.18%) who eventually received titles and of those who remained bourgeois (46; 18.70%). The engineer arm was almost entirely a bourgeois branch. Fewer than one noble general in 50 served initially in the engineers, whereas nearly one bourgeois general in ten did so.[18]

For nobles lacking the income needed for service in the guards units or desiring a completely professional career, line infantry regiments provided a firm basis for attaining high rank. For bourgeois officers of sufficient means and education, infantry and artillery regiments provided the best opportunities, although a few bourgeois generals managed to enter the army through one of the cavalry regiments.

In 1884 Maximilian von Mutius completed his training at one of the army's schools for officer candidates and departed for his regiment, where he was to receive his commission in the rank of second lieutenant. He traveled relentlessly throughout the night, pausing neither for sleep nor for relaxation. The reason for his haste, he noted later, was not mere eagerness to begin his duties as an officer. By arriving at his regiment the day following the end of his school, he received his commission a day or two earlier than his classmates. He thereby acquired a permanent advantage in later promotions because he stood above them on the seniority lists.[19]

Similarly, in 1869 Field Marshal Count von Moltke advised two of his young nephews who were considering military careers to join the army immediately, without further delay. The reason for acting with dispatch, he informed them, was that each passing year brought scores of men into the officer corps, each of whom would have seniority over those who delayed. His advice proved fateful. In 1914 one of these nephews, Helmuth von Moltke, led the German armies into World War I.[20] These two examples are illustrative of one of the most basic factors in any officer's career: the seniority principle.

Radical changes in the strict seniority system governing promotions before the disaster in 1806 had been a main objective of Prussia's reformers. With considerable justification they blamed the army's excessive reliance on promotions based on seniority for producing the superannuated and incompetent officer corps that had fared so poorly against Napoleon. At one point the Military Reorganization Commission went so far as to propose that seniority be entirely eliminated as a basis for promotions and that it be entirely discarded among the general officers.[21]

On this question, as on that of an officer's education, Boyen and his liberal colleagues were unable to remove the source of the problem, although they did achieve important reforms. In the 1820s the army adopted the concept of conditional seniority as the basis for promotions within the ranks of the officers. The new system, established by a commission headed by the future King William I, reaffirmed the principle that seniority was to be the basis of promotions. Thereafter, however, only those officers whose performance was satisfactory and who were judged suited for higher command became eligible for advancement. To this end, annual efficiency reports were prepared for each officer. These reports, the *Qualificationen* (reports of qualifications), contained comments on an officer's character, military capabilities and performance, personality, and any noteworthy personal attributes. They also rated officers on their suitability for promotion to the next higher rank and command position.[22] These reports became the official basis for the vast majority of the promotion decisions rendered each year by the Military Cabinet.[23]

This attempt to fuse the seniority principle with an evaluation of each officer's efficiency met with considerable success but was not without its problems. The regimental system continued to dominate even this aspect of an officer's career because each regiment had its own seniority list up to the rank of captain. Naturally this produced great inequities among the regiments. Some officers benefited from the situation, while the careers of others languished. On the performance side, the system was entirely dependent upon accurate evaluations by the various regimental commanders.

Unfortunately for many young officers, their superiors did not devote sufficient time and effort to these essential documents. A cabinet order of 1867 sharply warned regimental commanders to show greater diligence in preparing their reports.[24] By 1914 there were frequent complaints that many commanders wrote all their reports in the superlative, lest they unintentionally injure the careers of the officers in their regiments.[25] The effect, of course, was to blur the differences between capable and mediocre officers, because the reports of both types were often indistinguishable. Commanders for their part complained that they were buried in mountains of paper work connected with the reports.[26] As a result, the Military Cabinet's basis of promotions was of doubtful reliability in many cases. The Military Cabinet in turn had greater freedom to promote or pass over officers on grounds quite other than their purely military capabilities.[27]

The combination of seniority and performance evaluation gradually produced an inflexible dividing line in the promotion system. In the early years after 1820, officers who had been passed over, and who thereby fell significantly behind their contemporaries, were not compelled to leave the army, although many did so.[28] Eventually, however, the army forced officers who failed to attain promotion simultaneously with their contemporaries to retire. This was the origin of the much-feared *Majorsecke*.[29] By mid-century this juncture of an officer's career had become the fundamental dividing point between success and failure. At the same time, however, rapid advancement was unusual, and most successful officers could count on promotions only at regular intervals.

Unfortunately for most, the intervals between promotions could be quite lengthy. In the early decades of the century, seniority-based promotions combined with a surplus of officers in the small Prussian army to produce years of waiting before the critical Majorsecke. In 1815 an average officer could expect to remain a lieutenant for ten or eleven years. A further five to six years were normally passed in the rank of captain. By 1835, however, the persistence of older captains and majors in remaining on active duty had greatly reduced promotional opportuniities for younger officers. Advancement became primarily a matter of endurance as an officer's name slowly advanced upward on the seniority lists. An average lieutenant in 1835 had to wait 21 to 22 years for his promotion to captain and an additional 14 or more years before his promotion to major.[30]

By 1871 several factors, including heavy battle casualties, had eased the situation somewhat. Edwin von Manteuffel forced large numbers of old officers into retirement, thus creating vacancies for capable younger men.[31] Roon's reforms and expansion of the army created additional opportunities for young officers to advance.[32] In 1867 new policies added greater flexibility to the promotion process. Combined seniority lists for each branch of service replaced the old regimental lists. Through the rank of captain, three-fourths of all vacancies were filled on the basis of seniority alone; the remaining open slots were filled by special accelerated promotions. Officers who in this manner superseded their contemporaries were normally transferred to new regiments, even if their own regiments also had vacancies.[33]

Promotion rates improved slightly after 1870 but stagnated in the 1880s before again improving just before 1914. Officers reached the upper ranks only after prolonged periods of service.[34] Near the turn of the century, an officer could expect to become a lieutenant in his second year of service but then had to wait eight to ten years before promotion to first lieutenant. An additional four to six years passed before he could receive a promotion to captain. The typical officer remained in that rank for an additional ten years. At this point many careers terminated at the Majorsecke.[35] Those who turned the corner and reached the rank of major remained in that grade five to six years. Successful lieutenant colonels required only one and one-half years to attain the rank of colonel. Colonels remained stationary for about four years. At that point they retired or entered the ranks of the generals.[36]

Some officers exceeded the standard rates of promotion and advanced beyond their contemporaries for a variety of reasons.[37] Princes from ruling houses naturally did not tarry many years in the lower ranks. Mediatized families, however, did not enjoy excessive advantages as a result of their exalted rank. Nor did all nobles holding the dignities of prince or count automatically bound rapidly past their contemporaries.[38] General Staff officers usually advanced at a more rapid pace than did ordinary officers, as did those fortunate to serve as aides to royal princes. War Ministry officers sometimes, but not always, received accelerated promotions. Their inability to maintain parity with General Staff officers was a source of continuing friction between the two groups.[39]

For the officer with above average ability but ordinary family background, the most efficient way to attain high rank was through the General Staff, whose officers routinely received rapid promotions. Many, if not all, of Prussia's most famous generals attained their high rank through many years of service as General Staff officers. Perhaps this accounts for the widespread impression that the General Staff was the only escape from the shackles of the seniority system and the only way to become a general. One officer went so far as to assert that the only way to escape the "oxen's tour" of the normal officer was to attend the War Academy and to serve on the General Staff.[40] Such prominent officers as Julius von Verdy du Vernois and Count Alfred von Schlieffen were also of the opinion that the only way to become a general and attain high position was through the General Staff.[41] At least two recent scholarly studies have repeated this judgment.[42]

As Table 17 indicates, the widespread view that only General Staff officers had successful careers is erroneous. Only 621 of the 2,161 generals for whom information is complete ever served on the General Staff in any capacity. Most of these, moreover, were not long-term General Staff officers. Included in the 327 with limited General Staff experience are many individuals who served only as *kommandiert* (attached) officers. Such men spent no more than three years with the General Staff in a trial capacity, to see if they were suitable for such duty. Many of these officers served for only a few months during the annual tactical problems.[43] They were not at the time considered General Staff officers and did not wear the General Staff uniform, even during their duty in Berlin.[44] Some of the 327 listed as having limited General Staff experience had more than this limited exposure. But in each case the individual's career was of such a nature that it does not warrant the designation General Staff officer.[45]

Career General Staff officers were always a small portion of the total number of generals (Table 16). For the empire as a whole only about one general in eight (13.60%) was a General Staff officer. The proportion of these generals increased moderately from the 12.00 percent among the hold-over generals promoted before 1871 to the 14.41 percent among generals promoted from 1904 through 1914.[46] In fact, some successful officers had no desire to serve on the General Staff. General Alexander von Kluck, for example, turned down an appointment to the General Staff in 1872 because he preferred to remain closer to his regiment.[47]

An issue closely related to General Staff service was that of an officer's military education. Beyond the initial and quite flexible educational requirements described in the preceding chapter, the army made only modest demands of its officers. The only army-wide educational institution was the War Academy, first founded in 1810 as the Universal War School.[48] As originally envisioned by Scharnhorst and Clausewitz, the Universal War School was to be a technical academy for teaching officers subjects directly relevant to their profession. This concept met with considerable opposition from those who wanted a school with more universal goals and broader subjects, as opposed to a narrow school modeled on the German polytechnical academy (*technische Hochschule*)

Table 17
General Staff Service: Generals Listed by Decade of Promotion to Brigadier General

	Before 1871		1871–1881		1882–1892		1893–1903		1904–1914		Total	
	No.	%	No.	%	No.	%	No.	%	No.	%	No.	%
Typical Gen. Staff career[a]	21	12.00	35	9.23	57	12.64	83	17.40	98	14.41	294	13.60
Limited Gen. Staff experience[b]	32	18.29	56	14.78	67	14.86	71	14.88	101	14.85	327	15.43
No Gen. Staff experience	122	69.71	288	75.99	327	72.50	323	67.72	481	70.74	1,540	71.27
Total	175	100.00	379	100.00	451	100.00	477	100.00	680	100.00	2,161	100.00

[a]Typical General Staff career means a career predominantly with General Staff duty, with the normal rotation between staff and line duty.
[b]Limited General Staff experience includes those with some minimal service on the General Staff in a career primarily in ordinary troop duty.
Note: Information complete on 2,161 (88.46%) of 2,443 generals.

format. The first director of the school was General Rühle von Lilienstern, a firm partisan of the group opposed to Scharnhorst and Clausewitz. Accordingly, therefore, in its early years the War Academy emphasized mathematics, philosophy, history, and allied subjects over the purely military part of the curriculum.[49]

General Eduard von Peucker, who headed the War Academy from 1866 to 1870, directed a decisive return to the concepts of Scharnhorst and Clausewitz. Military subjects expanded at the expense of the more general courses and became obligatory for all students. Pedagogically, the method of instruction moved away from university-type lectures to procedures emphasizing practical exercises and allowing more active student participation.[50]

As the General Staff became more directly involved with the War Academy, the goals of the school underwent another change. Rather than offering a general education for a wide variety of officers, the War Academy became oriented toward the preparation of General Staff officers. In 1872 the academy came under the direct supervision of the chief of the General Staff. Not without reason did informed observers by 1890 describe the War Academy as a General Staff Academy.[51]

There can be no doubt that the War Academy became a central institution preparing young officers for successful careers and specifically for the General Staff. The role of the War Academy in preparing men for becoming General Staff officers has never been fully explored, although one recent historian has mistakenly stated that "nearly all senior officers had passed through the War Academy."[52] As will be seen (Table 18), it is also erroneous to maintain that after 1872 entry to the General Staff was "exclusively through the War Academy."[53]

Although attendance at the War Academy was hardly a prerequisite either for the General Staff or for attainment of the rank of general, the school was an important part of the careers of a large number of Prussia's generals. For the empire as a whole, slightly more than one general in three (34.01%) attended the War Academy. The proportion of generals with this education increased considerably between 1871 and 1914. Whereas barely one-fourth (26.96%) of the generals promoted between 1871 and 1881 had passed through the War Academy, about four generals in ten (40.79%) of those promoted after 1904 had done so.[54] An additional 82 generals were either in non-Prussian contingents during their early years as officers or for some other reason were not eligible for the War Academy. Under ordinary circumstances many of these officers would have attended. There were no such cases among the generals promoted after 1904, when attendance at the War Academy acquired increased importance.

The selection process for admission to the War Academy was a mixture of the traditional reliance upon the regimental system and the Scharnhorst

Table 18
War Academy Attendance: Generals Listed by Decade Promoted to Brigadier General

	Before 1871		1871–1881		1882–1892		1893–1903		1904–1914		Total	
	No.	%	No.	%	No.	%	No.	%	No.	%	No.	%
Yes	69	40.35	93	26.96	110	26.80	156	32.26	277	40.79	705	34.01
No	102	59.65	252	73.04	299	73.11	313	66.74	402	59.21	1,368	65.99
Total	171	100.00	345	100.00	409	100.00	469	100.00	679	100.00	2,073	100.00

Note: Information complete on 2,155 (88.21%) of 2,443 generals. Eighty-two generals had careers that precluded such an assignment, including many officers whose early years of service were in non-Prussian contingents. They have been excluded from Table 18 entirely.

Table 19
Military Education: Generals Listed by Original Unit of Service

	War Academy		No War Academy Training		Total	
	No.	%	No.	%	No.	%
Garde du Corps	3	37.50	5	62.50	8	100.00
Guard Cavalry	14	29.17	34	70.83	48	100.00
Line Cavalry	63	27.28	168	72.72	231	100.00
Guard inf.	134	40.24	199	59.76	333	100.00
Line inf.	370	37.68	612	62.32	982	100.00
Guard arty.	12	29.27	29	70.73	41	100.00
Line arty.	67	31.75	144	68.25	211	100.00
Engineers	16	17.39	76	82.61	92	100.00
Non-Prussian	26	21.49	95	78.51	121	100.00
Total	705	34.11	1,362	65.89	2,067	100.00

Note: Information complete on 2,154 (88.17%) of 2,443 generals. Eighty-seven generals have careers disqualifying them from consideration in Table 19.

ideals of emphasis on an individual's ability. A young officer desiring to further his career by studying at the academy had first to obtain the consent of his regimental commander. In granting the officer permission to apply for admission, the regimental commander certified that he was of good character and was suitable for this privileged assignment. The candidate then took the entrance examination in competition with officers from other regiments. Normally many more applied than could be admitted. The examinations covered history, mathematics, geography, military subjects, and French. Officers who failed to score high enough for admission could take the examination again the following year. A third attempt was not allowed. Many who failed to qualify the first time were successful on their second attempt.[55]

Although nearly all officers could in theory attend the War Academy if successful in the very competitive examinations, some applicants had better chances of acceptance than did others. Officers serving in the better regiments, particularly the guards units in the Berlin area, enjoyed significant advantages over those of their colleagues who toiled in the distant provincial garrisons. A regimental analysis of the generals who attended the War Academy and those who failed to gain admission (Table 19) further demonstrates the important differences between the various regiments and branches of the Prussian army.

Generals who spent their early years in cavalry regiments were significantly less likely to have attended the War Academy than were generals whose careers originated in most other types of units. Fewer than one guards cavalry general in three (30.36%) attended the War Academy. An even smaller proportion (27.27%) of the generals from line cavalry regiments passed through the academy. This is especially interesting because for many years following its founding, the War Academy automatically accepted all cavalry officers who applied for admission. This practice, which ended sometime before 1870 as competition for the available positions increased, was necessary because the nearly universally poor educations of cavalry officers left their regiments sorely in need of more learned officers.[56] Generals from most other types of units, whether elite or not, attended the War Academy in large numbers. Generals who entered the army in guards infantry regiments had the highest incidence (40.24%) of education in the War Academy. Those whose first units were line infantry regiments studied at the War Academy in nearly two cases in five (37.68%). The percentages of guards artillery officers (29.27%) and line artillery units (31.75%) indicate that on the whole artillery regiments were just as likely to have attended this military school as were their social superiors in the cavalry.[57]

When the generals are grouped according to their branch rather than by their first regiment a similar pattern emerges. Service in the non-cavalry branches was much more closely related to attendance at the War Academy than was the case for the cavalry.[58] The percentage of infantry generals who attended the War Academy increased steadily from the 28.23 percent among the 1871–81 promotions to 46.01 percent for the final decade.[59] During every decade the percentage for infantry officers was higher than that for cavalry officers, and was usually substantially greater. Artillery officers likewise were consistently more likely to have attended the War Academy than were cavalry officers, but only until 1904. Increased promotions in the artillery outstripped the available supply of officers with War Academy educations. Attendance at the War Academy was never very significant for engineer officers. The considerable fluctuation within their ranks during the final three decades reinforces the impression that success in this technical branch was but slightly related to the type of military education offered by the War Academy.

Limitations of the data and the scope of this study do not allow a conclusive statement on the composition of the War Academy. Nor does Table 19 necessarily prove that any particular percentage of officers from each type of regiment attended the school. Many, if not most, officers who attended the War Academy did not attain the rank of major general and thus do not appear in Tables 18 or 19. There are no studies of the composition of the student body of this important military institution.[60] It would appear, nevertheless, that the social policies of the regimental system had the indirect effect of favoring some types of officers over others, when and if officers from good units made the effort to attend the academy.

The advantages held by officers from regiments stationed in favorable locations were related both to their geographic disposition and to the nature of the units themselves. The guards regiments frequently had a surplus of lieutenants and could therefore exempt officers from duty to prepare for the examinations.[61] Officers stationed in Berlin, moreover, could attend lectures at the university and could draw upon a wide variety of materials for their studies. The intellectual climate of the city, with the War Academy and the General Staff as well as the university, was itself a stimulus to officers preparing for the academy.[62] In some guards infantry regiments, especially the Second Foot Guards, all or nearly all lieutenants took the examinations with the active encouragement of their superiors. Units stationed in other large cities offered similar advantages to aspiring young officers.[63]

The well-recognized advantages of officers in the better units and especially in the guards regiments may have given noble officers an advantage over their bourgeois colleagues. One recent historian has concluded that the admissions process may have been the object of tampering to ensure noble predominance. He has further asserted that contemporaries regarded the examinations with suspicion.[64] Although this would conform nicely with the army's well-known preference for promoting nobles to high positions, the available evidence hardly supports such a claim. Officers who graded the examinations were aware of the applicant's unit only, not his name. After 1893 even this information was withheld. This alteration in the grading procedure produced no significant changes in the proportion of officers accepted from the elite units.[65]

Aristocrats and others from elite units were overrepresented in the War Academy because their garrisons in Berlin or other large cities facilitated better preparation for the examinations. The army sponsored preparatory lectures for officers in the Berlin area. Provincial officers could take correspondence courses supplemented by occasional lectures, but these inadequate measures did not significantly improve their chances. Contemporaries were nearly unanimously of the opinion that officers in remote garrisons had very poor prospects on the entrance examinations.[66]

An examination of the relationship between social class and attendance at the War Academy does not indicate an excessive predominance of aristocratic types among the generals who studied there. Noble generals, regardless of unit and branch, attended the War Academy in about one case in three (33.58%).[67] Bourgeois generals had studied there in about the same ratio (34.80%). In the early decades of the nineteenth century, nobles constituted about one-half of the total number of officers. Their proportion declined thereafter, however, until in 1913 only about 27 percent of the lower-ranking officers were nobles.[68]

About twice as many noble generals (452) had studied at the War Academy than had bourgeois generals (253). Considering the heavy concentrations of nobles in guards regiments and other units in advantageous garrisons, this ratio of nobles to bourgeois is less impressive than at first glance. In the latter decades, moreover, newly promoted bourgeois generals came increasingly from the War Academy. Promotions during the final decade show no significant variation between nobles (40.82%) and bourgeois generals (40.76%). These generals were lieutenants in the 1880–90 period when bourgeois officers probably outnumbered nobles by approximately two to one. Nobles, therefore, did enjoy an advantage, but not one entirely out of proportion to their concentration in favorable garrisons. Unless more information becomes available on a larger number of War Academy students, including those who failed to attain the rank of brigadier general, the historian cannot properly maintain that deliberate favoritism and maladministration were evident in the War Academy's selection process.

Because neither the War Academy nor General Staff duty was characteristic of most Prussian generals, the question arises as to just what kinds of careers most did pursue. More detailed information on this point is contained in Table 20.

Elite units provided a declining percentage of Prussia's generals during the Imperial period.[69] On the one hand, nearly two in five (38.33%) of the hold-over generals had served primarily in elite units, even more than in line infantry regiments. By the final decade, however, this type of career was characteristic of only about one general in five (20.09%).[70] Ordinary infantry regiments, on the other hand, produced generals in moderately increasing percentages between 1871 and 1914. This is hardly surprising because very large numbers of officers served in line infantry regiments.

The socially less desirable units substantially increased their share of the generals as the decades passed. Still, only about one general in eight (12.00%) served primarily in artillery assignments. The increase in this type of general from only about one in twenty (5.55%) of the hold-over generals to about one in six (15.70%) among the final decade's total promotions reflected the increasing importance of artillery and the improved promotional opportunities for men with the appropriate skills. Engineer careers, on the other hand, were slightly less numerous among the generals promoted after 1904 than had been the case in earlier decades.

Among those generals whose careers were spent primarily in service other than with regiments, only the General Staff officers were numerically important. The steadily increasing numbers of such officers among the generals is hardly surprising considering the increased size of the General Staff and its influence within the army. Nevertheless, General Staff types

Table 20
Types of Careers: Generals Listed by Decade of Promotion to Brigadier General

	Before 1871		1871–1881		1882–1892		1893–1903		1904–1914		Total	
	No.	%	No.	%	No.	%	No.	%	No.	%	No.	%
Elite units	69	38.33	132	24.84	130	27.31	150	27.74	142	20.09	623	27.29
Line inf.	67	37.22	151	39.84	194	40.76	227	41.96	313	44.28	952	41.70
All arty.	10	5.55	32	8.44	66	13.87	55	10.17	111	15.70	274	12.00
Eng.	8	4.44	13	6.07	22	4.62	15	2.77	28	3.96	96	4.20
Gen. Staff	22	12.22	35	9.23	57	11.97	82	15.16	98	13.86	294	12.88
War Min.	0	—	5	1.32	5	1.05	3	.55	8	1.13	21	.92
Tech.	1	.56	0	—	0	—	3	.55	2	.28	6	.26
Adj./Hof.	3	1.68	1	.26	1	.21	6	1.10	1	.14	12	.53
Trains	0	—	0	—	1	.21	0	—	4	.56	5	.22
Total	180	100.00	379	100.00	476	100.00	542	100.00	707	100.00	2,283	100.00

Note: Information complete on 2,286 (93.57%) of 2,443 generals. Three generals are classified as having special careers not applicable to Table 20.

were only slightly more numerous in the final decade (13.86%) than they were among the hold-over generals (12.22%). These figures strongly reinforce the earlier conclusion that becoming a full-fledged General Staff professional was of great value to any individual but was hardly essential for a successful career.[71]

The War Ministry was hardly a favorable place for an enterprising officer to spend his career. Only 21 generals, less than 1 percent of the total, served primarily in the War Ministry. Given the extended conflicts between the War Ministry on the one hand and the Military Cabinet and the General Staff on the other, the failure of these officers to reach the ranks of the generals is understandable. Many influential officers, moreover, regarded the War Ministry as an administrative agency, a dumping ground for "specialists" and "technicians." These latter terms were derisively applied to persons not entirely suitable for military careers.[72]

Only a very few officers reached high office through technical careers. Although such men were generals in every sense of the term, they were in no way typical Prussian officers. They did not normally move back and forth from their specialties to troop duty, as did General Staff officers. The career of one of these generals, Ernst Lehmann, is illustrative of this point. Lehmann attained the rank of brigadier general in 1911. He had not attended the War Academy, nor had he enjoyed duty with any other special army agencies. His entire career was spent in weapons research. Lehmann reached the top because of his work, first, on the 1888 rifle, and, subsequently, on machine gun development. Another general, Wilhelm von Flotow, was one of the very few noblemen to be found in this purely technical type of career. Both Lehmann and von Flotow were rare specimens among Prussia's generals.[73]

Most of General von Flotow's aristocratic friends found technical careers of all types beneath their dignity. The army's ingrained social prejudices could only reinforce the nobility's disdain for such activities. Aristocrats, therefore, tended to pursue careers appropriate for their social standing and, as a consequence, are not randomly distributed among the various career categories (Table 21).[74] For the entire period, noble generals pursued careers classified as "elite" and "line infantry" in approximately equal proportions (38.09% and 39.96% respectively). Within these overall figures, however, some interesting changes are evident. The proportion of noble generals with elite careers declined substantially from a high of 44.04 percent of new promotions during the decade 1871–81 to a much smaller 31.09 percent during the final decade. Those with line infantry careers increased from 35.26 percent among the hold-over generals to 44.56 percent for the period 1904–14. Elite units thus provided successful careers for a decreasing percentage of the noble generals.

Table 21
Types of Careers: Generals Listed by Social Class and by Decade of Promotion to Brigadier General

	Before 1871		1871–1881		1882–1892		1893–1903		1904–1914		Total	
	No.	%	No.	%	No.	%	No.	%	No.	%	No.	%
Noble Generals												
Elite units	68	43.59	122	44.04	118	39.33	140	37.63	120	31.09	568	38.09
Line inf.	55	35.26	102	36.82	107	35.67	145	38.99	172	44.56	581	38.96
Arty.	5	3.21	12	4.33	26	8.67	15	4.03	29	7.51	87	5.84
Eng.	3	1.92	6	2.17	9	3.00	6	1.61	4	1.04	28	1.88
Gen. Staff	22	14.10	30	10.83	36	12.00	59	15.86	59	15.28	206	13.82
Other	3	1.92	5	1.81	4	1.33	7	1.88	2	.52	21	1.41
Total	156	100.00	277	100.00	300	100.00	372	100.00	386	100.00	1,491	100.00
Bourgeois Generals												
Elite units	1	4.35	10	9.80	12	6.82	10	5.85	22	6.88	55	6.94
Line inf.	10	43.47	48	47.07	87	49.43	81	47.37	144	45.00	370	46.72
Arty.	5	21.74	20	19.60	40	22.73	40	23.39	82	25.62	187	23.61
Eng.	5	21.74	17	16.67	13	7.39	9	5.26	24	7.50	68	8.59
Gen. Staff	1	4.35	6	5.88	21	11.93	25	14.62	35	10.94	88	11.11
Other	1	4.35	1	.98	3	1.70	6	3.51	13	4.06	24	3.03
Total	23	100.00	102	100.00	176	100.00	171	100.00	320	100.00	792	100.00

Note: Information complete on 2,283 (93.45%) of 2,443 generals.

93

Historians have made much of the nobility's tendency to concentrate in a relatively few elite units after 1870, allegedly using these sheltered regiments as aristocratic oases in an unpleasant bourgeois landscape.[75] This argument contains an important element of truth. However, there were relatively few such units, and they offered succor to only a few noble officers. As has already been noted, many of these aristocrats, especially in the cavalry regiments, were not serious officers in any case. Also, the very archetype of the Prussian officer, the former cadet, normally had little chance of finding an assignment in these regiments. Simply as a matter of sheer numbers, indeed, most nobles had no chance to serve in the elite regiments preserved for nobles. By concentrating playboy types and the wealthiest of the aristocracy in a few regiments, in fact, the system may have reduced their influence in the army while making them more visible to society at large.

Ordinary nobles, sons of officers and civil servants, and members of impoverished landed families had little chance of entering these units. Yet these types were the backbone, and even the majority, of the officer corps at the highest levels. Much research is still to be done on this point, but clearly the available evidence suggests that elite units dominated the army only in its public image.[76] Certainly the elite units did not provide a dominant share of the army's highest officers.

Old prejudices were slow in dying, especially when one considers the careers other than elite and line infantry among the noble generals. General Staff service among noble generals increased only marginally from the hold-over generals (14.10%) to the generals promoted after 1903 (15.28%). The latter figure was half again as large as that for 1871–81.[77] Only 35 noble officers reached the generalcy through careers classfied as artillery or engineers, or other service. Noble officers who did not qualify for the General Staff and who could not afford the cavalry had little choice but to pursue careers in line infantry units. They did so in ever-increasing numbers, although elite units continued to attract at least one in three even during the final decade.

Career patterns of bourgeois generals reflect their limited opportunities in many regiments and their corresponding predominance in the technical branches. During the entire period only 55 bourgeois generals (6.94%) served primarily in the cavalry or guards infantry regiments (Table 21). This was about one-sixth the proportion of noble generals with this type of career. Whereas only about one noble general in twenty (5.84%) pursued a career in the artillery, nearly one bourgeois general in four (23.61%) did so. In neither case did the career patterns among bourgeois generals show any significant change from 1871 to 1914. Bourgeois generals with line infantry careers increased slightly from the hold-over generals (43.47%) to the 1882–92 promotions but declined slightly be the decade 1904–14 (45.00%). About seven times as many bourgeois as noble generals came up in the engineers. General Staff careers, by contrast, were marginally less numerous among bourgeois generals (11.11%) as among their noble counterparts (13.82%).[78]

Career patterns on the whole provide another example of the importance of social divisions within the officer corps. Although ability was important in almost any officer's career, it is also clear that his social class had an important influence on the type of assignments he received and on the type of career he could hope to pursue.

In addition to social and purely military factors, the road to the generalcy was influenced by an officer's choice of a wife. Indeed, a poor choice of a nuptial partner might compromise or terminate even the most promising career. Just as not every young man was suited to serve as an officer, not every woman was worthy of becoming an officer's wife. Measures available to the army to prevent officers from acquiring unacceptable wives ranged from social pressure to outright legal prohibition of certain marriages.

In any consideration of marriage, the young officer had to bear two factors in mind. First, he had to be able to support a wife by meeting minimum private income requirements prescribed by army regulations. Equally important, he had to find a woman whose family circumstances were acceptable to the officer corps of his regiment and to the army. Failure to satisfy both requirements meant either continued bachelorhood or termination of his military career. Officers, in short, had to be prudent in their choices of mates and certain of their personal finances.

Marriage patterns among these wives demonstrate the complex role played by wives in a successful career. Noble generals tended to find noble spouses, although the practice was by no means universal. On occasion noble officers married above or below their station in the aristocratic order of rank. Whereas 108 generals held the rank of count or higher, only 89 wives were in that elevated category. In a similar fashion, 238 generals held the rank of baron, but only 128 wives were of that rank, including 24 who were married to bourgeois generals. Slightly fewer than one-third of all noble generals (32.58%) married bourgeois ladies. Because the percentage of noble generals with nonnoble wives varied only slightly, it would seem that the generals had no more difficulty in finding noble wives in the last prewar decade than during the years 1871–81.

Although the financial aspects of marriage will be discussed in detail later, the issue might profitably be mentioned at this point. The acquisition of bourgeois wives was closely related to the search for ladies of means to buttress shaky noble fortunes. Wealth could compensate for many a shortcoming in the bride's bloodline. Certainly there was nothing new in the practice, which could benefit both parties. Early in the nineteenth centry, King Frederick William III, noting the good social relationship between the officers of one of his cavalry regiments and a group of ladies

Table 22
**Wives' Social Class: Generals Listed by Class and Decade of Promotion to Brigad
ier General**

	Noble Generals		Bourgeois; Title after Promotion		Always Bourgeois		Total	
	No.	%	No.	%	No.	%	No.	%
Before 1871								
Royal & med.	6	4.55	0	—	0	—	6	3.90
Princess	1	.76	0	—	0	—	1	.65
Countess	7	5.30	0	—	0	—	7	4.55
Baroness	9	6.82	1	33.34	2	10.53	12	7.79
von	67	50.75	1	33.33	5	26.32	73	47.39
Bourg.	40	30.30	1	33.33	11	57.89	52	33.77
Foreign	2	1.52	0	—	1	5.26	3	1.95
Total	132	100.00	3	100.00	19	100.00	154	100.00
1871–1881								
Royal & med.	3	1.24	0	—	0	—	3	.90
Princess	0	—	0	—	0	—	0	—
Countess	15	6.22	0	—	0	—	15	4.48
Baroness	23	9.54	0	—	3	5.66	26	7.76
von	119	49.39	4	9.76	14	26.42	137	40.90
Bourg.	79	32.78	37	90.24	34	64.15	150	44.77
Foreign	2	.83	0	—	2	3.77	4	1.19
Total	241	100.00	41	100.00	53	100.00	335	100.00
1882–1892								
Royal & med.	4	1.54	0	—	0	—	4	1.05
Princess	0	—	0	—	0	—	0	—
Countess	15	5.77	0	—	0	—	15	3.93
Baroness	27	10.38	3	5.56	1	1.47	31	8.12
von	128	49.24	6	11.12	19	27.94	153	40.05
Bourg.	81	31.15	45	83.32	47	69.12	173	45.28
Foreign	5	1.92	0	—	1	1.47	6	1.57
Total	260	100.00	54	100.00	68	100.00	382	100.00

Table 22 (continued)

	Noble Generals		Bourgeois; Title after Promotion		Always Bourgeois		Total	
	No.	%	No.	%	No.	%	No.	%
1893–1903								
Royal & med.	5	1.46	0	—	0	—	5	1.07
Princess	0	—	0	—	0	—	0	—
Countess	15	4.37	0	—	0	—	15	3.21
Baroness	39	11.37	4	7.55	4	5.56	47	10.04
von	165	48.11	13	24.53	10	13.89	188	40.17
Bourg.	113	32.94	36	67.92	57	79.16	206	44.01
Foreign	6	1.75	0	—	1	1.39	7	1.50
Total	343	100.00	53	100.00	72	100.00	468	100.00
1904–1914								
Royal & med.	2	.57	0	—	0	—	2	.31
Princess	1	.28	0	—	0	—	1	.16
Countess	15	4.25	0	—	0	—	15	2.34
Baroness	30	8.50	4	8.16	2	.84	36	5.62
von	172	48.73	9	18.36	28	11.72	209	32.61
Bourg.	120	33.99	36	73.48	208	87.03	364	56.78
Foreign	13	3.68	0	—	1	.42	14	2.18
Total	353	100.00	49	100.00	239	100.00	641	100.00
Total all decades								
Royal & med.	20	1.50	0	—	0	—	20	1.01
Princess	2	.15	0	—	0	—	2	.10
Countess	67	5.04	0	—	0	—	67	3.38
Baroness	128	9.63	14	5.79	10	2.44	152	7.68
von	651	48.99	60	24.79	49	11.98	760	38.38
Bourg.	433	32.58	164	67.77	348	85.09	945	47.73
Foreign	28	2.11	4	1.65	2	.49	34	1.72
Total	1,329	100.00	242	100.00	409	100.00	1,980	100.00

Note: An additional 216 generals were bachelors at the time of their promotion to brigadier general. Information is complete for 2,196 (89.89%) of 2,443 generals.

from well-to-do bourgeois families, commented that "Meine gelben Kürassiere lieben die Fonds, und die Queslinburger Damen die vons."[79] Eventually the issue became more serious than humorous. One prewar observer, writing in a semiofficial history of the army, complained that the practice of marrying into extreme wealth by many officers was one of the main factors contributing to the increasingly extravagant standards of living in segments of the officer corps.[80]

Especially interesting is the high incidence of noble wives among the bourgeois generals. About one nonnoble general in five (20.34%) married a noblewoman, including 24 ladies holding the rank of baroness. Bourgeois officers won noble ladies from a variety of backgrounds. Friedrich Lange, a cavalry officer, married Countess Olga von Wrangel in 1882. Her father was of the Russian branch of the Wrangel family and had a distinguished career as a Czarist civil servant and diplomat. Other bourgeois oficers also found wives from distinguished aristocartic families. Paul Reichenau, while still a captain, married Magdalena Baroness von Plotho, whose father was a landowner and Landrat (official at the "Circle" level of government) in Prussian Saxony.[81] Lothar Heinzel, promoted to brigadier general in 1910, married a Countess Grote while still a first lieutenant. Her father was a civil servant, holding the exalted title of Geheimer Ober-Regierungs Rat (high assistant to district president) and also served as a Landrat.[82] Other bourgeois families were graced by prominent noble names, including von Below, von Krosigk, and von der Groeben.[83]

Although the percentage of bourgeois generals with noble wives may not at first glance be impressive, it must have been many times higher than the percentage among bourgeois males as a whole. It is especially noteworthy when one remembers that most of the weddings took place when the future generals were at most captains or majors. If a young noblewoman could not find a suitable spouse from the aristocracy, marriage to a bourgeois army officer was probably her best social prospect. In this respect the proportion of bourgeois-noble marriages probably reflects the prestige of the officer corps as well as bourgeois access to prospective brides in the aristocracy.

A sizable proportion of the generals had no wives at all. A total of 216 generals were bachelors at least until after their promotion to brigadier general. This total included 166 nobles (11.10% of the known noble generals) and 50 bourgeois generals (7.13% of the known cases). The financial demands of married life doubtless contributed to this high proportion of bachelors among the generals.[84]

A formidable procedure confronted those desiring to take a spouse. All officers needed the king's permission to marry. This request went initially to the regimental commander, who was free to approve or disapprove the prospective bride. He might also disapprove because of some factor in the officer's personal life. The request then went up the chain of command through the corps commander to the War Ministry.

The paper work necessary for the official approval included information on the bride's family name, the "class" of the father (his occupation), any previous husbands, for divorced women the grounds for the divorce and the necessary legal documents, information on the bride's "origins, upbringing, and education," and, finally, proof of a sufficient private income to support the marriage.[85] These regulations had their origins in cabinet orders of 1798 and 1802 and remained basically unchanged throughout the nineteenth century.[86] By 1900 such archaic regulations sometimes aroused intense resentment among younger officers.[87]

The most important of these requirements was the test for financial resources sufficient for a married Prussian officer. About 1900 a lieutenant had to show proof of a private income of at least 2,500 marks a year. Captains had to provide 1,000 marks annually beyond their official income. From the rank of major upward, there were no army-wide minimum requirements, although the regimental commanders retained their rights to set their own standards. Income derived from landed property, rural or urban, from mines, factories, and mercantile interests were acceptable only if the documents proved that the undertaking averaged the minimum income for at least the five previous years.[88] Either the officer or the prospective bride could provide the income. If a third party supplied the funds, a further agreement had to be concluded to guarantee to continue the education of the children of the marriage.[89]

Poorly paid officers frequently married women of less than perfect social standing whose financial assets compensated for other faults. Indeed, wealthy wives were a much sought-after commodity. Few officers were as skilled at heiress-hunting as was General Baron Gottlob von Scheffer-Boyadel. His first wife, the daughter of a wealthy industrialist, left him a fortune of 2 million marks. If that were not enough, his second wife supplied an additional 9 million marks from her father's vast fortune in the chemical industry.[90] In a similar fashion, General Hans von Winterfeldt married a certain Karoline von Bohlen und Halbach, sister of the industrialist Krupp von Bohlen und Halbach. On a lesser scale the future general Wilhelm Groener's marriage in 1899 was possible only because his wife had inherited considerable wealth from her father's business interests. Large numbers of officers were thus dependent upon their wives' resources to satisfy the official demands of private incomes.[91]

As was the case with the generals, occupational background was as important a factor as class in any assessment of their wives' social position. The search for eligible women produced a group of wives whose family backgrounds (Table 23) differed considerably from those of the generals. This is strikingly the case with regard to landownership. Slightly more than one-third of the wives (35.78%) were daughters of landowners, including 270 (19.52% of the total 1,383) who were without other occupations. This latter figure was nearly twice as high as that for landowner-only fathers of the generals (Table 11). Landed fathers among the generals' wives peaked during the decade 1882–92 and declined slightly by 1914. The large number of bourgeois wives in the "unknown" category probably causes the incidence of landownership to appear higher than it was in reality. As more of these fathers' occupations are identified, the overall percentage of landowners will doubtless decline somewhat.

Officer/fathers, by contrast, were much less common among the wives' fathers than among the generals' own fathers. Fewer than one wife in three (30.80%) had officer/fathers. Only about one wife in four (24.15%) came from a purely military family. This contrasts sharply with the 43.47 percent of the generals' fathers who were officers without other occupations.

Again relying on the same categories for the wives' fathers as were used for the generals' own families, it is apparent that government professionals were less common among the former group. About one wife in four (27.91%) came from a purely bureaucratic family. Fathers who were officers added another 24.15 percent for a total of 720 (52.06%) wives from families dependent upon government service for their livelihood. The corresponding figure for the generals' fathers was 65.86 percent.

Although many officers were forced to seek out women whose own resources would satisfy the army's requirements, the financial factor did not produce a large number of wives from undesirable occupational backgrounds.[92] Only about one wife in ten (9.47%) came from a business family. The academic, legal, and medical professions likewise produced only a handful of wives for Prussia's generals.[93] Diplomatic wives were rarities, but they could be quite valuable.[94]

Obviously most, if not all, generals found wives who measured up to the army's standards of social respectability. They did so for good reasons and could hardly have become generals had they failed. Officers whose female companions were of disreputable character were not encouraged to continue such relationships and could not bring such women into the distaff side of the officer corps. In extreme cases, persistence resulted in an early involuntary retirement. Count Ferdinand von Rhode, for example, was forced to leave the First Foot Guards Regiment in the 1860s when he insisted on marrying an unacceptable woman. Otto von Below remembered that even a general could be forced into early retirement because of an unsatisfactory marriage.[95] Usually such involuntary separations were masked by official explanations based on "health problems" to avoid indiscreet inquiries into the army's private business.[96]

Substantial wealth, even if slightly tainted, was a sufficient compensation for otherwise grave shortcomings. Although unbaptized Jews were not admitted to the officer corps, women of baptized Jewish families were

Table 23
Wives' Fathers' Occupations: Generals Listed by Decade of Promotion to Brigadier General

	Before 1871		1871–1881		1882–1892		1893–1903		1904–1914		Total	
	No.	%	No.	%	No.	%	No.	%	No.	%	No.	%
Royalty	6	4.38	3	1.17	3	1.12	3	.88	3	.79	18	1.30
Landowner	13	9.49	37	14.40	65	24.25	72	21.12	83	21.83	270	19.52
Landowner/officer	11	8.03	14	5.45	14	5.22	18	5.28	25	6.58	82	5.93
Landowner/general	3	2.19	3	1.17	0	—	3	.88	1	.26	10	.72
Landowner/civ. serv.	11	8.03	21	8.17	19	7.09	29	8.50	29	7.63	109	7.88
Officer	23	16.79	40	15.56	40	14.93	38	11.14	47	12.37	188	13.59
General	19	13.87	30	11.67	25	9.33	34	9.97	38	10.00	146	10.56
Civ. serv.	35	25.54	74	28.78	82	30.60	100	29.34	95	25.00	386	27.91
Business	9	6.57	23	8.95	13	4.85	32	9.38	48	12.63	125	9.04
Business/landowner	2	1.46	1	.39	0	—	1	.29	2	.53	6	.43
Academic	1	.73	1	.39	2	.75	3	.88	0	—	7	.51
Church	2	1.46	4	1.56	1	.37	3	.88	0	—	10	.72
Lawyer	0	—	0	—	0	—	1	.29	2	.53	3	.22
Doctor	1	.73	2	.78	0	—	3	.88	5	1.32	11	.80
Foreign dip.	0	—	2	.78	1	.37	0	—	2	.53	5	.36
Pruss. dip.	1	.73	1	.39	1	.37	1	.29	0	—	4	.29
Misc.	0	—	1	.39	2	.75	0	—	0	—	3	.22
Total	137	100.00	257	100.00	268	100.00	341	100.00	380	100.00	1,383	100.00

Note: Information complete on 1,383 (65.55%) of 2,110 known wives.

allowed to rescue impoverished officers from their pecuniary difficulties. In many cases the Jewish origins of these women were concealed and omitted from official records. The surviving genealogical sources rarely provide any information on such women. Nevertheless, examples and comments in the surviving material are sufficient to indicate that the practice of using Jewish money to salvage noble pride was not inknown in the officer corps.[97]

The final stage of an officer's career before he reached the generalcy was his time as a colonel. Normally this rank coincided with the position of regimental commander.[98] Mention has already been made of the enormous powers of this position. In addition to his purely military responsibilities in maintaining a combat ready unit, a regimental commander was responsible for officer replacements, for the moral and political attitudes of his officer corps, for their wives, and a host of other duties. Many generals looked back upon their years as a regimental commander as the most enjoyable and rewarding of their entire careers.[99] In no other position, many felt, was there such a combination of authority and direct involvement with their officers and men. For those who served as regimental commanders, a good performance was absolutely essential for further promotion. Not all officers served as commanders of regiments, and not all generals had that experience. An analysis of the types of assignments held by Prussia's generals while they were colonels will exhibit the role of the different types of regiments in providing regiments and will clarify the importance of that command position in a typical career.

Cavalry officers who became generals commanded guards cavalry regiments in relatively few cases (Table 24). Only 50 (6.78%) of the 339 generals with service as cavalry regimental commanders performed this duty in one of the guards cavalry regiments. Nevertheless, this was entirely out of proportion to the total number of colonels who commanded cavalry regiments. Throughout the empire the Prussian army had about 73 cavalry regiments, including eight guards cavalry regiments.[100] These eight guards regiments had a total of 102 commanders, all nobles. Apparently about one-half of these men made the promotion to brigadier general. A grand total of 796 different colonels commanded the 65 other cavalry regiments during the period. Because 289 generals had held such a command, only about one colonel in three (36.38%) who commanded a line cavalry regiment attained the rank of brigadier general or higher.[101]

Infantry regiments cannot be so closely compared with each other as could their cavalry counterparts. Almost every colonel who commanded a guards infantry regiment became a general. The nine such regiments that existed throughout the period, and the two new guards infantry regiments created in 1896, had a total of 154 commanders between 1871 and 1914. Fully 150 generals held such a regimental command. Even subtracting a few of the hold-over generals, it is obvious that more than 90 percent of all

Table 24
Regimental Command Position: Generals Listed by Decade of Promotion to Brigadier General

	Before 1871		1871–1881		1882–1892		1893–1903		1904–1914		Total	
	No.	%	No.	%	No.	%	No.	%	No.	%	No.	%
Gd. cav.[a]	7	4.00	10	2.66	8	1.70	14	2.27	11	1.58	50	2.14
Line cav.[b]	29	16.57	68	18.09	59	12.53	62	10.06	71	10.20	289	12.38
Gd. inf.[c]	20	11.43	21	5.59	30	6.37	41	6.66	38	5.46	150	6.43
Line inf.[d]	80	45.71	180	47.86	243	51.59	345	56.00	363	52.16	1,211	51.89
Gd. arty.[e]	1	.57	3	.80	7	1.49	9	1.46	10	1.44	30	1.29
L. arty.[f]	8	4.57	28	7.45	51	10.83	74	12.01	96	13.79	257	11.01
Other rgt.[g]	0	—	0	—	2	.42	3	.49	5	.72	10	.43
Gen. St.[h]	9	5.14	7	1.86	15	3.18	16	2.60	23	3.30	70	2.99
W.M.[i]	2	1.15	7	1.86	5	1.06	5	.82	12	1.72	31	1.33
Eng.[j]	6	3.43	24	6.38	16	3.40	20	3.25	22	3.16	88	3.77
Technical	2	1.15	0	—	3	.64	3	.49	10	1.44	18	.77
Fortress	1	.57	10	2.66	10	2.12	2	.32	2	.29	25	1.07
Other[k]	10	5.71	18	4.79	22	4.67	22	3.57	33	4.74	105	4.50
Total	175	100.00	376	100.00	471	100.00	616	100.00	696	100.00	2,334	100.00

[a]Gd. cav. = all guard cavalry regiments. [b]Line cav. = all line cavalry regiments. [c]Gd. inf. = all guard infantry regiments. [d]Line inf. = all line infantry regiments. [e]Gd. arty. = guard artillery regiments. [f]L. arty. = all line artillery regiments. [g]Other rgt. = railway or other special units. [h]Gen. St. = General Staff position. [i]W.M. = War Ministry. [j]Eng. = engineer units; normally not regiments. [k]Other = special assignments in rank of colonel. *Note:* Information complete on 2,399 (95.74%) of 2,443 generals. Five generals had careers of a nature making them inapplicable to Table 24.

colonels in guards infantry regiments attained the rank of brigadier general or higher.[102] Commanders of line infantry regiments were not so fortunate. Between 1871 and 1914 approximately 1,893 colonels commanded Prussia's 155 line infantry regiments.[103] Colonels who subsequently attained the rank of brigadier general or higher held 1,211 of these positions. It would appear, therefore, that about 60 percent of all commanders of line infantry regiments became generals.[104] Obviously elite units offered much more than mere social advantages to their members.

The comparable assignments of the other generals usually do not lend themselves to such comparative analyses. The artillery as a branch was in a constant state of change and growth after 1890 and broad comparisons are not possible. A total of 70 General Staff officers served only in General Staff positions while holding the rank of colonel and did not command regiments. Many others served as regimental commanders as well as holding General Staff assignments during their time in that rank. If a general performed both types of duties, he is listed under whatever kind of regiment he commanded. The 88 engineer officers are not listed as regimental commanders because there were very few regiments for them to command.[105]

Several factors important in career success, which have been previously discussed, coalesced into the final aspect to be discussed in this chapter. To a considerable extent Prussia's generals and the promotions to that select group were the product of the workings of an extensive "old-boy" network. For many officers this network of connections began even before they were born. For others, friendships established in the cadet corps provided useful contacts with influential persons in later years.[106] Men who studied together at the War Academy frequently became successful officers and were helpful to each other along the way. Many officers established good connections through their wives' families. The tightly knit regimental system was the source of many important friendships.[107] Especially in the guards cavalry and guards infantry regiments such an aristocratic old-boy network was of great value to many a career. Finally, specific assignments could give an officer access to the relatively small group of persons who wielded great influence. Service on the staff of a royal prince, friendship with an especially influential corps commander, or service with a senior officer who subsequently became very successful, were all routes to success through the old-boy network.[108] Success in the Prussian army was possible without such good connections, but only in exceptional cases. The career of nearly every general for whom full information is available offers evidence of one or more links to old friends, commanders, or relatives whose intervention was of substantial, if not decisive, importance in their successful careers.

7

Officers at the Summit

In January 1858, Prince Frederick William, later King and Emperor Frederick III, entered the ranks of Prussia's generals at the age of 26. This early promotion made the young Hohenzollern prince the youngest general among the more than 2,400 who served during the second empire. Several of his royal relatives also enjoyed very rapid promotions and advanced to the rank of brigadier general while quite young.[1] Ernst Crusius, at the other extreme in more ways than one, received his promotion to brigadier general after his sixty-third birthday. This artillery officer was thus the oldest man promoted to general during the empire.[2] Beyond a few such exceptional cases, however, promotional patterns based on age show no great variations among the various class and career categories. Within the framework of the seniority principle, only a few individuals could advance upward through the officer ranks more rapidly than was normal at that time.[3] Because of the leveling tendency of the system, therefore, even apparently small differences in the rates of promotion signify important policies of the Military Cabinet. This is equally true of the generals' ages at promotion to brigadier general. Differences in ages upon promotion are important indications of the types of officers favored by the Military Cabinet.

Even within the primary age groups, from age 50 through 55, the advantages enjoyed by noble officers are evident. The percentage of bourgeois promotions equaled that of aristocrats for the first time at age 55. By that age fully 56.01 percent of the noble generals had been promoted to brigadier general, whereas only 42.68 percent of their bourgeois peers had been similarly elevated. Only a very few noble generals (8.32%) received their promotions to brigadier general after age

56. By way of contrast, about one bourgeois general in five (20.18%) was 57 or older upon promotion to brigadier general. Noble officers had a median age of 52.73 years at their promotion to brigadier general; for bourgeois generals the median age was 54.11 years. This discrepancy indicates that the regimental system and the army's promotional policies favored nobles despite the workings of the seniority principle.

Variations in the generals' ages at promotion are more significant in light of the age differences upon commissioning for both groups. The median age at the time of commissioning as second lieutenant was 18.78 years for officers noble when promoted to brigadier general. General bourgeois at that point in their careers had a median age of 19.38 years when commissioned.[4] In this calculation the 142 generals who were bourgeois when commissioned but noble when promoted to brigadier general are counted as nobles. If they are subtracted from the latter group and counted as bourgeois, the median age for nobles drops to 18.75 years, and that for bourgeois generals drops to 19.36 years.

A comparison of the ages at commissioning with those at the generals' promotions reveals that noblemen who wore the king's uniform needed fewer years of service to reach the rank of brigadier general than did bourgeois officers. An average aristocratic officer was promoted to that rank 33.95 years after receiving his commission. A bourgeois general had typically needed 34.73 yeas to attain this same rank.

The Military Cabinet did not routinely promote most noble officers more rapidly than bourgeois officers regardless of ability, seniority, or other career-related factors. Especially in the lower ranks of lieutenant and captain, promotions were governed both by the seniority principle and the regimental system. Individual nobles with good connections and exceptional abilities received favorable treatment, as did many bourgeois officers who had influential friends, relatives, or patrons, or whose job performance set them clearly above their peers.

Noble officers advanced more rapidly because of a variety of advantages, ranging from the favorable circumstances inherent in elite units to the benefits conferred by attendance at the War Academy and the role played by influential senior commanders. An additional factor of considerable importance was the army's old-boy network, based on blood relations and personal acquaintance.

The advantages enjoyed by specific types of officers are nowhere more evident than in an analysis of age at promotion by types of careers pursued by the generals (Table 25).

Officers who served primarily in elite units, both cavalry and infantry, had a median age upon promotion to brigadier general of 52.28 years, a sharp contrast to the overall age average of 53.12 years. Elite careers thus produced the youngest group of brigadier generals of the three basic branch-related types of careers. Generals who served primarily in line

Table 25
Age at Promotion to Brigadier General: Generals Listed by Types of Careers,
Selected Careers Only

Age at Prom.	Elite		Line infantry		Artillery		General Staff	
	No.	%	No.	%	No.	%	No.	%
28	1	.16	0	—	0	—	0	—
30	1	.16	0	—	0	—	0	—
35	1	.16	0	—	0	—	0	—
38	1	.16	0	—	0	—	0	—
39	0	—	1	.11	0	—	0	—
41	1	.16	0	—	0	—	0	—
43	2	.33	0	—	0	—	3	1.01
44	3	.49	0	—	0	—	2	.68
45	2	.33	0	—	0	—	2	.68
46	10	1.63	5	.53	1	.37	7	2.36
47	21	3.43	2	.21	0	—	14	4.73
48	19	3.10	10	1.07	5	1.86	22	7.43
49	38	6.21	14	1.48	6	2.23	42	14.19
50	45	7.25	37	3.92	16	5.95	46	15.54
51	61	9.97	55	5.85	23	8.55	50	16.88
52	85	13.90	112	11.88	26	9.67	41	13.85
53	90	14.71	124	13.15	41	15.24	29	9.80
54	76	12.43	191	20.26	29	10.78	16	5.41
55	75	12.25	148	15.69	34	12.64	8	2.70
56	35	5.72	113	11.98	24	8.92	6	2.03
57	26	4.25	62	6.57	28	10.41	4	1.35
58	18	2.94	41	4.35	19	7.06	2	.68
59	1	.16	18	1.91	14	5.20	2	.68
60	0	—	10	1.06	3	1.12	0	—
Total	612	100.00	943	100.00	269	100.00	296	100.00
Median	52.28		53.38		54.13		50.75	

infantry regiments had a median age of 53.38 years upon reaching the generalcy. Artillery officers had a corresponding age of 54.13 years and thus were nearly two years older than were generals from elite units.

General Staff officers, with a median age at promotion to brigadier general of 50.75 years, were by a wide margin the youngest of the four career types listed in Table 25.[5] This was the result of continuing energetic efforts by the various chiefs of the General Staff to ensure that their officers received accelerated promotions. Among Count von Moltke's first official acts as chief was the presentation of such a demand to the Military Cabinet.[6] Waldersee continued this policy, which eventually became a standard practice of the Military Cabinet. As a result, General Staff officers who reached the rank of brigadier general were significantly younger than their fellow officers whose careers were spent primarily in regimental duty.[7]

An analysis of the generals' age distribution by types of careers bears out the impression created by a comparison of their median ages at promotion. Only a few artillery and line infantry officers (4.66% and 3.29% respectively) attained the rank of brigadier general by their fiftieth brithday. Nearly one elite general in six (16.48%) was this youthful upon promotion, as was nearly one General Staff general in three (31.08%). After age 54, when nearly all General Staff officers had either retired or become generals, more than half (56.23%) of the future artillery generals were still waiting for their promotion to brigadier general, as were about four line infantry officers in ten (41.55%). General Staff careerists thus enjoyed a remarkable advantage over all other types, including officers from elite units. They were virtual children compared with the graybeards whose promotions depended upon developments in the artillery units. The better promotional opportunities in the artillery after 1890 had some favorable influence on artillery officers' ages upon promotion but did not nullify the advantages held by officers serving on the General Staff and in elite units.

Military education, although closely related to General Staff duty, had a less significant effect on age at promotion than did the type of career pursued by an officer. Generals who attended the War Academy were, on the average, 52.29 years of age when promoted to brigadier general.[8] Their fellow officers who lacked this type of military education were 53.49 years old when promoted. The age discrepancy between generals with War Academy training and the General Staff officers of the same rank (50.75 years) is a further indication that the two were not synonymous. Many War Academy graduates did not qualify for a career in the General Staff, whereas, conversely, many General Staff officers had not attended the War Academy.

Other well-placed nobles, especially those in the cavalry, were older at promotion than some other types of officers. Princes rarely attended the War Academy. Cavalry officers also normally showed a strong reluctance to enter that competitive institution. Because these officers normally had better promotional opportunities stemming from their special personal situations and units of assignments, their careers had two factors working at cross-purposes. Their personal attributes favored early promotions, but their lack of military education at the War Academy was something of a hindrance. If such men were excluded from consideration, the median age of the generals who did not attend the War Academy would increase moderately. To this extent the above data understate slightly the value of War Academy education for officers from a line infantry or artillery regiment.

A bourgeois officer who succeeded in gaining a promotion to the rank of brigadier general had not yet overcome his final military obstacle course. Although it was no easy task for a nonnoble officer to reach that rank, advancement to higher levels of the generalcy was at least equally difficult. Class and social background continued to be a liability in the careers of most bourgeois officers. The Military Cabinet relied upon two methods to ensure that each succeeding rank beyond brigadier general remained as aristocratic as possible. Most obviously, any brigadier general, noble or bourgeois, could be retired at any point after his promotion and before he received a patent for the next higher rank. Even a senior brigadier general, with three or more years in grade, might be given a blue slip requesting his resignation rather than a congratulatory letter announcing a further promotion.

This very blunt method of ensuring continued noble predominance was not entirely satisfactory, however, because of the seniority system. If too many generals considered unsuited for the next higher rank reached the top of the seniority list for brigadier generals, it became very difficult to prevent their occupying the available positions. Gross exceptions to the seniority principle were allowed only in unusual cases. Massive interference would have threatened the principle. A much safer course of action was to prevent these imperfect officers from becoming senior brigadier generals. This in effect meant retiring them quickly, after a short term as brigadier general, while holding nobles on active duty for a longer period, thus giving the latter group a decided preponderance in the seniority lists. The army needed capable bourgeois brigadier generals to fill positions for which insufficient numbers of noble colonels were available. The practice of promoting the necessary number of bourgeois colonels to brigadier general and then retiring them before they could qualify for promotion and replacing them with additional bourgeois generals filled both needs: the important positions had capable officers, and the social goals were achieved as well.

Table 26 illustrates the practice of shortening the careers of most bourgeois generals relative to those of their noble colleagues, a practice with the side effect of inflating the total number of bourgeois generals. This in turn concealed the true nature of the situation by artifically inflating the bourgeois content of the generalcy. Whereas the latter produced the appearance of decreased social discrimination, in fact it was the result of a policy designed to do exactly the opposite.

Brigadier generals who served only one or two years in that rank almost always ended their careers at that level because the normal waiting period for the next promotion was more than three years. Slightly more than one

Table 26
Years as Brigadier General: Generals Listed by Class and by Decade of Promotion

Years as B.G.	Nobles		Bourgeois		Total	
	No.	%	No.	%	No.	%
Before 1871						
1	5	3.18	0	—	5	3.05
2	14	8.92	0	—	14	8.54
3	36	22.93	3	42.86	39	23.78
4	53	33.76	3	42.86	56	34.14
5	45	28.6	1	14.28	46	28.05
6+	4	2.55	0	—	4	2.44
Total	157	100.00	7	100.00	164	100.00
1871–1881						
1	39	12.83	12	18.18	51	13.79
2	36	11.84	14	21.21	50	13.51
3	38	12.50	5	7.58	43	11.62
4	39	12.83	10	15.15	49	13.24
5	80	26.32	17	25.76	97	26.22
6+	72	23.68	8	12.12	80	21.62
Total	304	100.00	66	100.00	370	100.00
1882–1892						
1	62	18.34	21	15.79	83	17.62
2	98	28.99	41	30.83	139	29.51
3	96	28.41	42	31.57	138	29.30
4	56	16.57	21	15.79	77	16.35
5	22	6.51	5	3.76	27	5.73
6+	4	1.18	3	2.26	7	1.49
Total	338	100.00	133	100.00	471	100.00
1893–1903						
1	45	10.64	30	14.35	75	11.87

noble brigadier general in three (35.75%) served for two years or less. Fully 44.94 percent of the bourgeois brigadier generals, including those who received titles, had such brief military lives in that rank. The bulk of both noble (48.87%) and bourgeois (49.36%) generals served either three or four years before moving up or out. With this amount of time in grade, they could either be promoted or retired, depending upon individual decisions by the Military Cabinet, without posing any problems on the seniority lists. Very few bourgeois officers (5.70%) survived longer than

Table 26 (continued)

Years as B.G.	Nobles		Bourgeois		Total	
	No.	%	No.	%	No.	%
1893–1903						
2	87	20.57	52	24.88	139	21.99
3	167	39.48	77	36.85	244	38.60
4	116	27.42	49	23.44	165	26.11
5	7	1.65	1	.48	8	1.27
6+	1	.24	0	—	1	.16
Total	423	100.00	209	100.00	632	100.00
1904–1914						
1	61	19.30	52	23.96	113	21.20
2	103	32.59	62	28.57	165	30.96
3	128	40.51	92	42.40	220	41.27
4	23	7.28	10	4.61	33	6.19
5	0	—	1	.46	1	.19
6+	1	.32	0	—	1	.19
Total	316	100.00	217	100.00	533	100.00
Total all decades						
1	212	13.78	115	18.20	327	15.07
2	338	21.97	169	26.74	507	23.36
3	465	30.22	219	34.64	684	31.53
4	287	18.65	93	14.72	380	17.51
5	154	10.01	25	3.96	179	8.25
6+	82	5.37	11	1.74	93	4.28
Total	1,538	100.00	632	100.00	2,170	100.00

Note: One hundred sixty-three generals are classified as having careers not relevant to this table. Most had either died while in this rank or were still brigadier generals in August 1914. Information complete on 2,333 (95.50%) of 2,443.

four years, whereas about one noble brigadier general in seven (15.03%) managed to do so.[9]

A decade-by-decade analysis of the time spent as brigadier general confirms the above picture in greater detail. The hold-over generals and the generals promoted between 1871 and 1881 had relatively few noble brigadier generals who served for only a year or two and then went into retirement (12.10% and 24.67% respectively). The same years saw a large number of nobles serving as brigadier generals for five or more years

(31.21% and 50.00% in the two time periods). A common complaint against William I was his tendency to keep his generals on active duty longer than was appropriate for their advancing years and longer than was healthy for the army.[10] Table 26 provides convincing evidence that this was indeed the case, both for nobles and for the small number of bourgeois brigadier generals.

During the decade 1871–81 even bourgeois brigadier generals served for five or more years in more than one case in three (37.88%).This caused extensive problems in the lower ranks, especially for colonels. These senior officers became progressively older while awaiting their promotions to brigadier general. As they remained on active duty, moreover, few positions became available to younger officers throughout the ranks.[11]

During the empire's second decade, promotion rates began to accelerate, but to the disadvantage of most bourgeois generals. Indeed, the overall tendency noted above first became evident between the years 1882 and 1892. A sizable 47.23 percent of noble brigadier generals and 46.62 percent of bourgeois officers in that rank were retained for only one or two years before their retirement. Only 7.69 percent of the nobles and 6.02 percent of the bourgeois brigadier generals were retained beyond their fourth year in that grade. Only a decade earlier, the percentages of brigadier generals with extended service had been more than six times as high as these figures.

By the empire's third decade, 1893–1903, the rapid retirement policy for bourgeois generals was in full operation. During this decade nearly four bourgeois generals in ten (39.23%) left active duty after only one or two years, and only one was retained beyond four years.[12] During the same period fewer than one noble brigadier general in three (31.21%) served for two years or less before retirement. Most brigadier generals, regardless of their class, fell into the primary promotion zones, with three or four years of service in grade before they retired or advanced to the rank of lieutenant general.

Information for the final decade is incomplete; the generals still on active duty in August 1914 have been excluded. One cannot safely speculate how many or which of these generals would have advanced in rank or retired. Nevertheless, more than 500 generals in this decade can be classified and appear in Table 26. There is strong, if inconclusive, evidence that by 1914 bourgeois generals were receiving better treatment. More than half (52.52%) were still sent into retirement after only one or two years and thus had no chance for further promotion. The corresponding figure for noble brigadier generals stood at 51.89 percent, indicating that a more rapid turnover was typical of both groups. To some extent, therefore, more equal opportunities were afforded bourgeois generals than had been the case in previous decades.

The Military Cabinet was even less inclined to accord nobles and bourgeois officers equal treatment in promotions beyond brigadier general

Table 27
Years as Lieutenant General: Generals Listed by Class

Years as Lt. General	Nobles		Bourgeois		Total	
	No.	%	No.	%	No.	%
1	85	12.76	38	22.75	123	14.77
2	113	16.97	37	22.16	150	18.01
3	116	17.42	40	23.95	156	18.73
4	139	20.88	31	18.56	170	20.40
5	99	14.86	16	9.58	115	13.81
6	41	6.16	4	2.40	45	5.40
7	27	4.05	0	—	27	3.24
8	17	2.55	0	—	17	2.04
9	16	2.40	1	.60	17	2.04
10	4	.60	0	—	4	.48
11	1	.15	0	—	1	.12
12	3	.45	0	—	3	.36
13	3	.45	0	—	3	.36
17	1	.15	0	—	1	.12
19	1	.15	0	—	1	.12
Total	666	100.00	167	100.00	833	100.00

than it was in the lower ranks. An analysis of the generals who made the jump from brigadier general to lieutenant general makes this social discrimination obvious. Fully 665 (79.74%) of the 834 lieutenant generals promoted during the empire had been nobles at the time of their promotion to brigadier general.[13] An additional 24 received titles after their promotion to brigadier general but before their next elevation. This raised the total number of noble lieutenant generals to 689 and their percentage of the total to 82.61 percent. For purposes of the following discussion, however, only the 665 who were nobles before promotion to brigadier general are counted as nobles.[14]

The patterns already noted above among the brigadier generals are even more in evidence among the lieutenant generals. More than four bourgeois lieutenant generals in ten (44.91%) served only one or two years in that rank (Table 27). An additional 23.95 percent served for three years. Nearly one noble lieutenant general in three (29.73%) served for two years or less; an additional 17.42 percent remained in that grade for three years. A total of 113 nobles (16.97%) held the rank of lieutenant general for six or more years, much longer than the time allowed nearly all bourgeois generals.

The five bourgeois generals who remained in the rank of lieutenant general for more than five years were exceptional cases. Their personal backgrounds make it abundantly clear that the typical bourgeois general could not have hoped to duplicate their careers. Three of the five exceptions were artillery officers. One of them, Karl von Hausmann, was a noble at the time of his promotion to the rank of lieutenant general. Another, Adolf von Schubert, received a title subsequent to his promotion to general of artillery. He was a General Staff officer and the son of a landowner from Posen. Both Hausmann and Schubert held special artillery positions that allowed them to spend extra years in this rank without being retired.[15] Friedrich Wiebe, the third artillery officer, had an almost ideal background for a man without a noble title. His father had been an officer, and he had married an officer's daughter. He had attended the War Academy but had not served on the General Staff.

The other two exceptions, both engineer officers, also possessed unusual personal attributes. Hans von Biehler, who received his title in 1871 before promotion to lieutenant general, had two positive assets in his background. He had married into the Uradel von Kleist family and his father-in-law was a Prussian general. The other engineer officer, Ludwig Dietrich, was of unusually humble origins. His father had been a lieutenant in the police in Westphalia and then a salt storage warehouse inspector. His mother, however, was of the Uradel Westphalian von Stockhausen family. His maternal grandfather was a landowner in Westphalia. His wife was the daughter of a bourgeois landowner from the province East Prussia.

Generals who made the promotion to lieutenant general and retired in that rank had accomplished a great deal and were justifiably proud of their careers. They need not have felt ashamed if they received no further promotions, for only a relative handful of officers advanced to the rank of full general. This grade was normally, but not always, reserved for those officers who commanded Prussia's army corps. The post of corps commander, whose incumbent was normally referred to simply as the commanding general, was especially powerful and influential.[16]

Generals in the Prussian army were nearly always nobles. In the Imperial period 195 (88.64%) of the 220 generals whose careers terminated in that rank had been nobles upon promotion to brigadier general. Many others, including those not counted as such in Table 28, received titles after their promotion to brigadier general but before their retirement.[17] As was the case with lieutenant generals, only those already noble upon promotion to brigadier general are counted as nobles in the following discussion.

The glittering and powerful rank of general was reserved for a very few officers, as Table 28 indicates. Although the time spent in this rank varied more widely than did the periods of time spent on active duty in the lower two levels of the generalcy, the earlier patterns were also characteristic of these officers. Whereas 44 percent of bourgeois generals retired after only two years in that rank, only 30.76 percent of the noble generals had such short periods of active duty after their promotions. Only two (8.00%) of the 25 bourgeois generals serviced for more than six years in that grade. A large number of nobles, however, enjoyed prolonged tours of six or more years (78 officers; 32.32% of the noble total), including more than one in ten (11.34%) who served ten or more years. Because each was a capable officer, the differences in time spent on active duty after promotion to the rank of general can have had no source other than favoritism on the part of the Military Cabinet and the Prussian kings.[18]

The amount of time spent in each officer grade in the generalcy was but one indicator of lingering social divisions within the ranks of the general officers. Also of some importance on this point is the last position held by the generals before their retirement. Some assignments were reserved for generals who were judged unsuited for higher command positions and higher rank and who, therefore, had no prospects of further promotion. Other positions were normally filled by generals destined for additional promotion and greater command responsibilities. Some positions were the exclusive property of generals best classified as technicians or specialists. The various assignments were closely related to a variety of career factors examined in earlier chapters, including social class, military education, and branch of service.

The Prussian army needed more brigade commanders than any other kind of general, with the predictable result that by far more brigadier generals served in that capacity than in any other. Brigade commander was the most basic position for capable officers destined for higher commands and was also the final duty position for most officers whose talents or other

Table 28
Years as General: Generals Listed by Class

Years as General	Nobles		Bourgeois		Total	
	No.	%	No.	%	No.	%
1	27	13.85	7	28.00	34	15.45
2	33	16.91	4	16.00	37	16.82
3	19	9.74	6	24.00	25	11.36
4	21	10.77	2	8.00	23	10.45
5	17	8.72	2	8.00	19	8.64
6	15	7.69	2	8.00	17	7.73
7	16	8.21	0	—	16	7.27
8	13	6.67	1	4.00	14	6.36
9	8	4.10	0	—	8	3.64
10	9	4.62	1	4.00	10	4.55
11+	17	8.72	0	—	17	7.73
Total	195	100.00	25	100.00	220	100.00

Table 29
Last Position: Generals Listed by Class

Last Position	Nobles		Bourgeois		Total	
	No.	%	No.	%	No.	%
Brig. comm.	745	46.86	347	55.62	1,092	49.33
Div. comm.	222	13.96	59	9.46	281	12.69
Corps comm.	104	6.54	5	.80	109	4.92
Army comm.	15	.94	1	.16	16	.72
Gen. Staff	12	.75	11	1.76	23	1.04
War Ministry	15	.94	10	1.60	25	1.13
Mil. Cabinet	4	.25	0	—	4	.18
Fort. comm.[a]	185	11.64	40	6.41	225	10.16
Fort. gov.[b]	73	4.59	6	.96	79	3.57
Diplomatic	4	.25	0	—	4	.18
Adjutant	26	1.64	5	.80	31	1.40
Technical	5	.31	11	1.76	16	.72
Insp. cavalry[c]	25	1.57	5	.80	30	1.35
Insp. inf.	5	.31	1	.16	6	.27
Insp. arty.	26	1.64	27	4.33	53	2.39
Insp. eng.	30	1.89	64	10.26	94	4.25
Insp. ldw.[d]	13	.82	6	.96	19	.86
Mil. schools	23	1.45	4	.64	27	1.22
Exam. comm./mil. courts[e]	20	1.26	7	1.12	27	1.22
Trains	5	.31	6	.96	11	.50
Other	11	.70	7	1.12	18	.82
a la suite[f]	22	1.38	2	.32	24	1.08
Total	1,590	100.00	624	100.00	2,214	100.00

[a]Fort. comm. = fortress commander [b]Fort. gov. = fortress govener [c]Insp. = inspector [d]ldw. = landwehr [e]Exam. comm. = examination commissions [f]a la suite = on special assignment, recuperating, etc.

personal attributes precluded further advancement. More than half (55.62%) of the 624 bourgeois generals in Table 29 ended their careers in that rank and position.[19] These bourgeois brigade commanders made up 31.78 percent of the total number of generals whose careers terminated in that assignment. This was quite close to the proportion of the entire group of bourgeois generals (30.33%). A higher proportion of bourgeois generals ended their careers in this, the lowest troop command, than was the case for nobles. The 745 noble generals whose careers terminated in the position of brigade commander were only 46.86 percent of all noble generals. This discrepancy was not the result of greater diversity in assignments for aristocrats, but rather was the result of promotion policies that advanced nobles to the better command positions.

The army's continuing preference for aristocratic officers may be clearly seen in the three columns in Table 29 for brigade commander. In descending order of appearance the next three columns are the ascending ranks in the positions of direct troop command: division, corps, and army.[20] The higher the command position, the fewer were the bourgeois officers advanced to fill the slots. Even considering the army's preference for aristocrats, one cannot help being impressed that only one bourgeois general held the office of army inspector during the Imperial period.[21] Only five bourgeois officers terminated their careers in so lofty a post as commanding general of an army corps.[22] By contrast, 119 nobles occupied these positions in their terminal years immediately before retirement. Nearly eight division commanders in ten (79.00%) were nobles, a figure that increases to 83.99 percent if one includes those generals who commanded corps or who served as army inspectors after their years as division commander.[23] Command positions beyond the division level were thus reserved almost exclusively for nobles.[24]

The distribution of the other terminal positions in Table 29 further indicates the personnel policies of the Military Cabinet and is a further index of the role played by factors other than military ability. The position of fortress commander was the final post for 225 brigadier generals.[25] This position was normally reserved for marginal brigadier generals, and few men who served in it advanced to higher rank or better positions.[26] About twice as high a proportion of nobles settled into these comfortable if terminal positions as did bourgeois generals. Fortress (or garrison) commanders usually spent two to four years in one of the many small installations before retiring.

Generals who served as commanders of larger installations were titled governors and frequently had higher rank as well as better positions.[27] Consequently, their prospects for further promotion were better. Many of them reached the rank of lieutenant general while in that assignment. It is therefore hardly surprising that only six bourgeois officers were among 79 generals who served their final years as governors of fortresses.[28] Forty bourgeois generals held the less favorable position as commander of a small fortress, where their careers ended in honor and obscurity.

Certain kinds of terminating positions were dominated by bourgeois officers, mostly along lines to be expected, considering the social prejudices of the army. Two-thirds of the generals holding positions as inspectors of engineers were bourgeois, as were equal proportions of those in technical positions.[29] Trains officers were predominantly drawn from nonnoble ranks, although to a lesser degree. Artillery inspectors were bourgeois in 27 of 53 cases.[30]

The reverse side of this coin was the number of positions reserved for aristocratic generals. Although fewer than 2 percent of all noble generals terminated their careers as inspectors of cavalry, these 25 aristocrats were a massive 83.33 percent of all men holding those positions. In a similar fashion, aristocratic generals dominated posts classified as diplomatic (4 of 4), adjutant to royalty or other princes (26 of 31), the Military Cabinet (4 of 4), and the honorary a la suite the army (22 of 24).[31]

Although the generals whose final positions were in General Staff posts were almost equally divided between nobles and bourgeois, it should not be concluded that preferential treatment played no role within that body nor that half of all General Staff generals were bourgeois. By far the majority of all General Staff generals ended their careers as brigade, division, or corps commanders and, therefore, appear in Table 29 under these categories. Bourgeois generals involved in technical General Staff duties tended to remain in certain staff positions and were usually not transferred to unit command positions. Aristocratic preference was a continuing factor in the selection and promotion of generals who served on the General Staff.[32]

A general's final assignment before retirement was related not only to his social class but also to the type of career he had pursued as a junior officer. This was a natural consequence of service in the differing branches having developed specialized skills required for many command positions. It was also the case, however, that certain types of careers gave officers better opportunities to reach the highest ranks and better prepared them for the more desirable positions. Correlation of the types of careers pursued by the generals with their final military positions will clarify the relationsip and will provide information about the kinds of officers preferred by the Military Cabinet for certain special assignments.

Because the position of brigade commander was normally reserved for officers holding the rank of brigadier general and a few colonels about to receive promotions to than rank, officers whose careers terminated as brigade commanders almost always ended their careers in the rank of brigadier general. Seen from this perspective, the advantages enjoyed by officers in elite units become manifest. Aside from engineer officers, men with elite careers were the least likely (47.37%) to have ended their careers as brigade commanders. Officers who plodded along in the so-called oxen's tour were not so fortunate. More than half of all line infantry and artillery generals had their professional lives terminated at this point (Table 30).

Seen from another perspective, however, the positions of officers with elite careers do not seem to have been substantially at variance with their total numbers among the generals. Of the 980 brigade commanders considered in Table 30, elite careers were characteristic of about one in four (28.57%), a percentage not greatly out of proportion to their total share of the generals (27.29%). Generals with line infantry careers, by contrast, made up 41.70 percent of all generals but fully 50.51 percent of those whose careers ended in the position of brigade commander.

Because of the increased responsibilities and higher rank associated with the position of division commander, the next promotion within the ranks of the general officers, the army naturally desired that only the most capable brigade commanders should advance to that assignment. Interestingly, generals from elite units did not reach this position proportionately more often than did officers with line infantry careers.[33] About one general in seven from each group ended his career while commanding a division. Artillery generals and General Staff officers, on the other hand, varied substantially from the above figures. Only 16 artillery generals (6.93% of those officers) ended their careers as division commanders. About one General Staff general in four (23.32%) terminated in this position, a proportion much higher than those of the other career groups. The advantages derived from a successful career in the General Staff are, therefore, again evident in the high command positions. Because of the social and career disadvantages of the engineer branch, as well as the limited relevance of such a career to infantry and cavalry divisions, only a single general with this background closed his career as a division commander during the entire period.[34]

Only a select few attained the next highest rung on the command ladder of the Prussian army—corps commander, one of the most powerful offices. The unique nature of this position and the enormous influence wielded by those holding it merit it a further examination. The commanding generals' prestigious positions in the provinces falling within their corps areas put them on a footing at least equal with the highest civilian authorities, the *Ober-Präsidenten* (head of government of a Prussian province).[35] A corps commander in theory as well as in practice had no superior other than the king himself.[36] Commanding generals possessed the right of direct access to the king and frequently intervened with the Military Cabinet in personnel matters at all levels of their commands. They normally outranked the war minister and were responsible to him only for purely administrative matters. It is small wonder that Eugen Richter labeled the special position of corps commander a "legal-mystical" concept.[37]

Gott behüt mich vor der Grenze,
Gottlieb Häseler, August Lentze.

This jingle, popular in the army around the turn of the century, referred to the massive reputations of the army's two most feared and respected corps commanders.[38] It could have applied to other commanding generals who used their authority to mold an entire army corps in their own image.

Table 30

Last Position: Generals Listed by Career Pattern, Selected Careers Only

Last Assignment	Elite Careers		Line Infantry Careers		Artillery Careers		Engineer Careers		General Staff Careers	
	No.	%	No.	%	No.	%	No.	%	No.	%
Brig. comm.	280	47.37	495	58.25	137	59.32	9	10.12	59	23.32
Div. comm.	80	13.53	118	13.88	16	6.93	1	1.12	59	23.32
Corps comm.	45	7.60	22	2.59	1	.43	0	—	37	14.62
Army insp.	5	.85	2	.24	0	—	0	—	9	3.56
Gen. Staff	2	.34	0	—	0	—	0	—	21	8.30
War Ministry	6	1.02	4	.47	2	.86	2	2.25	4	1.58
Military Cab.	1	.17	0	—	0	—	0	—	3	1.19
Fort. comm.[a]	69	11.68	119	14.00	11	4.76	1	1.12	12	4.74
Fort. gov.[b]	26	4.40	30	3.53	1	.43	1	1.12	15	5.93

Diplomatic	2	.34	0	—	0	—	1	1.12	1	.40
Adjutant	14	2.36	3	.35	3	1.30	0	—	3	1.19
Technical	0	—	3	.35	6	2.59	0	—	0	—
Insp. cav.^c	22	3.73	1	.11	0	—	0	—	6	2.36
Insp. inf.	2	.34	3	.35	0	—	0	—	0	—
Insp. arty.	2	.34	1	.11	38	16.45	1	1.12	4	1.58
Insp. eng.	2	.34	7	.82	3	1.28	72	80.91	2	.79
Insp. ldw.^d	3	.51	14	1.65	0	—	0	—	1	.40
Mil. Schools	6	1.02	5	.59	3	1.30	0	—	7	2.77
Exam. comm./mil. courts^e	4	.68	14	1.65	3	1.30	0	—	6	2.36
Trains	2	.34	0	—	3	1.30	1	1.12	1	.40
a la suite^f	14	2.36	4	.47	1	.43	0	—	0	—
Other	4	.68	5	.59	3	1.30	0	—	3	1.19
Total	591	100.00	850	100.00	231	100.00	89	100.00	253	100.00

^aFort. comm. = fortress commander. ^bFort. governer = fortress governer. ^cInsp. = inspector. ^dLdw. = landwehr. ^eExam. comm. = examination commissions. ^f a la suite = on special assignment, recuperating, etc.

The army managed to conceal most of its internal problems, but a few examples have surfaced to illustrate the extent to which commanding generals could intimidate and dominate their officers. The career of Julius von Bose, a fine officer who did not suffer fools lightly, provides one such illustration. General von Bose, commander of the Ninth Army Corps in Kassel, found that one of his subordinates, a prince of Mecklenburg, did not possess all the qualities expected of a Prussian officer, especially one under his command. After a series of particularly unpleasant scenes during the annual maneuvers in 1875, General von Bose proceeded to Berlin, presumably to confer with the Military Cabinet and William I. Four days later the *Militär-Wochenblatt* (Military Weekly) announced that the unfortunate prince was no longer a Prussian officer. Such was the wrath and influence of an angry commanding general.[39]

Count Gottlieb von Haeseler, perhaps the most colorful Prussian general between 1871 and 1914, was the archetype officer and commanding general. He was also the most famous officer in the army during these years, except for the various war ministers, chiefs of the General Staff, and a few other such celebrities. The son of a Prussian officer who owned two estates in Brandenburg, Haeseler was of impeccable aristocratic and military origins. Of a Prussian noble family, his mother, born von Schönermarck, was the daughter of a Prussian general. Haeseler's branch was cavalry, but he became a career General Staff officer despite lack of training at the War Academy. His personality bore the stamp of the rigid upbringing he experienced in the cadet corps. For 14 years, from 1890 until 1903, Haeseler provided the 16th Army Corps with some of the most decisive personal leadership in the peacetime history of the Prussian army.[40]

Although somewhat less renowned than Count von Haeseler, August von Lentze cut no mean figure in his years as commanding general. Born in Westphalia (1832) of a bourgeois Prussian colonel, Lentze likewise was a General Staff officer, but unlike Haeseler was a graduate of the War Academy. As was the case with many bourgeois officers, Lentze's paternal grandfather and father-in-law had pursued careers in the church and civil service. In 1896, while a general, Lentze received a title of nobility. He commanded the 17th Army Corps from 1890 until early 1902. His career was, therefore, an example of what an exceptionally capable bourgeois officer could achieve; but it is equally illustrative of the necessary proper background and career development required for any officer to attain such an exalted position.[41]

Despite the complexity of the factors governing promotions, assignments, and retention of officers on active duty, nobles clearly enjoyed significant advantages in all these areas. Aristocrats were slightly younger upon promotion, attained higher ranks, received the better assignments, and dominated the most important command positions. Most bourgeois generals were confined to a limited variety of positions and had great difficulty in attaining the higher ranks beyond brigadier general. Many of the bourgeois generals whose rank, position, or longevity equaled those of their noble peers possessed unusual personal characteristics. In nearly every case either a family connection with the nobility or with the officer corps set them apart from the typical German civilian.

Numerous military attributes also contributed to rapid promotions or attainment of the higher ranks and the better command positions. General Staff service was the most efficient road to the rank of brigadier general. It was also the most demanding. Service in elite regiments also gave many officers, most of whom were aristocrats, promotions at early ages. War Academy graduates enjoyed a similar although less marked advantage. Generals whose early careers were spent in service in elite regiments also had considerably greater chances to command divisions or corps than did officers from ordinary units. General Staff officers were even more privileged in this respect.

Although the General Staff provided the army with a large number of generals, and an even larger proportion of those who wrote memoirs, only a minority of the generals ever wore the red trousers. Bourgeois General Staff officers enjoyed the advantages of such careers, and many who commanded divisions and corps and reached the rank of full general or higher were General Staff officers. Their visibility has caused historians to regard the General Staff as an institution largely free of the social prejudices so prevalent in other segments of the officer corps. Such an assumption, however, runs against much of what we know about the army's personnel and promotion policies.

8

The Demigods:
General Staff Generals,
1871–1914

Few confrontations in the career of Otto von Bismarck were more acerbic and created more lasting resentment than the chancellor's epic struggle with Helmuth von Moltke and the General Staff during the Franco-Prussian War.[1] Far more than a personal conflict between two of King William's titans, and running much deeper than a purely tactical question involving specific military problems, the extended and bitter quarrel involved fundamental issues of the primacy of civilian over military control of the Prussian army's operations.[2] Ultimately Bismarck emerged the victor and coined the famous phrase about Moltke's arrogant staff, the demigods, whose defiance of civilian authority and contempt for diplomacy had endangered the entire war effort.[3] The General Staff continued to be a problem for the political leadership of Prussia and Germany and has, therefore, been a central concern of historians studying Wilhelmian Germany.[4]

The men who served the Prussian army as General Staff generals occupied a central role in Prussian history. The 113 generals who held General Staff positions after promotion to the rank of brigadier general were the military elite of the General Staff as well as of the army. All were career General Staff officers and were handpicked by the chiefs of the General Staff for the important positions they held.[5] In addition to their service on the General Staff many of these generals went on to command brigades, divisions, and corps before their careers ended. They were, therefore, the elite of the officer corps—the most fertile minds and the best staff officers in the army.[6]

The following social profile arranges biographical information on the 113 General Staff generals under various headings similar to those utilized in the earlier chapters.[7] Chronological divisions are based on the service periods of the four prewar chiefs of the General Staff. Count Helmuth von Moltke, who commanded the Prussian army in the victorious wars of 1866 and 1870–71, served as chief of the General Staff from 1857 until October 1888. His successor, Count Alfred von Waldersee, served from the latter month until his dismissal by Emperor William II on July 2, 1891. Count Alfred von Schlieffen followed Waldersee and served until January 1, 1906, retiring after completion of the fateful campaign plan that immortalized his name. The last prewar chief was Helmuth von Moltke, nephew of the legendary victor of Königgrätz and Sedan. The younger Moltke (frequently referred to here and elsewhere as Moltke II) performed as chief of the General Staff until he collapsed under the strain of battle of the Marne in September 1914.[8]

Count Helmuth von Moltke, of an Uradel Danish and Mecklenburg family, was one of the most complex military figures of the nineteenth century. He had become a Danish officer quite by accident, as he told it, and entered Prussian service because of the better promotional opportunities in that state's large army. Moltke fits few, if any, of the stereotypes of a Prussian officer. Although an infantryman, his General Staff service afforded long periods away from the provincial surroundings of most of Prussia's garrison towns. Largely self-educated, he possessed considerable talents as a writer and amateur artist. He was a humanist and a deeply cultured man who might have become a distinguished historian had he not chosen a military career. Despite this diversity of talents, Moltke was a thoroughgoing aristocrat and harbored a lingering distrust of bourgeois types in the army.[9] Although he was himself not reared in a landed family, Moltke used his postwar financial grant, bestowed upon him by a grateful government, to purchase an estate in Silesia. Few, if any, Prussian officers commanded the enormous respect accorded Moltke by his fellow soldiers.

Count von Moltke's chosen successor, Count Alfred von Waldersee, was an extraordinary officer whose prejudices and political activities have overshadowed his considerable military talents. His superiors recognized his potential very early, and he always retained the respect of most of the army's officers.[10] In a truly unusual promotion, Waldersee made the jump from second lieutenant directly to captain and thus acquired an enormous advantage over his contemporaries. Waldersee deeply hated Catholics and Jews and was alarmed by the influx of officers from bourgeois backgrounds considered to be other than old-Prussian.[11]

Unfortunately for his career, Waldersee's blunt manner of expressing himself soon added the name of Emperior William II to his long list of enemies, chief among whom was Bismarck. Although Waldersee originally had high hopes for the young kaiser, and like many of his fellow officers breathed easier with the death of Frederick III, he was too good a judge of character and of men to maintain his illusions for long. A series of unpleasant scenes with William II in the presence of large groups of officers soon resulted in his "promotion" to commanding general of the Tenth Army Corps in Altona.[12] His short service period as chief of the General Staff left no lasting personnel changes but saw a disastrous extension of the army's intervention in politics and diplomacy.[13]

Count Alfred von Schlieffen succeeded Waldersee in July 1891 and quickly put an end to the army's most blatant attempts to influence German diplomacy. Although Schlieffen had no great respect for Emperor William II, he did refrain from criticizing William's ridiculous conduct at the annual maneuvers.[14] Few of Prussia's leaders have enjoyed so firm and universal a reputation as has Schlieffen. Historians are virtually unanimous in their verdict that Schlieffen was "the classic example of the 'technician' to whom pre-conceived notions of the social structure of the officer corps took second place to purely military considerations."[15] Gerhard Ritter described Schlieffen as a "completely non-political officer."[16]

Certain it is that Schlieffen avoided direct interference in politics and foreign policy and discontinued Waldersee's constant demands for preventive war against France and Russia. He had a deep interest in politics, however, and conferred frequently with Friedrich von Holstein. Schlieffen in private conversations was quite critical of Chancellor von Bülow, William II, and the foreign office in general.[17] Tall, slender, with a monocle, and usually in the uniform of the First Guard Dragoon Regiment, Schlieffen could have passed for the archetypal officer so often pictured in *Simplicissimus*. As shall be seen, his General Staff appointments indicate a strong preference for old-Prussian aristocrats and belie his reputation for indifference to social considerations.[18]

Schlieffen's successor, Helmuth von Moltke, was one of the most unfortunate of the many poor personnel selections made by William II. The kaiser chose Moltke against the advice of the chief of the Military Cabinet, Count Dietrich von Hülsen-Haeseler, probably because of the famous name and because Moltke had been his aide for several years.[19] Beyond these two very questionable attributes, Moltke had few assets to recommend him for one of the most important positions in the empire. His selection was greeted with disbelief in the officer corps, especially among those who had known him in earlier years. Schlieffen was amazed and without doubt considered his successor completely unqualified for the assignment.[20] Moltke himself knew that he was unequal to the tasks involved in his new station and feared that he was not the man to lead the army in case of war.[21] Almost completely lacking in the training and experience necessary for the position, Moltke was a guards infantry officer by career and was acquainted with General Staff work mainly through many years of service as an aide to his illustrious uncle.[22]

For the empire as a whole, 84 generals (83.18%) were nobles at the time of their appointment to the General Staff (Table 31). The nine additional

Table 31
Social Class of General Staff Generals: Generals Listed by Chief of Staff

Class	Moltke I		Waldersee		Schlieffen		Moltke II		Total	
	No.	%	No.	%	No.	%	No.	%	No.	%
Noble when appointed	31	88.58	7	77.78	35	79.54	21	84.00	84	83.18
Bourgeois, title later	2	5.71	1	11.11	3	6.82	3	12.00	9	7.97
Bourgeois	2	5.71	1	11.11	6	13.64	1	4.00	10	8.85
Total	35	100.00	9	100.00	44	100.00	25	100.00	113	100.00

generals who subsequently received titles (including seven while still on
active duty) raised the proportion of nobles to 91.15 percent. There was a
small decline in the percentages of noble generals from Moltke I (88.58%)
to Moltke II (84.00%).[23]

A comparison of the General Staff generals with all generals serving
during the Imperial period reveals that the General Staff was consistently
more aristocratic than was the larger group of generals.[24] The General
Staff generals appointed under Moltke I and Waldersee may usefully be
compared to all generals appointed during the first two decades and the
hold-over generals in Table 1.[25] Count Moltke and Waldersee appointed
aristocratic generals to the General Staff in 38 of 44 cases (86.36%).[26]
During approximately the same period, in the army at large about four
general officers in five (837 of 1,051; 79.64%) were nobles. During these
years, then, General Staff generals were moderately more heavily drawn
from the nobility than were their fellow generals as a whole.

This prevalence of nobles on the General Staff increased sharply in
subsequent years. Count Schlieffen's appointments came from the ranks of
the aristocrats in 35 (79.54%) of 44 cases. During approximately the same
years, that is during the decade 1893–1903, the Prussian army's new
promotions to the rank of brigadier general were nobles in only 434
(67.08%) of 647 cases. The aristocratic margin of difference in favor of the
General Staff, therefore, was nearly twice as great as it had been under
Moltke I and Waldersee. Schlieffen, in other words, continued to appoint a
high ratio of nobles despite their being present in decreasing proportions
among available officers. The relative position of the two groups of
generals showed the same tendency during the tenure of Moltke II. Of the
latter's appointments 21 (84.00%) were nobles. During the final decade of
the empire, fewer than six generals in ten (57.86%) held titles of nobility
before their promotions to brigadier general.

Historians have frequently noted that by 1913 only about half of all the
officers serving on the General Staff were nobles. This figure is normally
contrasted with the corresponding percentage for earlier years and is used
to illustrate the increasing bourgeois representation in nearly all parts of
the officer corps.[27] This presentation, however accurate in itself, may be
quite misleading. The total General Staff figures from 1913 include many
lieutenants and captains who served for trial periods of about three years in
minor staff positions and then returned to ordinary troop duty. Most of
these men never became genuine General Staff officers. Because of that
fact, and because of their low rank, they had little if any effect on the
General Staff. The most influential positions remained firmly in aristocratic hands, to an even greater extent than was the case for Prussia's generals
as a whole.

Of the myriad distinctions within Prussia's and Germany's nobility, one
of the most fundamental was based on antiquity of title.[28] Of the four

chiefs of the General Staff, Count Schlieffen demonstrated the strongest preference for sons of Prussia's oldest and most prestigious families.[29] More than one of his appointments in three (35.29%) were of Uradel extraction, and more than six in ten (61.76%) held patents of nobility dating to 1700 or earlier. Only five of Schlieffen's thirty-four noble General Staff generals held titles of imperial creation (Table 32).

General Staff generals were of consistently younger aristocratic stock than were Prussia's generals as a whole. This was true of the appointments of each of the four chiefs of the General Staff and for the entire period, during which only 26.38 percent of the General Staff generals were from Uradel families; 48.89 percent of all generals possessed such blue blood. Again, during Schlieffen's tenure the differences in Uradel titles between General Staff generals and all generals were the smallest (35.29% for Schlieffen and 52.35% for the decade 1893–1903) of the four chiefs. Thus Schlieffen demonstrated a definite preference for General Staff generals whose noble pedigree was similar to his own.

The 19 General Staff generals whose titles were of post-1870 creation provide further insights into the elitist nature of the General Staff. Of the 1,315 new titles awarded by Prussia's kings during the second empire, 506 went to Prussian army officers, including 169 generals and 75 colonels.[30] These 19 General Staff generals constituted only 3.75 percent of the officers receiving titles and only 7.79 percent of the colonels and generals who became nobles. Despite their obviously good standing with the monarchs who ennobled them, noble generals with titles awarded after 1870 were a disadvantaged group and only infrequently received appointments to the General Staff.[31]

Given the aristocratic nature of Prussia's ruling elite, it is hardly surprising that the General Staff sample consists largely of men whose family origins lay in the German nobility. From 1871 to 1914 more than two General Staff generals in five not only inherited their titles from a noble father but had a noble mother as well.[32] Schlieffen's appointments reflected the greatest incidence (50%) of generals so well insulated from possible bourgeois contamination. In addition, slightly more than one General Staff general in four possessed a noble father and a bourgeois mother. Within the General Staff this parental distribution became increasingly common as the decades passed and after 1905 surpassed all other configurations. The percentage (71.43%), large as it is, of General Staff generals with noble fathers is not a full measure of these officers' parental nobility. An additional eight generals (7.62%) sprang from bourgeois fathers and noble mothers. Thus, nearly eight General Staff generals in ten had a parental connection with the nobility. The inescapable conclusion is that the aristocratic General Staff successfully resisted the bourgeois challenge to its social exclusivity throughout the Imperial period.

As previously noted, wives were yet another potential attribute in a society in which one's social standing was of great importance. Indeed, the acquisition of a wife possessing great wealth or a good family was adequate compensation for other social or personal shortcomings. The women who married noble General Staff generals were dramatically less aristocratic at birth than were their husbands. Barely half (54.55%) of the aristocratic generals found wives of their own social class.[33] The available data confirm the existence of a strong preference among noble generals for bourgeois wives from good families over noble ladies whose family circumstances might be financially less than desirable.[34] Other than the very small number of new appointments during Waldersee's brief tenure, Schlieffen's generals again led the way in aristocratic content. Nearly two of his noble generals in three (64.70%) had noble wives, a percentage substantially higher than those for the generals appointed by Count Moltke and his nephew.

Bourgeois General Staff generals exhibited a similar pattern of socially mixed marriages. The 15 married bourgeois General Staff generals had 12 bourgeois and three noble wives. Thus the bourgeois General Staff generals found wives who, as a group, were marginally more aristocratic than were the wives of all bourgeois generals (16.74%) during the entire Imperial period.[35] Schlieffen's bourgeois generals possessed noble wives in a greater proportion than did bourgeois appointments of the other chiefs except Waldersee.[36] The percentage of Schlieffen's bourgeois appointments with noble wives was also considerably greater than was the corresponding figure among all generals promoted during the decade 1893–1903 (16.74%). Considering the prestige attached to service on the General Staff, it should not be surprising that a number of bourgeois generals who wore the red trousers found noble wives. If a noble lady sought a spouse among the ranks of Prussia's officers, a young General Staff officer was probably her best bet for a bright future.

It has been shown in Chapter 2 that the army consistently sought men from certain backgrounds and excluded persons for others. The General Staff, certainly the army's military and intellectual elite, showed the same preference and to an even greater extent. Because the General Staff required a relatively small number of officers, it could be even more selective than could regimental commanders in choosing officer candidates and than could the Military Cabinet in promoting officers at all levels.

About one General Staff general in six (16.98%) was the son of a landowner. Count Moltke appointed the highest ratio of generals from landed families (23.52%; Table 33), and after 1891 their proportion of the total plummeted. Only one landowner's son became a General Staff general after 1905—a miniscule 4.55 percent of the total serving from 1906 until the outbreak of World War I.[37]

Table 32
Dates of Titles of Noble General Staff Generals: Generals Listed by Chief of Staff

Date of Title	Moltke I		Waldersee		Schlieffen		Moltke II		Total	
	No.	%	No.	%	No.	%	No.	%	No.	%
Uradel	6	20.69	2	28.58	12	35.29	4	19.05	24	26.38
1401–1500	2	6.90	0	—	1	2.95	2	9.52	5	5.49
1501–1600	3	10.25	1	14.28	4	11.76	0	—	8	8.79
1601–1700	5	17.25	1	14.28	4	11.76	1	4.76	11	12.09
Subtotal	16	55.17	4	57.14	21	61.77	7	33.33	48	52.75
1701–1800	4	13.79	0	—	4	11.76	5	23.80	13	14.29
1801–1869	3	10.34	1	14.28	4	11.76	3	14.29	11	12.09
1870–1914	6	20.69	2	28.58	5	14.71	6	28.58	19	20.87
Total	29	100.00	7	100.00	34	100.00	21	100.00	91	100.00
Unknown	2		0		1		0		3	

Note: Information complete on 91 (96.18%) of 94 generals noble when appointed.

Table 33
Fathers' Occupations: General Staff Generals Listed by Chief of Staff

	Moltke I		Waldersee		Schlieffen		Moltke II		Total	
	No.	%	No.	%	No.	%	No.	%	No.	%
Landowner	2	5.88	1	11.11	1	2.44	1	4.55	5	4.72
Landowner/officer	4	11.76	0	—	5	12.19	0	—	9	8.10
Landowner/civil serv.	2	5.88	1	11.11	1	2.44	0	—	4	3.77
Landowner subtotal	8	23.82	2	22.22	7	17.07	1	4.55	18	16.59
Civil servant	7	20.59	1	11.11	14	34.15	9	40.91	31	29.24
Officer	19	55.89	5	55.55	18	43.90	10	45.45	52	49.06
Other	0	—	1	11.11	2	4.88	2	9.09	5	4.72
Total	34	100.00	9	100.00	41	100.00	22	100.00	106	100.00

Note: Information complete on 106 (93.80%) of 113 fathers.

Even more striking is the almost complete absence of landed fathers whose sole occupations were in agriculture.[38] Of the 18 landowning fathers, 13 were civil servants or officers as well as landowners, leaving only five General Staff generals who were sons of purely agricultural fathers. Half the landowning fathers of generals appointed by Moltke I were also officers, as were five of the seven landed fathers of Schlieffen's appointments. Because all of these landed fathers were full-time officers for at least 20 years, a question arises as to their true occupations. Some may have been active officers only until they inherited their fathers' land, but others doubtless were career officers. The same reservation applies equally to those fathers who were civil servants as well as landowners.[39]

General Staff generals of the Imperial period were primarily sons of the old officer class. Half (49.06%) of the 113 generals had fathers who were officers without other visible occupations or means of support. Although the percentage of these fathers declined from its peak under Moltke I, fathers who were officers always formed the largest occupational category. Nine additional generals (8.49%) were sons of landed officers. When they are added to the fathers whose occupations were solely military, it may be seen that 57.55 percent of the General Staff generals were following in their fathers' footsteps when they entered the army.

A significant and increasing proportion of the General Staff generals were sons of civil servants. For the empire as a whole, 21 (29.24%) generals had fathers who were civil servants without other discernible occupations or income. The percentage of fathers in this category increased dramatically between 1888 and 1914. An additional four generals were sons of civil servants who owned land. The combined ratios of these categories were significantly higher immediately before World War I than they had been just after the Franco-Prussian conflict. By 1914, generals who were sons of civil servants had become the second largest occupational category, exceeded only by those who were sons of officers.

When the sons of officers are combined with sons of bureaucrats, it is apparent that more than nine General Staff generals in ten were offspring of fathers at least partially dependent on the government for their income or social position. Nearly eight fathers in ten (78.30%) were government professionals without other visible means of support. Except for the decrease among the very few generals appointed by Waldersee, the percentage of General Staff generals with fathers whose income depended primarily if not exclusively on government employment rose steadily throughout the period. The correlation between high position on the General Staff and a family tradition of royal service was approximately equal to that of membership in the nobility.

In a consideration of factors more under the control of the officers involved, few were so fortunate as was the later General and War Minister Karl von Einem, who managed to marry the daughter of his division commander.[40] All young officers who married, of course, had to find acceptable women and were best advised to choose wives whose personal attributes might contribute to their careers. An examination of the occupational backgrounds of the wives of the General Staff generals will reveal the preferences of these officers and will complete the overall picture of this segment of the total body of generals (Table 34).

Daughters of landowners were the most frequent marital partners of General Staff generals during the second empire. While most landed connections among the generals' families were declining, it is possible that the proportion of landowners' daughters among the wives may have increased.[41] Another variation from the previous findings on the generals' own families is the few wives' fathers with mixed occupations.[42] Only six of the twenty-six landed men among the fathers-in-law were also either officers or civil servants. The apparent reciprocal preference of officers for women from landed families and of such ladies for General Staff officers was a reflection of the high social standing of both occupations. If a noble landowner's daughter could not marry the son of another landowner, the next logical choice might well have been an officer. For a young officer, noble or bourgeois, the acquisition of a wife with landed connections had the potential of opening useful lines of access to influential noblemen.

Wives of the General Staff generals were far less likely to have had fathers who were officers than were the generals themselves. About three wives in ten (29.58%) were daughters of officers. This was hardly more than half as many officers as were to be found among the generals' own fathers. Schlieffen's appointments had married into military families more frequently (32.55%) than had the generals selected by the other chiefs of Staff.[43] In selecting such men Schlieffen had again chosen officers whose family backgrounds were similar to his own.[44]

The proportion of the wives' fathers who were civil servants was even less consistent with the ratios among the generals' own families. Of the wives, 25 (32.15%) were daughters of civil servants, including four who also owned land. The percentage of wives in this category steadily decreased from its peak under Moltke I to its lowest point among the generals appointed after 1905. This downward trend was quite the reverse of that among the generals' fathers and paternal grandfathers.[45] The army's enhanced social standing after the wars of unification may have allowed officers marrying in subsequent years to choose daughters of landowners or higher officers rather than daughters of various types of civil servants.

A tradition of family service to the crown was present in a large majority of the wives' families. Nearly two wives in three (64.74%) were the offspring of men whose careers were wholly or partially involved with state service. The number of fathers-in-law in this category declined, however, during the imperial years, reaching its low point among the generals

Table 34
Occupations of Wives' Fathers: General Staff Generals Listed by Chief of Staff

	Moltke I		Waldersee		Schlieffen		Moltke II		Total	
	No.	%	No.	%	No.	%	No.	%	No.	%
Landowner	3	14.28	3	50.00	9	26.47	5	50.00	20	28.17
Landowner/officer	0	—	0	—	2	5.88	0	—	2	2.82
Landowner/civil serv.	3	14.28	0	—	1	2.94	0	—	4	5.63
Civil servant	8	38.10	2	33.33	9	26.47	2	20.00	21	29.58
Officer	6	28.57	1	16.67	9	26.47	3	30.00	19	26.76
Business	1	4.77	0	—	4	11.77	0	—	5	7.04
Other	0	—	0	—	0	—	0	—	0	—
Total	21	100.00	6	100.00	34	100.00	10	100.00	71	100.00

appointed by Moltke II. The proportion of government professionals among the wives' fathers was much lower than among the generals' fathers (90.56%) and paternal grandfathers (82.72%). It should be observed, nevertheless, that the wives were from basically the same levels of society that produced the generals, except that more wives came from landed families.

An overview of the total picture for the occupational background of the General Staff generals reveals a group of talented officers whose backgrounds were anything but diverse. Only five General Staff generals had fathers whose professions were not in the army, bureaucracy, agriculture, or a combination of the three.[46] These five generals were a mere 4.72 percent of the 106 known cases. For the entire group of Prussian generals in the same period, the situation was somewhat different. Generals with fathers whose occupations were other than old-Prussian constituted about 7 percent of the total during the period. From this perspective the General Staff was slightly more narrow in its social base than was the entire group of general officers.

The occupational backgrounds of the grandfathers were not greatly different for the two groups of generals. Paternal grandfathers of General Staff generals were of old-Prussian occupational backgrounds in 90.13 percent of the known cases. Among the entire body of generals, the figure was equally impressive—93.72 percent. Also by this measure, then, General Staff generals were no more diverse in their family backgrounds than were typical Prussian generals between 1871 and 1914.[47]

Count von Schlieffen's appointments are an exception to the overall relationship between General Staff generals and their colleagues in the wider army. His appointments were drawn more heavily from military families and less frequently from landed families than were the generals promoted during the decade 1893–1903.[48] Nearly six of Schlieffen's appointments in ten (56.09%) were sons of officers. During the 1893–1903 period, however, fewer than half (47.19%) of all generals had military fathers. Schlieffen's appointments came from landed fathers in about one case in six (17.07%). The entire group of generals during the same period contained sons of landowners in about one case in four (25.59%).

The overwhelming majority of the General Staff generals were born in Prussia (Table 35). Only 11.65 percent were born in non-Prussian Germany, and a small 3.88 percent, outside the empire's frontiers. These proportions underwent no significant variations between 1871 and 1914. Slightly fewer than six General Staff generals in ten (58.26%) were born in the eastern provinces. The percentage of generals in this category reached its peak (65.00%) under Schlieffen and declined moderately among the generals appointed to the General Staff by Moltke II. His figure of 59.08 percent, nevertheless, was higher than that for the generals appointed by his illustrious uncle. This trend was quite the opposite of the broad

Table 35
Region of Birth: General Staff Generals Listed by Chief of Staff

Region	Moltke I		Waldersee		Schlieffen		Moltke II		Total	
	No.	%	No.	%	No.	%	No.	%	No.	%
Eastern Prussia	17	51.52	4	50.00	26	65.00	13	59.08	60	58.26
Western Prussia	11	33.33	1	12.50	8	20.00	7	31.82	27	26.21
Other German	4	12.12	2	25.00	5	12.50	1	4.55	12	11.65
Foreign	1	3.03	1	12.50	1	2.50	1	4.55	4	3.88
Total	33	100.00	8	100.00	40	100.00	22	100.00	103	100.00

Note: Information complete on 103 (91.15%) of 113 General Staff generals.

demographic movement in Germany, where the proportion of the population living east of the Elbe declined from about 33 percent in 1870 to about 31 percent in 1910, the year of the last prewar census.

General Staff generals were slightly more heavily drawn from the eastern provinces than was the entire group of Prussian generals. While General Staff generals came increasingly from the eastern areas in the later years of the empire, the reverse was true of the larger group of generals. Schlieffen's appointments, of whom 65.00 percent were from east of the Elbe, were noticeably more east-Elbian by birth than were the generals promoted between 1893 and 1903. Only 55.42 percent of the latter generals were born in the eastern provinces. Moltke I's appointments, by contrast, were less east-Prussian by birth (51.52%) than were the generals promoted between 1882 and 1892 (54.69%). The General Staff increasingly became a preserve of the eastern nobility in the latter decades of the empire.

When the bourgeois generals are considered separately from the nobles, a somewhat different picture emerges. The places of birth are known for 15 of the 19 bourgeois General Staff generals. Of these 15, seven (46.67%) were born in eastern Prussia.[49] Because only one of these generals was the son of an officer, the close connection between possession of bourgeois civilian fathers and noneastern birthplaces is obvious. Sons of nobles and officers tended to be born in the eastern areas, whereas sons of civilians and nonnobles were predominantly born in the western provinces or other German states. Five of the fifteen bourgeois generals were born in non-Prussian German states. It is probably the case, therefore, that family and occupational backgrounds were more important than geographic origins. Although successful bourgeois generals did not have to be from the eastern provinces, the study has established that in most cases they possessed other attributes that apparently overcame any geographic handicaps they may have had.

Another consideration in determining the extent of Prussian dominance in the General Staff is the source of family titles of nobility. Although applicable only to noble generals, this factor was of considerable importance in social and career success. Information has been assembled on the origins of the titles of nobility with geographic divisions drawn between Prussian, non-Prussian German, and foreign titles (Table 36).[50]

Despite the multitude of ancient and frequently extinct states, imperial cities, bishoprics, and other agencies that had granted titles long before Brandenburg or Prussia had become prominent centers of political and military power, a majority (61.80%) of the General Staff generals possessed titles originating in Prussia. Prussian dominance of the General Staff reached its peak under Schlieffen and declined slightly after 1905. About one title in five was of non-Prussian origins. The number of titles in this category remained fairly constant from the 20.69 percent under Moltke I through Schlieffen's 24.24 percent but dropped off sharply after 1905.

Table 36
Sources of Noble Titles: Noble General Staff Generals Listed by Chief of Staff

	Moltke I		Waldersee		Schlieffen		Moltke II		Total	
	No.	%	No.	%	No.	%	No.	%	No.	%
Prussian	19	65.51	3	42.86	23	69.70	13	65.00	58	65.17
Non-Pr. German	6	20.69	2	28.57	8	24.24	2	10.00	18	20.22
Foreign	4	13.80	2	28.57	2	6.06	5	25.00	13	14.61
Total	29	100.00	7	100.00	33	100.00	20	100.00	89	100.00

Note: Information complete on 89 (94.68%) of 94 noble General Staff generals.

The reduction was due partially to the number of noble generals appointed by Moltke II who held titles created after 1800, nearly all of which were Prussian.[51]

That possession of a non-Prussian German title was only marginally more common than possession of a foreign title is probably a reflection of the cosmopolitanism and aristocratic cohesiveness of much of Germany's nobility.[52] The proportion of noble generals whose titles were of foreign origin is curiously large (Table 36). One noble General Staff general in seven (14.61%) had a title of a foreign state. Of course, by 1870 many of these families had considerable traditions of Prussian state service and many had received Prussian recognition of their foreign titles.[53] Some families, however, remained substantially foreign, especially those from the Russian and Austrian border areas.[54]

A comparison of the titles of the General Staff generals with those of all Prussian generals reveals that the General Staff was of substantially stronger Prussian origins than was the larger group.[55] Barely half (52.80%) of the noble generals in the entire period held Prussian titles.[56] The discrepancy, moreover, increased as the years passed. The figures for Prussian titles among Moltke I's appointments were nearly equal to the corresponding percentages for all noble generals serving in the first two decades of the empire.[57] Schlieffen's General Staff appointments, however, held Prussian titles in two cases in three. All generals promoted between 1893 and 1903 held Prussian titles in fewer than half the known cases (49.51%). General Staff generals picked by the younger Moltke were almost as heavily Prussian as were Schlieffen's generals and were equally disproportionate to the larger group of generals of the corresponding decade.[58]

The role of religion as a factor in career success, as well as a basis for personal morality and social and political values, has been discussed in an earlier chapter. This important aspect of a general's background was no less significant for General Staff generals than it was for their colleagues in elite or line regiments. The chiefs of the General Staff were religious men and usually chose General Staff generals whose religious inclinations were thoroughly Evangelical (Table 37).[59]

General Staff generals were of the Evangelical church to an overwhelming degree. Of the 113 General Staff generals, 81 listed their religion as Evangelical, 88.04 percent of the total. Only six were Catholics. These were a far smaller proportion of the generals than were their brethren a part of the entire Prussian or German populations. Schlieffen's General Staff generals were by a narrow margin the most predominantly Evangelical of the four groups of officers. His staff appointments were also marginally more heavily drawn from the Evangelical faith than were all generals promoted between 1893 and 1903.[60]

Schlieffen's personal religious beliefs fully accepted and even strongly advocated the Prussian system of a union between throne and altar.[61] In

Table 37
Religion: General Staff Generals Listed by Chief of Staff

	Moltke I		Waldersee		Schlieffen		Moltke II		Total	
	No.	%	No.	%	No.	%	No.	%	No.	%
Evangelical	23	82.15	7	87.50	31	91.18	20	90.91	81	88.04
Lutheran	3	10.71	0	—	2	5.88	0	—	5	5.43
Catholic	2	7.14	1	12.50	1	2.94	2	9.09	6	6.52
Total	28	100.00	8	100.00	34	100.00	11	100.00	92	100.00

Note: Information complete on 92 (81.42%) of 113 General Staff generals.

taking the abitur examination in 1853, the young Alfred von Schlieffen wrote a comparative essay on patriotism in pagan and Christian lands.[62] Even at this early stage in his life, Schlieffen saw the church and state as twin pillars of the nation. He was very intolerant of anyone who used religious orthodoxy as a justification for criticism of the official church or of the monarchy.[63] It is easily understood, then, that as chief of the General Staff Schlieffen preferred members of the state church.[64]

The highest officers on the General Staff clearly constituted a social elite as well as the most capable group of officers in the army. In nearly every category General Staff generals were more aristocratic than was the entire group of generals. More than eight General Staff generals in ten were nobles at the time of their appointment. A large proportion of the bourgeois General Staff generals had important family connections with the aristocracy. Despite the General Staff's reputation as a haven for capable officers of diverse backgrounds, the General Staff generals formed a very homogenous and highly aristocratic group.

From a different perspective, occupational and geographic backgrounds, the traditional old-Prussian types clearly dominated the General Staff. Only five of the 106 known fathers were of backgrounds other than the social circles historically the bases of the officer corps. Equally significant is the absence of substantial numbers of generals from landed families. Only 18 of the 106 known fathers owned land, and only one general appointed to the General Staff after 1905 had such a father.

Finally, some concluding attention must be focused upon Count von Schlieffen. The evidence concerning this aristocratic officer has hardly upheld his reputation as a narrow-minded specialist concerned only with military matters, excluding all social and political factors. On the contrary, Schlieffen appointed a group of generals that proved the most aristocratic and the most Prussian of the four sets of General Staff generals. His generals had the highest percentage of nobles, of noble parents, of Uradel titles, of Protestants, and of generals born in the eastern provinces. It is inconceivable that Schlieffen's generals were selected entirely on their ability and that these aristocrats were the best officers available. Schlieffen probably preferred men of a social background similar to his own and selected this type of officer to serve on his staff. The army's long process of aristocratic selection provided him with enough capable officers to fill the necessary positions, and fill them with old-Prussians he did.

9

Conclusions

From the days of Frederick William I to the beginning of World War I, the Prussian army remained an aristocratic institution. This was especially the case in the army's highest and most important command positions. In social terms, in fact, the history of the army in the nineteenth century is the story of the military aristocracy's attempts to retain its dominance in an expanding officer corps and to exclude undesirables. In official eyes the army's special relationship to the monarchy and its position in the Prussian state depended on the continued political reliability and thus the social composition of the officer corps. The army preferred aristocrats and those bourgeois young men whose family circumstances placed them among the nation's privileged social groups. An elaborate system of officer selection, largely based on tradition, but modified to meet the army's social requirements and the increased need for officers, excluded outsiders or prevented them from attaining high rank. Consequently, Prussia's general officers as a group were of remarkable social homogeneity. In the face of continued challenges from internal reformers, democratic politicians, and finally, the leaders of social democracy, the officer corps repeatedly closed ranks and maintained its traditional values, social policies, and political credo.

The most fundamental fact of the army's relationship to Prussian society was its continued reliance on men who were noble by birth or who had acquired titles to fill the majority of the best command positions. Although after 1860 the army was unable to maintain numerical aristocratic predominance among the lower ranks, it stubbornly resisted the advance of bourgeois officers into the higher ranks. Nearly seven generals in ten were nobles when promoted to the rank of brigadier general. The considerable expansion of the infantry and technical branches and an increasing shortage of nobles available to fill the vacancies had the inevitable result of lessening aristocratic dominance even among the generals. Nevertheless, even in the final ten years before World War I, nearly six Prussian generals in ten were nobles before their promotion.

The aristocratic content of the Prussian army, as defined in this study, probably was greater than in any other major European army. Although a recent historian has argued that the class origins of Britain's officers changed only slightly between 1854 and 1900, the social fluidity of the "aristocracy and landed gentry" render most of those men less aristocratic than their Prussian counterparts.[1] Likewise, although a respected scholar has emphasized that 87 percent of Russian infantry generals in 1914 were "of noble origin," a careful occupational study has demonstrated that nearly half the infantry officers were descendants of serfs. Few such men acquired titles and commissions in Prussia, and even fewer became generals.[2] Although available data on the French army are not directly comparable to the information presented here, the most comprehensive recent study clearly establishes that relatively few high French officers were of noble origins. Nobles, in fact, did proportionally better in the National Assembly than in the French army.[3]

The generals' geographic roots reflect a relatively greater diversity than do their social origins. More than eight generals in ten were born in Prussia, but fewer than six in ten came from the eastern provinces. This latter figure, nevertheless, was a complete reversal of the overall population distribution of Prussia and Germany. Religious and occupational factors reinforced the geographic influences in favoring officers whose homes were in the eastern provinces. Prussia's Protestant population was heavily concentrated in the eastern areas, which also contained numerous garrisons whose officers produced many sons destined for the officer corps. This was also the case for the large number of generals who were born in the Berlin-Potsdam area.

Religious orthodoxy was another important attribute expected of Prussian officers, and only about one general in ten was not a member of the state church. The army forced its enlisted men to attend religious services, and officers likewise found themselves in attendance at official ceremonies on frequent occasions. Prussia's brand of Protestantism reinforced the union of throne and altar and was seen as a counterweight to materialism, socialism, and other dangerous movements of the century. Under these circumstances it is hardly surprising that officers were expected to take their religious obligations seriously and that, by far, the vast majority felt compelled to maintain at least formal ties to the official religion. Many officers, moreover, were deeply religious and found in their Protestant faith an effective antidote to the intellectual challenges of Marxists and other enemies of the established order. Catholics especially were frequently identified with the Reich's opponents and only rarely pursued successful military careers.

As for the frequently discussed issue of Jewish participation, or lack of same, the Prussian officer corps was in the front ranks of the anti-Semites, but it was hardly unique. No Jew could reasonably expect to receive a commission in the Russian army.[4] The Austro-Hungarian army stood at the opposite end of the spectrum.[5]

Good social standing had little to do with wealth in itself. Men from certain occupational groups, in the army's view, were quite likely to present good officer material regardless of their financial situation. Other groups were entirely unproductive in this respect, especially if their place in society was based solely on commercial or other wealth not ordinarily associated with agriculture. "Peasants with money" remained peasants and belonged in the enlisted ranks, not in the officer corps. The question of an officer's family background became increasingly important as the army had to accept large numbers of bourgeois officers. This is not to deny, of course, that new wealth gained a considerable foothold in the officer corps. Even in 1914, however, Prussia's industrial and commercial establishments lacked strong representation among the ranks of the army's generals.

Landowning families provided the army with a substantial number of generals during the Imperial period but hardly enough to dominate the officer corps numerically. The percentage of generals from landed families declined noticeably between 1871 and 1914. By the last decade before World War I, only about one new general in four had a landowning father. Most of these were either officers or civil servants as well as landowners. Only about one general in ten was the son of a purely agricultural father.

The army promoted sons of officers and high civil servants into its highest positions in a strong majority of the total cases. These solid old-Prussian types of families had traditionally provided a large number of Prussia's officers, and it was from these elements that the army drew the bulk of its general officers. The business and academic communities produced very few generals although the number from these backgrounds increased between 1871 and 1914. Families occupied in other professions, such as law and medicine, were almost entirely absent from the ranks of Prussia's generals. All things considered, the upper levels of the officer corps remained a remarkably homogenous group. Old-Prussian types were nearly as dominant in 1914 as they had been in 1870, despite some internal shifts within the occupational categories.

The generals' families showed a strong tendency to become employed in the service of the Prussian state, either in the bureaucracy or in the army. Nearly two-thirds of the generals had fathers who were civil servants or officers without other visible means of support. They were therefore at least two generations removed from the land, and many were even further removed. The resulting total dependence on the good graces of the Prussian monarch and his government thus gave these families more than mere ideological grounds for supporting official policies on political and social questions. In such cases as the furor over the proposed canal bill, army officers and bureaucrats without land to rely upon and whose careers demanded support of official policy usually complied while their agricultural countrymen resisted bitterly.

The officer corps did not weather the storms of the nineteenth century without considerable internal change and some strains. During the latter half of the century and until 1914, large numbers of wealthy young men joined the army in search of social prestige and resplendent uniforms. Their presence combined with rising standards of living began to raise serious questions about the role of wealth in the officer corps. The War Ministry was unable to prevent many regiments from acquiring excessively luxurious standards of living. These units, mainly cavalry and guards infantry regiments, eventually demanded such large amounts of private income that only the wealthy could afford to serve in them.

This ultimately had serious effects on the internal cohesion of the officer corps and greatly damaged the army's image. The cavalry branch became a pleasant diversion for wealthy military playboys at the same time that its military usefulness diminished. Serious officers of modest means had no choice but to enter the infantry because many, if not all, artillery regiments also acquired expensive tastes. Because the regiments and their commanders retained control over most officer replacements, the army's weak War Ministry was unable to act effectively to curb this serious defect. The consequence was an increasing gap between the different kinds of regiments in their social content and lifestyles. This was evident in the contempt for the cavalry displayed by many infantry and some General Staff officers.

For those young men deemed worthy to enter the officer corps, career success was dependent upon several factors. Reasonably efficient performance of duty, acceptable personal and political conduct, favorable reports by superior officers, and, above all, good relations with the Military Cabinet were the basic ingredients of success. General von Schwienitz's comments on the power of the Military Cabinet in the middle years of the nineteenth century remained valid throughout the Imperial period.

The seniority system established the rate of normal advancement for the majority of the officer corps. These standards could be exceeded only under special circumstances. Only a few of the available openings each year were reserved for accelerated promotion of especially gifted officers.[6] Attendance at the War Academy and service on the General Staff were very helpful but were by no means essential for successful careers. Influential high commanders frequently interceded with the Military Cabinet on behalf of relatives or friends. Those who lacked connections with the Military Cabinet, personal or professional, had to wait patiently as their names moved slowly up the seniority lists. Beyond the rank of captain, such men were dependent upon God's mercy, as one officer remarked. Even for officers who possessed considerable talents and good connections, the road from the first commissioning to promotion to brigadier general was quite lengthy—more than 30 years' duration in most cases. At every step and at every grade, the seniority system at least partially protected average officers from the threat of rapid advances by their juniors.

Women played an important role in the careers of many Prussian officers, a fact given insufficient attention in most treatments of the officer corps. Aristocratic mothers provided many bourgeois officers with the essential family ties to the nobility that their fathers lacked. About one bourgeois general in six had such a noble mother, a fact of some importance for the growth of the bourgeois elements with the officer corps. In a number of cases bourgeois mothers, who happened to have fathers, brothers, or other relatives in the officer corps, gave their sons advantages over other bourgeois young men who lacked any ties with the aristocracy or the military establishment. It was for good reason that the army developed stringent regulations governing an officer's marriage. Disreputable women were unsuitable companions and unacceptable wives for Prussia's officers. If an officer insisted on marrying a woman whose background was not what the officer corps demanded, he normally had to resign his commission and leave the army. Regimental commanders had the primary tasks of investigating and approving the character and background of their officers' potential wives; the commanding generals and the War Ministry had the king's final blessing.[7]

Many officers, nonnobles and aristocrats alike, used good marriages to further their careers, either by marrying into prominent noble families or by finding wives from military families. About one bourgeois general in five married a noble woman, and about three generals in ten married daughters of career officers. Wealthy ladies, even of Jewish origins, brought their own important assets to impoverished officers. Frequently young officers were able to marry only because their wives possessed the substantial financial resources required by army regulations. In both personal and professional terms, women were an important ingredient in military careers. At the very least officers had to find wives who met the army's minimum standards of social acceptability.

Prussia's generals hardly correspond to their most frequent stereotype, the Junker officer. Although the generals had strong family ties to Prussia's aristocracy and were frequently born east of the Elbe river, only a few had direct family connections with landowners in the eastern provinces. Even fewer had both fundamental traits of a Junker—landed fathers and birth in the eastern provinces. Fewer than one general in ten may be properly classified as a Junker. An adequate characterization of the generals is much more complex.

In fact, Prussian generals on the whole probably had weaker direct connections to their state's landed elite than did the generals of other

European armies. A limited sample of British generals, for example, reveals that in 1913 more than one in three were from landed families. One study concluded that about 18 percent of the Russian generals examined owned property themselves. Although the data on the French army are not directly comparable, Barge's study found that as late as 1905 nearly one general in four had an "agricultural" father.[8]

A typical Prussian general may be said to have existed in reality only in the broadest of terms. Such an officer was noble at birth, was likely to have had a noble mother, and probably married a noble woman. A typical general was Prussian by birth and was likely to have been born in the eastern provinces, if one includes the Berlin-Potsdam area in that category. The typical general was the son of a Prussian officer rather than of a landowner or civil servant. Generals themselves rarely owned land. All landed connections, except for those through wives from landowning families, decreased markedly during the empire.

Beyond these few very broad generalizations, however, the complexity of the officer corps defies any sweeping conclusions. There existed not one officer corps of very similar individuals but rather two or even three distinct groups of officers within the larger body.

The aristocratic officers of the cavalry regiments, and especially of the guards cavalry regiments, stood clearly apart from the rest of the officer corps. Nearly all generals who began their careers in one of the guards cavalry regiments were nobles. Only 40 of the 286 generals who entered the army in a cavalry regiment of any kind were bourgeois. The very substantial private income required of cavalry officers further emphasized the distinctiveness of that branch. Those cavalry regiments whose officers were largely bourgeois had even higher standards than did some of the aristocratic cavalry regiments. All cavalry units demanded private incomes far beyond that necessary for most infantry regiments.

Cavalry regiments, and again the guards cavalry regiments above all, were distinct from the rest of the officer corps because of their professional outlook as well as their social background. Cavalry officers attended the War Academy in small numbers and felt no need to subject themselves to the intellectual rigors of the General Staff.[9] The careers of generals in the cavalry reflect this aristocratic disdain for military education and intellectual attainment. It simply was not necessary for cavalry officers to depart their comfortable units or to compete against the other branches for the best professional opportunities. Cavalry officers became generals without such exertions.

Officers of the guards infantry units occupied a middle ground between those of the cavalry and line infantry regiments. The officer corps of these were less aristocratic than those of the guards cavalry but were substantially more aristocratic than those of line infantry units. Correlation of social class and original unit of service shows that the generals faithfully reflected these relationships of the lower levels of the army. Most guards infantry officers were men of some private wealth, however, and stood closer to the cavalry than to line infantry regiments in their overall social position, origins, and wealth.

Guards infantry officers stood most clearly apart from officers of the cavalry regiments in their career patterns. Nearly four generals in ten whose early years were spent in guards infantry units attended the War Academy, a proportion substantially greater than that of their successful peers in the cavalry. Guards infantry regimental commanders were routinely promoted to general officers in far greater numbers than were cavalry officers. Although their social standing was nearly equivalent to that of the guards cavalry officers and although their wealth and social origins were closer to the cavalry than to line infantry regiments, guards infantry officers were far more professional in their aspirations and in their determination to reach the top. They and the line infantry officers formed the core of the army.

The second type of officer in the army was the most common—the officer whose entire career was spent in the provincial garrisons scattered throughout Prussia. These officers were predominantly nobles, although not to the extent that cavalry and guards infantry officers were. Most possessed very modest financial resources, and some were almost entirely without private income. Their lifestyles were accordingly much more in the customary tradition of Prussian officers. Relatively few sons of landowners served in the infantry, and easily two-thirds of the infantry generals were sons of officers and civil servants without land.

Artillery generals differed significantly from the above two types in several important respects. Artillery generals were predominantly bourgeois in their social origins. They were, however, possessed of considerable wealth in most cases, especially later in the period. A few prominent nobles found their way into the guards artillery regiments, but most noble officers who could afford the artillery preferred to serve in the infantry if their purses could not bear the burdens of cavalry duty. The social prejudice encountered by artillery officers is reflected in their greater ages at promotion and longer time spent in the army before elevation to the rank of brigadier general. Artillery officers were more likely to have attended the War Academy than were cavalry officers and frequently served on the General Staff. Once they attained the rank of brigadier general, however, the old social prejudices again came to the fore. Very few artillery officers commanded military units larger than a brigade, and fewer than 5 percent commanded fortresses just before their retirement. Generals with infantry or elite careers were two to three times as likely to have enjoyed the latter command and to have commanded a division or corps. Although these artillery officers had the money to establish expensive standards of living in their units, they lacked the social and professional influence and power to attain equality with their social superiors in the cavalry and infantry regiments.

The General Staff corresponds to its reputation even less than the Junker stereotype applies to the officer corps or the generals as a whole. The General Staff did indeed provide many capable bourgeois officers with otherwise unattainable opportunities for advancement. This does not mean, however, that the General Staff was free of social prejudice or favoritism. The army's central planning authority remained an aristocratic institution to an even greater extent than did the officer corps as a whole. This was especially true for the generals who served while Schlieffen was chief of the General Staff. All four chiefs were old-Prussian types of distinguished lineage. Their key General Staff personnel reflected their social preferences for men who were remarkably like themselves. There are numerous well-known cases of capable bourgeois officers whose General Staff careers elevated them to prominent positions in the army. These men were a minority of the General Staff officers as well as of the generals as a whole.

The War Academy and General Staff were not the sole, or even the most prevalent, types of service leading to promotion to high rank. Many capable officers, including most of the army's most famous commanders and nearly all who wrote memoirs after 1900, were General Staff officers. They were a minority among the General Staff officers, however, and may in no way be seen as typical generals. General Staff officers felt themselves distanced from the rest of the army, as indeed they were if their careers, rates of promotion, and their image in the rest of the army are any indications. Drawn from all the basic branches, General Staff officers were the army's military elite, and, as is now evident, were a social elite as well. Some were wealthy; others were not. Examples of great wealth and extreme poverty are to be found in the youthful days of General Staff officers. Their superior ability in military affairs has always been unquestioned; their social standing was on almost as high a plane.

The officer corps was thus a homogenous group when compared with Prussian society as a whole. Most members of that society could not have hoped to become a Prussian officer as long as the army relied on a relatively narrow definition of social acceptability. Nevertheless, the historian should not be blind to the important internal differences within the officer corps. All officers were not equal. Nor were they identical in their social origins and career patterns. Although they stood shoulder to shoulder against the government's political enemies, the officers were themselves split into several groups according to social status, wealth, and career patterns. The archetypal Prussian officer existed only in the imaginations of hostile contemporaries and in the minds of some subsequent historians.

The regimental system remained the foundation of the entire army. The regiment, with its powerful commander and self-recruiting officer corps, enforced the army's standards for officer replacements. Individual regiments frequently exceeded the army's recommendations in demanding aristocratic officer candidates, excessive private incomes, very narrow social backgrounds, or whatever else they wished. If a young man were rejected by any individual regiment, he had no choice but to apply to another. No central authority, and certainly not the War Ministry, could intercede in his behalf. Promotions up to the rank of captain, likewise, were based on the regimental system. Elite regiments offered better opportunities for appointments to the War Academy and the General Staff. Officers remained fiercely loyal to their original regiments and zealously prevented outsiders from gaining admittance whenever possible.

The Prussian army grew with the cadet branch of the Hohenzollerns, helped shape the dynasty and the state, prospered when the family prospered, and suffered when the monarch suffered. The fate of the monarchy, as Bismarck noted, was inextricably bound up with that of the army and its officer corps. Neither the monarchy nor the army could adapt sufficiently to the new situation created by the vast economic, political, and social changes of the nineteenth century. Both institutions still possessed considerable reserves of strength in August of 1914, but the massive casualties of the opening months of the war virtually destroyed the old officer corps just as four years of extended warfare fatally weakened the monarchical state of the Hohenzollerns. By November 1918, the army and the king had both become intolerable to the great mass of the German people. Born together, the old Prussian state and its officer corps expired together in that fateful month.

Notes

Chapter 1

1. This statement has most recently been quoted by Michael Balfour, *The Kaiser and His Times* (New York: W. W. Norton, 1964), p. 178. Admiral von Tirpitz claimed to have heard Bismarck's pronouncement to the Kaiser. See his *Erinnerungen* (Leipzig: K. F. Koehler, 1920), pp. 93–94. It is also printed in Prince Otto von Bismarck, *Die gesammelten Werke*. 19 vols. (Berlin: Verlag für Politik und Wirtschaft, 1924–1932), IX: 489.

2. Arthur Rosenberg, *Imperial Germany: The Birth of the German Republic, 1871–1918*, trans. Ian F. D. Morrow (Boston: Beacon Press, 1970 [1931]), p. 1.

3. Gordon A. Craig, *Germany 1866–1945* (New York: Oxford University Press, 1978), pp. 1–2, makes this point emphatically and convincingly. Manfred Messerschmidt, *Militär und Politik in der Bismarckzeit und im wilhelminischen Deutschland* (Darmstadt: Wissenschaftliche Buchgesellschaft, 1975), pp. 32–34, discusses the essential constitutional points and has a useful bibliography. As he points out, there is no doubt among constitutional historians that Prussia and the Prussian army were the "hard core" of the constitutional structures of 1867 and 1871. Wolfgang Sauer, "Das Problem des deutschen Nationalstaats," in *Probleme der Reichsgründungszeit 1848–1879*, ed. Volker Berghahn (Köln: Kiepenheur & Witsch, 1968), p. 470, concludes that Bismarck's system was dependent upon the army and that the military apparatus was the core of the entire state.

4. Prussia, Kriegsministerium, *Rang und Quartierliste der königlich preussischen Armee*, 42 vols. (Berlin: E. S. Mittler & Son, 1870/71–1914). This title varies and the series includes the Württemberg army in later years. The Ranglisten list each officer by his last name under his regiment or other unit of assignment. The Prussian rank was *Generalmajor*. To avoid confusion of this with the U.S. rank of major general, which corresponds to the Prussian *General-Leutnant*, the term brigadier general will be used as the translation of Generalmajor.

5. Kurt von Priesdorff, ed., *Soldatisches Führertum*, 10 vols. (Hamburg: Hanseatische Verlagsanstalt, 1936–1942), contains many such honorary generals. So does Bogislav von Kleist, *Die Generale der königlich preussischen Armee von 1840–1890*, 3 vols. (Leipzig: Zuckschwerdt & Möschke, 1895). [Thus the official army Rangliste for each year is the best source for accurate lists of generals.]

6. On the incorporation of the smaller contingents see Klaus-Dieter Kaiser, *Die Eingliederung der ehemals selbständigen Norddeutschen Truppenkörper in die preussische Armee in den Jahren nach 1866* (Ph.D. dissertation, Free University of Berlin, 1972, privately printed). An important new study is Rolf Wilhelm, *Das Verhältnis der süddeutschen Staaten zum Norddeutschen Bund (1867–1870)* (Husum: Mathiessen Verlag, 1978).

7. In addition to the above works, Baron Ottomar von der Osten-Sacken und von Rhein, *Preussens Heer von seinen Anfängen bis zur Gegenwart*, 3 vols. (Berlin: E. S. Mittler & Sons, 1914), III: 119–28, 271–87, examines the military conventions.

8. Only one Prussian officer, the war minister, took an oath to the Prussian constitution and none pledged loyalty to the German constitution. On the oaths of the officers of the smaller armies, see Lieutenant General Friedrich von der Boeck (retired), *Deutschland: Das Heer* (Berlin: Verlagsbuchhandlung Alfred Schall, 1903), p. 17.

9. The discrepancies between the army's demands and the Reichstag's willingness to provide funds are beyond the scope of this study. Gordon Craig, *The Politics of the Prussian Army, 1640–1945* (New York: Oxford University Press, 1956), pp. 219–23, 225–26, 228, 242–45, has an excellent summary.

10. There is no comprehensive monograph on the Prussian army in the nineteenth century, but numerous surveys are relevant. Craig, *Prussian Army*, remains the best. Others include Curt Jany, *Geschichte der königlich preussischen Armee*, 4 vols. (Berlin: Verlag von Karl Siegismund, 1933), an important source of basic information and now virtually a primary source; Herbert Rosinski, *The German Army* (Washington, D.C.: The Infantry Journal, 1944); Gerhard Ritter, *The Sword and the Scepter: The Problem of Militarism in Germany*, trans. Heinz Norden, 4 vols. (Coral Gables: University of Miami Press, 1964–73), especially I and II; Emil Obermann, *Soldaten, Bürger, Militaristen. Militär und Demokratie in Deutschland* (Stuttgart: J. G. Cotta'sche Buchhandlung Nachfolger n.d. [1955?]); and Baron L. Rüdt von Collenberg, *Die deutsche Armee von 1871 bis 1914* (Berlin: E. S. Mittler & Son, 1922).

11. On Frederick William I, see Robert Ergang, *The Potsdam Führer: Frederick William I, Father of Prussian Militarism* (New York: Columbia University Press, 1941).

12. Craig, *Prussian Army*, p. 11. See also the classic essay by Otto Hintze, "The Hohenzollern and the Nobility," in *The Historical Essays of Otto Hintze*, ed. Felix Gilbert (New York: Oxford University Press, 1975), pp. 52–60.

13. William O. Shanahan, *Prussian Military Reforms, 1786–1813* (New York: AMS Press, 1966 [1944]), p. 29.

14. Craig, *Prussian Army*, pp. 22–36, is excellent on the weaknesses of the army in 1806. Peter Paret, *Yorck and the Era of Prussian Reform, 1807–1815* (Princeton: Princeton University Press, 1966), is also a fundamental source.

15. On the reformers and their failure to effect permanent change in the army, see Shanahan, *Prussian Military Reforms,* passim; Walter M. Simon, *The Failure of the Prussian Reform Movement, 1807–1819* (Ithaca: Cornell University Press, 1955), especially pp. 145–240; Paret, *Yorck,* concentrates on military tactics but has a final chapter that is one of the most important examinations of reformers in Prussia and of historians' treatment of them. Also useful is the same author's *Clausewitz and the State* (Oxford: Clarendon Press, 1976). Guy Stanton Ford, *Stein and the Era of Reform in Prussia, 1807–1815* (Princeton: Princeton University Press, 1922), devotes considerable space to military reforms. Manfred Messerschmidt, "Die preussische Armee," in *Handbuch zur deutschen Militärgeschichte 1648–1939,* ed. Friedrich Forstmeister and Hans Meier-Welcker (Munich: Bernard & Graefe, 1962–1976), IV, part 2, has an excellent bibliography on military aspects of the reforms.

16. In addition to the above sources, one might turn to Manfred Messerschmidt, "Die politische Geschichte der preussisch-deutschen Armee," in *Handbuch zur deutschen Militärgeschichte,* IV, part 1; and his *Militär und Politik.* Martin Kitchen, *A Military History of Germany* (Bloomington: Indiana University Press, 1975), is of less value.

17. Representative of the East German view are Horst Bartel and Ernst Engelberg, eds., *Die grosspreussisch-militaristische Reichsgründung 1871,* 2 vols. (Berlin: Akademie Verlag, 1971), especially II; Ernst Engelberg, ed., *Diplomatie und Kriegspolitik vor und nach der Reichsgründung* (Berlin: Akademie Verlag, 1971).

18. Fritz Fischer, *Krieg der Illusionen. Die deutsche Politik von 1911 bis 1914* (Düsseldorf: Droste Verlag, 1969), places much emphasis on the army's involvment in plotting an aggressive war. Much of the literature on the "Fischer debate" discusses the attitude of prominent military figures. On the question of the army's social and armaments policies see Volker Berghahn, *Germany and the Approach of War in 1914* (New York: St. Martin's Press, 1973); and his *Der Tirpitz Plan. Genesis und Verfall einer innenpolitischen Krisenstrategie unter Wilhelms II* (Düsseldorf: Droste Verlag, 1971), pp. 249–71. Michael Stümer, ed., *Das kaiserlich Deutschland. Politik und Gesellschaft 1870–1918* (Düsseldorf: Droste Verlag, 1970), has excellent sections on this question. Count Otto zu Stolberg-Wernigerode, *Die unentschiedene Generation. Deutschlands konservative Führungsschichten am Vorabend des Ersten Weltkrieges* (Munich: R. Oldenbourg, 1968), has a chapter on the officer corps.

19. No comprehensive study of the social make-up of any level of the officer corps exists. Karl Demeter's remarkable *Das deutsche Offizierkorps in Gesellschaft und Staat 1650–1945,* 4th ed. (Frankfurt am Main, Bernard & Graefe, 1965 [1930]), is the best by far. Franz Karl Endres, *The Social Structure and Corresponding Ideologies of the German Officer Corps before the World War,* trans. S. Ellison (New York: Columbia University Press, 1937), is very brief and unbalanced. Martin Kitchen, *The German Officer Corps, 1890–1918* (Oxford: Clarendon Press, 1968), has a short section on the social composition of the officer corps but offers nothing new either in evidence or in interpretation. Nikolaus von Preradovich, *Die Führungsschichten in Oesterreich und Preussen 1804–1918* (Wiesbaden: Franz Steiner Verlag, 1955), has some very general information. Günther Martin,

"Gruppenschicksal und Herkunftschicksal, zur Sozialgeschichte der preussischen Generalität 1812–1918" (Ph.D. dissertation, Saarbrücken, 1970), examines only commanding generals and is severely limited by methodological shortcomings. Gotthard Breit, *Das Staats-und Gesellschaftsbild deutscher Generale beider Weltkriege im Spiegel ihre Memoiren* (Boppard am Rhein: Harald Boldt Verlag, 1973), is useful but very limited in its perspective.

20. Ritter, *Sword and Scepter*, I: 181.

21. The Military Cabinet receives fuller treatment in Chapter 6.

22. Count Alfred von Waldersee, Edwin von Manteuffel, Paul von Hindenburg, and Erich Ludendorff are the best-known, but by no means the only, examples. World War I saw the realization of nearly all of the worst possibilities of political interference by the military. See the indispensable study of Wilhelm Deist, *Militär und Innenpolitik im Weltkriege 1914–1918*. 2 vols. (Düsseldorf: Droste Verlag, 1970), I.

23. Rudolf Schmidt-Bückeburg, *Das Militärkabinett der preussischen Könige und deutschen Kaiser* (Berlin: E. S. Mittler & Son, 1933), pp. 28–30; Ritter, *Sword and Scepter*, I: 168. Friedrich Meinecke, *Das Leben des Generalfeldmarschall Hermann von Boyen*, 2 vols. (Stuttgart: J. G. Cottasche Buchhandlung Nachfolger, 1899), remains the standard work on this pivotal figure. But see also Eberhard Kessel, "Zu Boyens Entlassung," *Historische Zeitschrift* 175 (1953): 41–54.

24. The war minister became and remained the only officer in the army who took an oath to the constitution.

25. Baron Fritz Adolf Marschall von Bieberstein, *Verantwortlichkeit und Gengenzeichnung* (Berlin: Verlag von Franz Vahlen, 1911) is the most thorough study of the constitutional and legal complexities. Friedrich Hossbach, *Die Entwicklung des Oberbefehls über das Heer in Brandenburg, Preussen, und im deutschen Reich von 1655–1945* (Würzburg: Holzner Verlag, 1957), pp. 29–50, is useful. Eckart Busch, *Der Oberbefehl. Seine rechtliche Struktur in Preussen und Deutschland seit 1848* (Bopard am Rhein: Harald Boldt, 1967), pp. 7–47, surveys the major issues.

26. Craig, *Prussian Army*, p. 195.

27. It was at this point, in 1866, that the epic confrontation between Bismarck and Moltke began in earnest. This bitter quarrel between King William's most illustrious servants receives fuller treatment in Chapter 7.

28. Moltke's comment is in his history of the Franco-Prussian War, *Gesammelte Schriften und Denkwürdigkeiten des General-Feldmarschalls Grafen Helmuth von Moltke*, 8 vols. (Berlin: E. S. Mittler & Son, 1892–1918), III: 423–24.

29. Schmidt-Bückeburg, *Militärkabinett*, p. 58.

30. Manteuffel's fall was the result of a campaign by Bismarck. See ibid., p. 92. Wilhelm Gradmann, *Die politischen Ideen Edwin von Manteuffels und Ihre Auswirkungen in seiner Laufbahn* (Düsseldorf: Dissertations Verlag G. H. Nolte, 1932), is a useful treatment of Manteuffel.

31. Schmidt-Bückeburg, *Militärkabinett*, p. 72; Marschall von Bieberstein, *Verantwortlichkeit*, pp. 223–24.

32. Schmidt-Bückeburg, *Militärkabinett*, p. 80.

33. Count Alfred von Waldersee, *Denkwürdigkeiten des Generalfeldmarschalls Alfred Grafen von Waldersee*, H. O. Meisner, ed. 3 vols. (Stuttgart: Deutsche Verlags-Anstalt, 1925), I: 220, amply states Waldersee's attitude.

34. On Kameke's personality, see Schmidt-Bückeburg, *Militärkabinett*, pp. 126–27. Chlodwig Hohenlohe-Schillingsfürst, who was not unfriendly toward Kameke, referred to him as a military *Streber*. See Hohenlohe-Schillingsfürst, *Denkwürdigkeiten des Fürsten Chlodwig zu Hohenlohe-Schillingsfürst*, Friedrich Curtius, ed., 2 vols. (Stuttgart: Deutsche Verlags-Anstalt, 1907), II: 68.

35. It was during one of these exchanges that Eugen Richter made his well-known attack on the Garde du Corps, calling them parade troops. Also at issue was the Reichstag's demand for a reduction in the officers' immunity from communal taxation. Kameke wished to compromise on this issue. See Ritter, *Sword and Scepter*, II: 120–23.

36. The best accounts of what was a massive constitutional crisis are Schmidt-Bückeburg, *Militärkabinett*, pp.137–51; Craig, *Prussian Army*, pp. 227–31; and Frederic B. M. Hollyday, *Bismarck's Rival: A Political Biography of General and Admiral Albrecht von Stosch* (Durham: Duke University Press, 1960, pp. 206–9. For an entirely different evaluation of Paul Bronsart von Schellendorff's part in the drama see Friedrich von Bronsart, "Die alte Kaiser und sein Kriegsminister von Bronsart," *Historische Vierteljahresschrift* 31 (1937–1939): 293–306.

37. After 1883 the following officers had the right of direct access to the king of Prussia; the chiefs of the Military Cabinet and the General Staff, the war minister, all corps commanders, the president of the Military Court, general inspectors of foot artillery, engineers, and of armies, a variety of officers in the king's personal entourage, and numerous naval officers.

38. The Military Cabinet consisted of ten or fewer officers and a small number of civilian assistants.

39. The position of the chief of the Military Cabinet and his enormous power is discussed more fully in Chapter 6.

40. Some information is missing for many generals. The percentages of completion normally appear in the tables.

41. The *Gotha* appeared under various titles between 1796 and 1942. The volumes are divided according to rank, with the von families divided according to date of title: e.g., *Gothaisches Genealogisches Taschenbuch der Uradeligen/ Briefadeligen/Freiherrlichen/Gräflichen/Fürstlichen Häuser* (Gotha: Justus Perthes, 1764–1942). Hans Friedrich von Ehrenkrook et al., eds., *Genealogisches Handbuch des Adels* (Glücksburg: C. A. Starke Verlag, 1951 to date), is a continuation of the *Gotha*, but concentrates on living relatives within the same format. Other useful sources are Baron L. von Zedlitz-Neukirch, ed., *Neues preussisches Adels Lexicon oder genealogische und diplomatische Nachrichten*, 6 vols. (Leipzig: Gebrüder Reichenback, 1837); and Ernst Kneschke, ed., *Neues allgemeine deutsches Adels-Lexicon*, 9 vols. (Leipzig: Friedrich Vogt, 1860–1870).

42. Bernard Koerner et al., eds., *Genealogisches Handbuch bürgerlicher Familien: ein deutsches Geschlechterbuch*, 174 vols. (Görlitz: C. A. Stark Verlag, 1904 to date), is arranged by geographic areas, principally relying on the pre-1914 provinces and various regional designations.

43. *Wer Ist's*, 10 vols. (Leipzig: Verlag von H. L. Degener, 1905–1935), lists the person's name, place of birth, father's occupation, mother's name, and basic educational and career information.

44. Kurt von Priesdorff, ed., *Soldatisches Führertum*, 10 vols. (Hamburg: Hanseatische Verlagsanstalt, 1936–1942), gives the generals' full names, date and place of birth, fathers' occupations, and mothers' names. The entries also have full career information, including all military assignments and dates of promotions. They also frequently contain sections from the officer efficiency reports. The published volumes conclude with officers who retired about 1893. Priesdorff had prepared the typescript for an additional ten or so volumes, and some were ready for the printer when war interrupted the project. These manuscripts were lost in the confusion following the war and have not been fully recovered. The *Bundesarchiv/ Militärarchiv* has obtained the existing copies. These cover the years 1908 through 1914. In this study they are cited as BA/MA, Priesdorff Manuscripts. I am indebted to Dr. Peter-Christian Stahl, formerly director of the military archives, for permission and assistance in using these very valuable papers.

45. A typical Stammliste provides basic career information and some details of the officers' personal background.

Chapter 2

1. Leopold von Ranke, *Leopold von Ranke, Neue Briefe,* Bernard Hoeft and Hans Herzfeld, eds. (Hamburg: Hoffmann and Campe Verlag, 1949), p. 496.

2. The rank of Generalmajor is rendered as brigadier general, its best equivalent in English.

3. Ulrich Trumpener, "Junkers and Others: The Rise of Commoners in the Prussian Army, 1871–1914," *Canadian Historical Journal* 16 (April 1979): 29–47, stresses the bourgeois component of the generalcy while raising the basic issue of quantification.

4. It was indeed a *Besonderheit* (unusual occurence), as one distinguished historian has noted, when a bourgeois officer became a general without at some point acquiring a noble title. See Manfred Messerschmidt, "Die preussische Armee," p. 61.

5. It would be interesting to see if these generals were representative of all Prussian generals serving between 1819 and 1870.

6. The years have been arranged into four 11-year "decades," the term used to describe the periods in this study.

7. Demeter, *Offizierkorps,* p. 59, cites the study by Prince Karl zu Isenburg, "Zur Statistik des deutschen Adels," *Deutsches Adelsblatt* 55 (1937), based on the *Gotha* nobility handbooks, which surely understated the nobility's total numerical strength.

8. Hermann Rumschöttel, *Das bayerische Offizierkorps 1866–1914* (Berlin: Duncker & Humboldt, 1973), pp. 62–63. Rumschöttel leaves no doubt that nobles received preferential treatment in promotions.

9. See Joachim Fischer, "Das württembergische Offizierkorps 1866–1918," in *Das Deutscher Offizierkorps 1860–1960.* Edited by Hubert Hoffman (Boppard: Harald Boldt Verlag, 1980).

10. Craig, *Prussian Army,* pp. 5–14, has a good account.

11. Prussia, Kriegsministerium, ed., *Militärische Schriften weiland Kaiser Wilhelms des Grossen Majestät,* 2 vols. (Berlin: E. S. Mittler & Son, 1897), passim,

has ample evidence of William's interest and considerable expertise in military affairs.

12. Karl von Einem, *Erinnerungen eines Soldaten 1853–1933* (Leipzig: Verlag K. F. Koehler, 1933), p. 36.

13. William I, *Militärische Schriften*, II: 344–79.

14. Friedrich von Bernhardi, ed., *Aus dem Leben Theodor von Bernhardis*, 7 vols. (Leipzig: Verlag von S. Hirzel, 1895), IV: 166.

15. See William's letter to Roon, May 9, 1844, in William I, *Militärische Schriften*, I: 495; Count Alfred von Blumenthal, ed., *Tagebücher des General-Feldmarschalls Graf von Blumenthal aus den Jahren 1866 und 1870/71* (Berlin: C. G. Cotta'sche Buchhandlung Nachfolger, 1902), passim, details William's interest in promotions.

16. On the changed relationship between the monarch and the army during the rule of William II, see Deist, *Militär und Innenpolitik*, xv.

17. The emperor's physical handicap made the numerous signatures a major production. He perservered in spite of the difficulties. See *Bundesarchiv/Militärarchiv* (hereafter cited as BA/MA), Nachless von Mutius, N 195/2, p. 171.

18. This was the view of Count Dietrich von Hülsen-Haeseler, chief of the Military Cabinet between May 1901 and his sensational death in November 1908. See Prince Bernhard von Bülow, *Denkwürdigkeiten*, 4 vols. (Berlin: Ullstein, 1930), II: 183–84.

19. The decree is printed in part in Hans Meier-Welcker, ed., *Offiziere im Bild von Dokumenten aus drei Jahrhunderten* (Stuttgart: Deutsche Verlags-Anstalt, 1964), p. 197. The order came out on March 29, 1890. See also Craig, *Prussian Army*, pp. 234–35.

20. On the size of the army see Wiegand Schmidt-Richberg, "Die Regierungszeit Wilhelms II," in *Handbuch zur deutschen Militärgeschichte*, V: 90.

21. Demeter, *Offizierkorps*, pp. 28–29, has the overall figures.

22. Julius von Hartmann, *Lebenserinnerungen, Briefe, und Aufsätze* 2 vols. (Berlin: Verlag von Gebrüder Paetell, 1882), I: 127. Complaints about the practice of rapidly advancing young princes may be found in Heinrich Otto Meisner, ed., *Denkwürdigkeiten des General-Feldmarschalls Alfred Grafen von Waldersee*, 3 vols. (Stuttgart: Deutsche Verlags-Anstalt, 1925), II: 209, 341; and G. von Gleich, *Die alte Armee und ihre Verirrungen*, 2nd ed. (Leipzig: Verlag K. F. Koehler, 1919), p. 64.

23. For his hapless military performance, the grand duke earned the sharp criticism of a young General Staff officer, Count Alfred von Schlieffen. See Count Alfred von Schlieffen, *Graf Alfred Schlieffen. Briefe*, Eberhard Kessel, ed. (Göttingen: Vandenhoeck & Ruprecht, 1958), pp. 252–54, 257–58; and Hollyday, *Bismarck's Rival*, pp. 72–79.

24. The prince's nonmilitary career is given in detail in Priesdorff, *Soldatisches Führertum*, no. 2523.

25. After one visit to the Habsburg court and dinner with Francis Joseph and his entourage, General Otto von Below (title dating to early thirteenth century) complained of the company and the dinner, which smacked of the parvenu—surely an unusual complaint about the Hapsburg court. See BA/MA Nachlass von Below, N 87/43, p. 533.

26. Baron Richard von Strombeck, *Fünfzig Jahre aus meinem Leben* (Leipzig: Friedrich Wilhelm Grunow, 1894), pp. 138–39.

27. The well-known Dohna tale is recounted by Lord D'Abernon, *An Ambassador of Peace: Lord D'Abernon's Diary*, 3 vols. (London: Hadder & Stoughten, 1929), II: 210–211, who correctly concluded that the nobility's "obsequiousness to royalty is tempered by their reverence for the *Almanach de Gotha*."

28. Hans von Kretschmann, *Kriegsbriefe aus den Jahren 1870/71*, ed. Lily Braun (Berlin: Meyer & Jessen, 1911), p. 7.

29. Einem, *Erinnerungen*, p. 7.

30. Exceptions would be members of the ruling and mediatized houses, who normally stood clearly above even the most ancient lower-ranking families.

31. Uradel families normally lacked specific patents of nobility but were able to cite ancient documents as proof that they had been nobles before 1400. Many Briefadel families also lacked a specific patent conferring nobility.

32. Useful introductions to the nobility are Albert Goodwin, ed., *The European Nobility in the Eighteenth Century* (London: Adam and Charles Black, 1953); Joachim von Dissow, *Adel im Übergang* (Stuttgart: W. Kohlhammer Verlag, 1961); and Stolberg-Wernigerode, *Unentschiedene Generation*. Two important new studies are Peter-Michael Hahn, *Struktur und Funktion des brandenburgischen Adels in 16. Jahrhundert* (Berlin: Colloquium Verlag, 1979); and Hans Reif, *Westfälischer Adel, 1770–1860: Vom Herrschaftsstand zur regionelen Elite* (Göttingen: Vandenhoeck & Ruprecht, 1979). A solid East German contribution, although with no mention of military affairs, is Klaus Vetter, *Kurmärkischer Adel und preussische Reformen* (Weimar: Herman Böhlaus Nachfolger, 1979).

33. Some generals have been excluded for reasons explained at the bottom of Table 4. During World War I the army's very highest ranks were opened to men of common birth. By 1918 a total of seven such men attained the rank of colonel-general or field marshal.

34. Lamar J. R. Cecil, *The German Diplomatic Service, 1871–1914* (Princeton: Princeton University Press, 1976), p. 203.

35. A reason for the higher proportion of older families among the generals was undoubtedly that diplomatic careers required greater personal financial sacrifices to meet the expenses of the service. The question of the expenses involved in a military career will be discussed in Chapter 5.

36. Karl Friedrich von Steinmetz, *General-Feldmarschall von Steinmetz, aus Familienpapieren dargestellt*, Hans von Krosigk, ed. (Berlin: E. S. Mittler & Son, 1900), pp. 72–73.

37. Other examples of well-placed mothers exercising influence on behalf of their sons may be found in BA/MA Nachlass von Mutius, N 195/1, p. 64; Nachlass Chales de Beaulieu, N 187/1, p. 23; Prince Krafft zu Hohenlohe-Ingelfingen, *Aus meinem Leben*, 4 vols. (Berlin: E. S. Mittler & Son, 1907), IV: 7; Ernst Buchfink, *Feldmarschall Graf von Haeseler* (Berlin: E. S. Mittler & Son, 1929), p. 1.

Chapter 3

1. Some specifically military examples of these geographical prejudices, which were closely tied to cultural and religious differences, may be found in Waldersee,

Denkwürdigkeiten, I: 243; BA/MA Nachlass Lequis, N 30/13; BA/MA Nachlass von der Leyen, N 154/1, p. 15.

2. Emil Obermann, *Soldaten, Bürger, Militäristen, Militär und Demokratie in Deutschland* (Stuttgart: J. G. Cotta'sche Buchhandlung Nachfolger, n.d.), pp. 14–16, has a good introduction to these differences and their importance in the officer corps. See also Frank B. Tipton, Jr., *Regional Variations in the Economic Development of Germany during the Nineteenth Century* (Middletown, Connecticut: Wesleyan University Press, 1976).

3. One interesting feature of Prussian history was the ability of the monarchs to attract talented officers from other states.

4, For further details on the careers of all types of non-Prussian officers, see the author's "Non-Prussian Officers in the Prussian Army, 1867–1914," *Red River Valley Historical Journal* 6, No. 2 (Winter 1981): 4–32.

5. Klaus-Dieter Kaiser, "Die Eingliederung der ehemals selbständigen Norddeutschen Truppenkörper in die preussische Armee in den Jahren nach 1866" (Ph.D. dissertation, Free University of Berlin, 1972).

6. Eduard von Fransecky, *Denkwürdigkeiten des preussischen Generals der Infanterie Eduard von Fransecky*, Walter Bremen, ed. (Bielefeld & Leipzig: Verlag von Velhagen und Klasing, 1901), p. 1.

7. Kaiser, "Die Eingliederung," pp. 42–50.

8. For Tresckow's role in the amalgamation process, see Thilo Krieg, *Hermann von Tresckow, General der Infanterie und General-Adjutant Kaiser Wilhelms I* (Berlin: E. S. Mittler & Son, 1911), pp. 72–75.

9. Meier-Welcker, *Offiziere in Dokumenten*, pp. 189–90.

10. Theodore Hamerow, *The Social Foundations of German Unification*, 2 vols. (Princeton: Princeton University Press, 1969, 1972), II: 415.

11. For the destruction of the war memorial, ordered by General von Schwartzkoppen, see *Denkwürdigkeiten aus dem Leben des General-Feldmarschalls Kriegsministers Grafen von Roon*, ed. Count Waldemar von Roon, 3 vols. (Breslau: Verlag von Eduard von Trewendt, 1897), III: 148–49. Ernst Keostring, BA/MA Nachlass Koestring, N 123/6, pp. 14–15, records the continuing hostility of his Hanoverian family toward Prussia. Hans von Beseler's letter to his mother, September 20, 1887, Nachlass Beseler, N 30/52, records the same sentiments. Waldersee, *Denkwürdigkeiten*, I: 46–47, records his dislike for Hanoverian officers who were insufficiently Prussian for his tastes. Wilhelm Keitel later remembered that a Prussian officer frequently could not wear his uniform at home in Hanover. See BA/MA Nachlass Keitel, N 54/1, p. 8.

12. Einem, *Erinnerungen*, pp. 31–32.

13. Blumenthal, *Tagebücher*, p. 163, relates the general's fear of lingering Austrian influence in the southern states, a sentiment echoed by Waldersee, *Denkwürdigkeiten*, I: 24. William I, *Militärische Schriften*, I: 475, has evidence of the monarch's long-standing mistrust of southerners. Similar particularist views may be found in Einem, *Errinerungen*, pp. 9, 11, 31–32; Baron Paul von Schoenaich, *Mein Damaskus, Erlebnisse und Bekenntnisse* (Berlin-Hessenwinckel: Verlag der neuen Gesellschaft, 1926), p. 43; Friedrich von Bernhardi, *Denkwürdigkeiten aus meinem Leben* (Berlin: E. S. Mittler & Son, 1927), p. 257. Baron Hugo von Freytag-Loringhoven, *Menschen und Dinge wie ich sie in meinem Leben sah* (Berlin: E. S. Mittler & Son, 1923), pp. 82–83, mentions the hazards of

encountering a superior officer whose particularist prejudice might threaten an entire career.

14. BA/MA Nachlass von Stülpnagel, N 5/27, p. 9.

15. Waldersee, *Denkwürdigkeiten*, II: 147–48.

16. Kurt von Bülow, *Preussischer Militarismus zur Zeit Wilhelms II, aus meiner Dienstzeit im Heer* (Schweidnitz: Hugo Reisse, 1930), p. 35.

17. Franz von Lenski, *Lern-und Lehrjahre in Front und Generalstab* (Berlin: Verlag Bernard & Graefe, 1939), pp. 18–19. For prejudice against Bavarians, see Kretschmann, *Kriegsbriefe*, pp. 247–48.

18. Einem, *Erinnerungen*, pp. 11, 31–32, for his political conservatism and monarchism. Likewise, August von Goeben said that he soon acquired an enthusiasm for Prussia. See Gebhard Czernin, *Das Leben des Königlich preussischen Generals der Infanterie August von Goeben*, 2 vols. (Berlin: E. S. Mittler & Son, 1895), I: 1.

19. On the western nobility, see Heinz Reif, *Westfälischer Adel, 1770–1860. Vom Herrschaft zur Regionalen Elite* (Göttingen: Vandenhoeck & Ruprecht, 1979).

20. Franz von Lenski, *Aus den Leutnantsjahren eines alten Generalstabsoffiziers* (Berlin: Verlag Georg Bath, 1922), p. 12.

21. BA/MA Nachlass von der Leyen, N 154/1, p. 15.

22. Waldersee, *Denkwürdigkeiten*, I: 243.

23. BA/MA Nachlass Lequis, N 30/13, p. 7. By this Lequis meant total devotion to the Prussian state.

24. More than 200 generals were born in Prussian Saxony, nearly 11 percent of the total.

25. The Mecklenburg and Danish nobility were closely intertwined. Many families, such as the Moltke or Bülow clans, may be placed in either category.

26. For example, the official schedule of the activities for the annual "Kaiser maneuvers" usually included a compulsory church service on Sunday mornings, with the uniform of the occasion carefully regulated. One such printed schedule survives in BA/MA Nachlass von Waldersee, N 182/11. Helmuth von Moltke, *Erinnerungen, Briefe, Dokumente, 1877–1916*, ed. Eliza von Moltke (Stuttgart: Der kommende Tag Verlag, 1922), p. 111, has another example where officers received an invitation, not to be refused, to attend an Evangelical church service with William I. The Lutherans in Table 9 were a splinter group that refused amalgamation with the state church. Many others within the Evangelical church revered Luther as opposed to Calvin as the founder of Protestantism. Von Rabenau, *Die deutsche Land-und Seemacht und die Berufspflichten des Offiziers*, 4th ed. (Berlin: E. S. Mittler & Son, 1914), p. 35, explains the obligations of soldiers and officers to attend Sunday church regularly.

27. Reinhard Höhn, *Die Armee als Erziehungsschule der Nation. Das Ende einer Idee* (Bad Harzburg: Verlag für Wissenschaft, Wirtschaft und Technik, 1963), pp. 220–80, has an extensive and excellent account.

28. The exchange is recorded in BA/MA Nachlass von Stülpnagel, N5/27, p. 10.

29. On Moltke's religious views see Eberhard Kessel, *Moltke* (Stuttgart: K. F. Koehler Verlag, 1957), p. 191; and Höhn, *Armee als Erziehungsschule*, pp. 209–213.

30. Erich Ludendorff, *Mein militärischer Werdegang. Blätter der Erinnerung an*

unser stolzes Heer (Munich: Ludendorffs Verlag, 1935), p. 6. Ludendorff, of course, was a notorious anti-Catholic. See also Hans Pommer, *Zwanzig Jahre im Reichslande* (Frankfurt am Main: Neuer Frankfurter Verlag, 1914), p. 44.

31. Klaus Epstein, *Matthias Erzberger* (Princeton: Princeton University Press, 1959), p. 69.

32. Lysbeth Walker Muncy, "The Prussian *Landräte* in the Last Years of the Monarchy: A Case Study in Pomerania and the Rhineland in 1890–1918," *Central European History* 6, No. 4 (December 1973): 326; Cecil, *German Diplomatic Service*, p. 96; Herwig, *Naval Officer Corps*, p. 42.

33. Excluded from Table 10 are generals who died on active duty and those still on active duty when the war began in 1914. The latter cannot be accurately classified as to high rank and thus have been omitted.

34. Information based on research not presented in tables. The Catholic part of the generals in selected provinces was as follows: eastern Prussia, 36 Catholics of 1,067 generals born there; western provinces, 40 of 552; Hesse, 4 of 43; Baden, 6 of 43; Saxony, none of 18; Württemberg, none of 5.

35. Rumschöttel, *bayerische Offizierkorps*, pp. 236–38. Again the problem is murky because of a lack of precisely comparable data. The proportion of Protestant officers in the Bavarian army probably increased during the imperial years.

36. Joachim Fischer, "Das württembergisch Offizierkorps 1866–1918" (unpublished paper, Büdinger Gespräche, 1977), pp. 6–7.

37. On William I and Catholics, see Demeter, *Offizierkorps*, p. 219; William's letter to Ambassador von Bunsen (London), September 5, 1851, in Erich Brandenburg, ed., *Briefe Kaiser Wilhelms des Ersten* (Leipzig: Insel Verlag, 1911), p. 94; William to Major von Orlich, December 29, 1852, in William I. *Briefe, Reden, Schriften*, I: 330. On William II, see John C. G. Röhl, *Germany without Bismarck: The Crisis of Government in the Second Reich, 1890–1900* (Los Angeles: University of California Press, 1967), pp. 133–35; Ekkehard-Teja Wilke, *Political Decadence in Imperial Germany: Personnel-Political Aspects of the German Government Crisis, 1894–1897* (Urbana: University of Illinois Press, 1967), p. 87.

38. See Demeter, *Offizierkorps*, p. 214.

39. Lenski, *Lern-und Lehrjahre*, p. 12. Arndt instead became governor of Metz in 1894.

40. Ibid., pp. 12–13, for information on the old cabinet order.

41. There were occasional exceptions among the large landowners. Perhaps the best-known of these was Count von Hutten-Czapski, who had a fairly promising career in the army before his early resignation. Two new studies treat the Polish question. See John Kulczycki, *School Strikes in Prussian Poland, 1901–1907: The Struggle over Bilingual Education* (New York: Columbia University Press, 1981); and Richard Blanke, *Prussian Poland in the German Empire, 1871–1900* (New York: Columbia University Press, 1981).

42. A representative sampling of anti-Catholicism among officers may be found in the following: BA/MA Nachlass von Beseler, N 30/52.

43. The excellent article by Werner T. Angress, "The Prussian Army and the Jewish Reserve Officer Controversy before World War I," *Leo Baeck Institute Yearbook* 17 (1972): 19–42, reviews the literature. Alexander von Kluck, *Wanderjahre-Krieg-Gestalten* (Berlin: Verlag R. Eisenschmidt, 1929), describes the treatment meted out to Jewish officers in 1870 and the army's attitude toward them. Kitchen, *Officer Corps*, pp. 139–46, estimates that by 1878 and 1909,

respectively, Jews had been excluded from the active and reserve officer corps. Angress estimates that there were about 25–30 Jewish reserve officers in 1914. All, however, were baptized.

44. Waldersee, *Denkwürdigkeiten*, is filled with examples of his prejudices. Ulrich von Stosch, ed., *Denkwürdigkeiten des Generals und Admirals Albrecht von Stosch* (Stuttgart: Deutsche Verlags-Anstalt, 1904), p. 39, contains his position. He was, he said, not a liberator of the Jews because they were un-Christian and un-German (letter of July 13, 1856).

45. Hohenlohe-Ingelfingen, *Aus meinem Leben*, IV: 309.

46. Excluded from this consideration are the memoirs written after 1918, when racial comments became fashionable. Typical earlier comments on Jews may be found in Blumenthal, *Tagebücher*, p. 7; and Paul Bronsart von Schellendorff, *Paul Bronsart von Schellendorff, Geheimes Kriegestagebuch 1870–71*, Peter Rassow, ed. (Bonn: Athenäum Verlag, 1954), p. 30.

47. Schlieffen to his sister Anna, August 10, 1860, Schlieffen, *Briefe*, p. 125.

48. Otto Liman von Sanders was also of Jewish descent. His grandfather had converted to the Evangelical faith. His father was an east-Elbian landowner and his wife, the daughter of a Prussian officer. He was in no way a Jew by the definition used by the Prussian army.

49. Mossner's father is mentioned in Demeter, *Offizierkorps*, p. 217. The general himself is listed in the *Gothaisches Genealogisches Taschenbuch der Briefadeliger Häuser*, I (1907): 546, but without a hint of his Jewish origins.

50. BA/MA (Library): Berkun and Krüger, eds., *Stammliste des Infanterie Regiments von Alvensleben Nr. 52*. The handwritten comments are partly in German and partly in English.

51. Angress, "Jewish Reserve Officer Controversy," p. 33.

52. Fritz Stern, *Gold and Iron: Bismarck, Bleichröder and the Building of the German Empire* (New York: Alfred A. Knopf, 1977), p. 174.

53. Rumschöttel, *bayerische Offizierkorps*, pp. 245–251. Demeter, *Offizierkorps*, pp. 218–19; Kitchen, *Officer Corps*, p. 46.

54. Cecil, *German Diplomatic Service*, pp. 95–96.

55. Preliminary research indicates that no Jews served in the active or reserve officer corps in Württemberg between 1871 and 1914. See Fischer, "württembergisch Offizierkorps," pp. 8–9.

Chapter 4

1. See, for example, Obermann, *Soldaten, Bürger, Militaristen*, p. 101.

2. Baron Richard von Strombeck, *Fünfzig Jahre aus meinem Leben* (Leipzig: Friedrich Wilhelm Grunow, 1894), p. 145; and Hollyday, *Stosch*, pp. 260–61.

3. Baron Colmar von der Goltz, *The Nation in Arms*, trans. Philip A. Ashworth (London: W. H. Allen, 1887), pp. 36–41, argues the case at length.

4. Messerschmidt, "preussische Armee," pp. 11–12. For the diverse elements in the post-Napoleonic officer corps see the comments of Julius von Hartmann, *Lebenserinnerungen, Briefe und Aufsätze*, 2 vols. (Berlin: Gebrüder Paetel, 1882), I: 88–89, 104; and Jany, *Armee*, IV: 118. On the reformers see Peter Paret, *Yorck and the Era of Prussian Reform, 1807–1815* (Princeton: Princeton University Press,

1966); and Walter Simon, *The Failure of the Prussian Reform Movement, 1807–1819* (Ithaca: Cornell University Press, 1955).

5. William to General von Natzmer, March 21, 1857, in *Kaiser Wilhelms des Ersten, Briefe, Reden, und Schriften*, ed. Ernst Werner, 2 vols. (Berlin: E. S. Mittler & Son, 1906), I: 408.

6. General von Kameke, "Denkschrift über Luxus in der Armee und die damit verbunden Gefahren," reproduced in Demeter, *Offizierkorps*, p. 332.

7. Friedrich von Bernhardi, *Denkwürdigkeiten aus meinem Leben* (Berlin: E. S. Mittler & Son, 1927), p. 263.

8. See, for example, the formulation of the concept by War Minister Albrecht von Roon in *Denkwürdigkeiten aus dem Leben des General-Feldmarschalls Kriegsministers Grafen von Roon*, ed. Count Waldemar von Roon, 3 vols. (Breslau: Verlag von Eduard Trewendt, 1897), II: 542; and Baron Ottomar von der Osten-Sacken und von Rhein, *Preussens Heer von seinen Anfängen bis zur Gegenwart*, 3 vols. (Berlin: E. S. Mittler & Son, 1897), II: 7.

9. For contemporary use of the term, see Kitchen, *Officer Corps*, p. 50.

10. The reader must bear in mind the long time between commissioning and promotion to brigadier general, normally about 30 years.

11. Fathers who served in the army for only a short time have not been counted as officers. The vast majority of officer/fathers served for 15 or more years and attained the rank of captain. Most were at least majors. Fathers who served in the capacity of Landrat have been counted as civil servants.

12. A study of French generals has revealed that "agricultural" fathers declined sharply between 1889 and World War I. See Walter S. Barge, "The Generals of the Republic: The Corporate Personality of High Military Rank in France, 1889–1914" (unpublished Ph.D. dissertation, University of North Carolina, 1982), Table I-28.

13. Michael Balfour, *The Kaiser and His Times* (New York: W. W. Norton, 1964), pp. 17–18, 29.

14. Fritz Stern, *Gold and Iron: Bismarck, Bleichröder, and the Building of the Great German Empire* (New York: Alfred A. Knopf, 1977), p. 160.

15. The references are, respectively, to Lysbeth Walker Muncy, *The Junker in the Prussian Administration under Wilhelm II, 1888–1914* (Providence: Brown University Press, 1944), p. 31; and Barbara Tuchman, *The Proud Tower* (New York: The Macmillan Company, 1966), p. 355. Other examples of the assumed dominance of landed officers may be found in Volker Berghahn, *Der Tirpitz-Plan, Genesis und Verfall einer innenpolitischen Krisensstrategie unter Wilhelms II* (Düsseldorf: Droste Verlag, 1970), p. 234; and the same author's *Approach of War*; Rumschöttel, *bayerische Offizierkorps*, p.43. More recently, Hans-Jürgen Puhle has made the same argument. See his "Pruessen: Entwicklung und Fehlentwicklung," in *Preussen im Rückblick*, ed. Puhle and Hans-Ulrich Wehler (Göttingen: Vandenhoeck & Ruprecht, 1980), p. 28.

16. A Junker of 1800 might differ considerably from one of 1860 or 1900. Normally the term is used without any such discrimination, rendering it almost useless for precise historical writing. Ulrich Trumpener, "Junkers and Others: The Rise of Commoners in the Prussian Army, 1871–1914," *Canadian Journal of History* 14 (April 1979): 29–47, gives no past or present definition but generally assumes that all old noble families were Junker types.

17. Muncy, *Junker in Administration*, p. 440. This pioneering study remains unique in its area.

18. Count Otto zu Stolberg-Wernigerode, *unentschiedene Generation*, pp. 168–69. Walter Görlitz, *Die Junker. Adel und Bauer im deutschen Osten* (Glücksburg: C. A. Starke, 1956), does not define the term but usually assumed a direct landed connection. Abraham J. Peck, *Radicals and Reactionaries: The Crisis of Conservatism in Wilhelmine Germany* (Washington, D.C.: University Press of America, 1978), pp. 8, 39, seems to assume a direct agrarian connection, as does Geoff Eley, *Reshaping the German Right: Radical Nationalism and Political Change after Bismarck* (New Haven: Yale University Press, 1980), p. 294. Demeter, *Offizierkorps*, pp. 12–13, clearly uses the term synonymously with nobles, without any necessary reference to landownership. Hanna Schissler, "Die Junker, zur Sozialgeschichte und historischen Bedeutung der agrarischen Elite in Pruessen," in *Preussen Im Rückblick*, p. 89, emphasizes the inherency of the landed connection as the basis for a meaningful discussion of the term.

19. Information based on research not presented in tables.

20. Count Helmuth von Moltke, *Essays, Speeches and Memoirs of Count Helmuth von Moltke*, trans. Charles F. McClumph, C. Barter, and Mary Herms, 2 vols. (New York: Harper & Brothers, 1893), II: 83.

21. Ernest K. Bramsted, *Aristocracy and the Middle Classes in Germany* (Chicago: University of Chicago Press, 1964 [1937]), p.178.

22. Muncy, *Junker in Administration*, pp. 77, 117.

23. BA/MA Nachlass von der Leyen, N 154/1, p. 14.

24. BA/MA Nachlass von der Schulenburg, N 58/1, p. 7.

25. Max van den Bergh, *Das deutsche Heer vor dem Weltkriege* (Berlin: Sanssouci Verlag, 1934), p. 103.

26. Excluded are generals whose fathers were officers for only a brief period.

27. It might be noted that the continuity of military families in the Prussian army exceeded that of most other European armies. Fragmentary information indicates that around the turn of the century about one-fifth of France's generals had fathers who had been officers but that only a minute proportion of the latter were themselves generals. See Barge, "Generals of the Republic," pp. 36–37. Likewise a study of a limited sample of British generals for the years 1870, 1897, and 1913 revealed that about one-fourth to one-third had military fathers. See C. B. Otley, "Militarism and the Social Affiliations of the British Army Elite," in *Armed Forces and Society: Sociological Essays*, ed. Jacques van Doorn (The Hague: Mouton, 1968), p. 90. Otley errs, however, when he argues (p. 92) that officering was as hereditary in the British army as in the Prussian.

28. Demeter, *Offizierkorps*, pp. 19–25, cites archival sources (since destroyed) to the effect that in 1862–1866 perhaps one new officer in five was the son of a landowner, but that by 1900–1910 this had declined to between 8 percent and 10 percent.

29. Hermann Vogt, *Das Buch vom deutschen Heer* (Bielefeld: Velhagen & Klasing, 1886), pp. 147–49. A subsequent chapter discusses the cadet corps. There were no special provisions for sons of landowners although the king could intervene in any individual case.

30. The important question of how large a private income (Zulage) was required will be examined in Chapter 5. This complex issue is basic to an

understanding of the differences between the branches of the army and their social standing.

31. In this respect, then, army officers were quite different from their cousins serving in the diplomatic service or the bureaucracy. In both these cases a substantial private income was essential. See Cecil, *German Diplomatic Service*, pp. 39–41. This subject will receive further consideration in a subsequent chapter.

32. An exception is Friedrich von der Gablentz, "Das preussischdeutsche Offizierkorps," in *Schicksalsfragen der Gegenwart*, ed. Bundesministerium für Verteidigung, 7 vols. (Tübingen: Niemeyer, 1958), III: 47, 71. Peter Paret, *Clausewitz and the State* (Oxford: Clarendon Press, 1976), also comments on this point with reference to Clausewitz's father.

33. Most officers were reluctant to criticize the army's procedures because, among other reasons, they were subject to military courts even after retirement. Two exceptions were G. (anonymous) *Das Ende der Offizierslaufbahn* (Berlin: Verlag R. Felix, 1902), pp. 32–33; and, later, (anonymous), *Das alte Heer, von einem Stabsoffizier* (Charlottenburg: Verlag der Weltbühne, 1920), p. 27.

34. Adolf Keim's dismissal was the occasion for an extensive press commentary. Apparently he was forced into retirement because of disfavor over a book on infantry tactics and because he was too close to Caprivi. See August Keim, *Erlebtes und Erstrebtes, Lebenserinnerungen* (Hanover: Ernst Letsch Verlag, 1925), pp. 94–95.

35. It was a mark of the distance separating the wealthy aristocrats of the foreign office from the army's nobles that only three sons of Prussian diplomats became generals. By contrast, the foreign office frequently recruited former officers and assigned active officer to embassies. See Cecil, *German Diplomatic Service*, pp. 112–13. No directly comparable data are available on the occupations of the diplomats' fathers.

36. A few examples should suffice. Emil Priwe, the son of a tax collector, became a brigadier general of artillery in 1891. His grandfather, wife's father, and maternal grandfather were all civil servants of higher position than his father. Ferdinand Bliedung, son of a prison inspector, became brigadier general of infantry in 1900. Other details of his family are obscure. Max Gallwitz (ennobled in 1913) became brigadier general of artillery in 1902. His father had been a tax collector, but his wife was the daughter of a bourgeois Silesian landowner. He reached the generalcy after extensive General Staff service.

37. Schack's letter to Manteuffel, May 19, 1862, is quoted in Demeter, *Offizierkorps*, pp. 18–19.

38. Hans Rosenberg, *Bureaucracy, Aristocracy, and Autocracy: The Prussian Experience, 1660–1815* (Boston: Beacon Press, 1966 [1958]).

39. John C. G. Röhl, *Germany without Bismarck: The Crisis of Government in the Second Reich, 1890–1900* (Berkeley and Los Angeles: University of California Press, 1967), p. 147.

40. Muncy, *Junker in Administration*, pp. 39, 224.

41. By contrast, fewer than 3 percent of the bourgeois envoys in the diplomatic service were sons of landowners. See Cecil, *German Diplomatic Service*, pp. 180–81.

42. Hans Rosenberg, "Die Pseudo-democratisierung der Rittergutsbesitzerklasse," in *Moderne duetsche Sozialgeschichte*, ed. Hans-Ulrich Wehler (Berlin:

Kleins Druck und Verlagsanstalt, 1968), pp. 290–91; Hans-Jürgen Puhle, *Agrarische Interessenpolitik und preussischer Konservatismus im wilhelminischen Reich 1893–1914* (Hanover: Verlag für Literature und Zeitgeschehen, 1966), p. 18. By 1900 probably fewer than half the *Rittergüter* in the eastern provinces were still in noble hands.

43. Ludendorff's father had also been an active officer. His mother was from a very respectable noble family. The Ludendorff's family lifestyle was as aristocratic as a typical landowning noble family's. In fact, they were nobles in all but name. See Henny von Templehoff, *Mein Glück im Hause Ludendorff* (Berlin: Druck und Verlag August Scherl, 1919).

44. They may have left the army after a short time, as their noble counterparts apparently did. It is also possible that many nobles regarded these bourgeois fathers as peasants. There is little if any reliable information on this point. A total of 225 sons of bourgeois landowners were raised to the rank of knight during the empire. Many and probably most of these men remained on the land, however, and few seemed to have been career officers. See Lamar Cecil, "The Creation of Nobles in Prussia, 1871–1918," *American Historical Review* 75, no. 3 (February 1970): 765–66, 770–71.

45. Sons of bourgeois landowners might be exceptions, if these men were not of the undesirable elements accepted only because of the necessities of the Napoleonic wars. In such individual cases the grandfather's occupation would be a decisive factor.

46. John W. Wheeler-Bennett, "Men of Tragic Destiny: Ludendorf and Groener," in *Essays Presented to Sir Lewis Namier*, ed. Richard Pares and A. J. P. Taylor (London: Macmillan, 1956), pp. 510–11.

47. There were sharp increases in the incidence of businessmen among the grandfathers of generals promoted after 1893 and then again after 1903.

Chapter 5

1. BA/MA Nachlass von der Leyen, N 154/1, p. 8, has interesting comments on this point.

2. In a cabinet order of 1867, William I reminded his regimental commanders that the selection of suitable officers was their "first duty." They were held responsible if "undesirable elements" entered their units. See Meier-Welcker, *Offiziere in Dokumenten*, p. 190. In 1899 William II reaffirmed this responsibility. See Waldersee, *Denkwürdigkeiten*, II: 424.

3. Demeter, *Offizierkorps*, p. 32.

4. Schlieffen, *Briefe*, pp. 83, 85; BA/MA Nachlass Chales de Beaulieu N 187/1, p. 23.

5. Wilhelm von Schweinitz, ed., *Denkwürdigkeiten des Botschafters General von Schweinitz*, 2 vols. (Berlin: Reimar Hobbing, 1927), I: 16; BA/MA Nachlass von Stülpnagel, N 5/27, p. 29. On William's relationship to the unit see Count Richard von Pfeil, *Vor vierzig Jahren* (Schweidnitz: Verlag von L. Heege, 1911), pp. 93, 194.

6. This procedure dated to the very early days of the Prussian army. Its nineteenth-century format was established in a cabinet order of 1817. In 1861

William I reaffirmed the procedure and stipulated that if even one negative note were cast the candidate could not become an officer without the intervention of the corps commander. See Meier-Welcker, *Offiziere in Dokumenten*, pp. 175–76, 181–87.

7. van den Bergh, *Heer*, pp. 116–17.

8. BA/MA Nachlass von Schlieffen, N 43/99.

9. von Rabenau, *Die deutsche Land-und Seemacht und die Berufspflichtung des Offiziers*, 4th ed. (Berlin: E. S. Mittler & Son, 1914), p. 347.

10. BA/MA Nachlass Chales de Beaulieu, N 187/1, pp. 24, 40.

11. Infantry regimental adjutants frequently but not always had to have a horse. See von Liebert, *Leben*, p. 43.

12. Cecil, *German Diplomatic Service*, p. 105, cites the example of two horses costing 7,000 marks. Chales de Beaulieu's experience is recorded in BA/MA Nachlass Chales de Beaulieu, N 187/2, pp. 63, 144. Hans Pommer, *Zwanzig Jahre im Reichslände* (Frankfurt am Main: Neuer Frankfurter Verlag, 1914), pp. 39–41, recalled the dangers posed to an officer's honor and integrity by horse dealing. Von Liebert, *Leben*, p. 43, mentions the difficulties in affording a horse despite the official assistance.

13. von Rabenau, *Land-und Seemacht*, p. 58, has the details. Any officer could purchase horses through the army's remount system.

14. van den Bergh, *Heer*, p. 134; Pommer, *zwanig Jahre*, p. 35. Max von der Leyen, BA/MA Nachlass von der Leyen, N 154/1, p. 17, speaks of the extraordinary costs of a compulsory ball at the Berlin palace. Officers had to wear special uniforms and arrived in carriages rented for the occasion. See also the report of the anonymous author of *Das End der Laufbahn* (Berlin: Verlag R. Felix, 1902), p. 75, on excessive social expenses.

15. Messerschmidt, "preussische Armee," p. 26, cites the pay scales first established in 1808. Cavalry officers received an additional 39 marks. See also Felix Priebatsch, *Geschichte des preussischen Offizierkorps* (Breslau: Priebatschs Verlagsbuchhandlung, 1919), p. 36.

16. Waldersee, *Denkwürdigkeiten*, I: 7; Hans Mohs, ed., *General-Feldmarschall, Alfred Graf von Waldersee in seinem militärischen Wirken*, 2 vols. (Berlin: R. Eisenschmidt, 1929), I: 16. Fransecky, *Denkwürdigkeiten*, p. 75, gives the same figure for his pay at mid-century.

17. Hermann Vogt, *Das Buch vom Deutschen Heere* (Leipzig: Verlag von Velhagen & Klasing, 1886), pp. 126–29, has a full basic pay table. Messerschmidt, "preussische Armee," p. 225, has a more limited version of the same. Waldersee, *Denkwürdigkeiten*, I: 52, gives the pay of officers assigned to an embassy. Waldersee remarked that by Prussian standards he received "very good pay" while at the embassy.

18. BA/MA Nachlass Chales de Beaulieu, N 187/1, pp. 41–42. Then Second Lieutenant Chales de Beaulieu complained that he had little money left for his personal expenses.

19. van den Bergh, *Heer*, p. 119; Freiherr von Gall, ed., *Fircks Taschenkalender für das Heer, 1909* (Berlin: Verlag von A. Bath, 1909), pp. 405–6; Rabenau, *Land und Seemacht*, pp. 20–21.

20. van den Bergh, *Heer*, p. 118, said that pay increases for lieutenants removed the worst problems and reduced the financial suffering in the officer corps.

21. BA/MA Nachlass von der Leyen, N 154/1, p. 15.

22. Gerhard Bry, *Wages in Germany, 1871–1945* (Princeton: Princeton University Press, 1960), p. 51; Werner Sombart, *Die deutsche Volkswirtschaft im neunzehnten Jahrhundert*, 3rd ed. (Berlin: Georg Bondi, 1913), pp. 434–35.

23. On the division schools see *Lebenserinnerungen des königlich preussischen Generalleutnants Otto von Hoffmann*, ed. Colonel Von Hoffman (Oldenburg: Schulzesche Hof-Buchhandlung, 1907), p. 21; Messerschmidt, "preussische Armee," pp. 96–97; Meier-Welcker, *Offiziere in Dokumenten*, pp. 72–73.

24. William I, *Militärische Schriften*, I: 62–63.

25. Demeter, *Offizierkorps*, p. 96.

26. Between 1824 and 1840 there were only about 600 cadets in any single year. Fewer than 100 entered the army each year. Osten-Sacken, *Preussens Heer*, II: 239, has the details.

27. Ibid., II: 112.

28. American historians have almost completely ignored the cadet corps, and their European counterparts have done little more. There exists no scholarly study of the cadet corps in English.

29. Alfred Vagts, *A History of Militarism, Civilian and Military*, rev. (New York: The Free Press, 1959 [1937]), p. 171. Scharnhorst, Gneisenau, and Humboldt wanted outright abolition of the cadet corps, while Boyen desired a fundamental reform without abolition.

30. Egmont Zechlin, *Bismarck und die Grundlegung der deutschen Grossmacht* (Stuttgart: J. G. Cotta'sche Buchhandlung, 1960), p. 181.

31. The eight voranstalten were at Cöslin, Potsdam, Wahlsatt, Bensberg near Cologne, Plön, Orianstein, Karlsruhe, and Naumburg. See von der Boeck, *Heer*, p. 259. Gross-Lichterfelde had about 1,000 students and each provincial institute 160–200. On the main school see Walter Deussen, *Ernstes und Heiteres aus dem Kadettenleben zur Gross-Lichterfelde* (privately printed: Zentralkartei ehem. kgl. preussischer und kgl. sächsischer Kadetten, 1967 [1921]).

32. Gleich, *Alte Armee*, pp. 63–64, who generally favored the cadet corps, admitted its educational shortcomings. Von Leibert, *Leben*, p. 13, also a defender, agreed on its shortcomings. Wilhelm Keitel, BA/MA, Nachlass Keitel, N 54/2, pp. 81–82, criticized the academic side of cadet schooling. General Heinrich von Brandt, *Aus dem Leben des Generals der Infanterie z. D. Dr. Heinrich von Brandt*, 3 vols. (Berlin: E. S. Mittler, 1868), II: 7, a teacher in the cadet corps, complained of the poor quality of his students. Von der Goltz, *Denkwürdigkeiten*, p. 27, mentions the inadequacy of the academic subjects. A few officers, notably Heinz Guderian, *Erinnerungen eines Soldaten* (Heidelberg: Kurt Vowinckel, 1951), p. 11, insisted that the cadet corps was equivalent to civilian schools.

33. von Schoenaich, *Mein Damaskus*, p. 18, says that most of his instructors were war invalids who needed light duty. Otto von Below, BA/MA Nachlass von Below, N 87/37, p. 67, also mentions such teachers.

34. Cadets who qualified for budgeted positions paid little if any tuition. Persons eligible for such scholarships included sons of officers killed in action or who died on active duty, sons of active officers, sons of pensioned officers, sons of nonpensioned officers who were deceased veterans, sons of honorary officers who held their commissions for 25 years or more or who had served for 25 years on active duty, and, if positions were still available, sons of civilians who had performed dangerous service for the king.

35. Strombeck, *Fünfzig Jahre*, p. 13, states that he himself was such a case. For the cadet corps' harsh discipline, see Fransecky, *Denkwürdigkeiten*, p. 61; von der Goltz, *Denkwürdigkeiten*, p. 8; von Leibert, *Leben*, p. 15. For an officer's arrogant pride in his cadet years, see BA/MA Nachlass von Stülpnagel, N 57/27, p. 23.

36. Lieutenant General Wilhelm von Holleben, "Die wissenschaftliche Grundlage für den Offizier und die Reorganisation des Kadetten Korps," *Jahrbücher für die Deutsche Armee und Marine* (1902), 2: 465–66.

37. Lieutenant Colonel Thilo von Trotha, "Offizierberuf und Offizierlaufbahn," *Jahrbücher für die Deutsche Armee und Marine* (1910), 1: 17, adds the caution that once in the cadet corps a young man was unsuited by his education for any other career.

38. By contrast, French generals were highly educated, although not at the most expensive private schools. Three-fourths of the French generals in Barge's sample had at least one baccalaureate, and probably 85 percent were members of the educated elite of French society. See Barge, "Generals of the Republic," Chapter 2, pp. 6–11.

39. The army, therefore, lagged far behind the navy. By 1914 about 90 percent of the navy's new officers possessed the abitur. Although direct comparisons are imprecise because of lack of comparable data, Herwig's *German Naval Officer Corps*, pp. 46–49, indicates that most naval officers had better educations than Prussia's generals.

40. Frederick E. Bolton, *The Secondary Schools of Germany* (New York: D. Appleton, 1900), has the details.

41. Demeter, *Offizierkorps*, pp. 90–91.

42. Information based on data not presented in tables. For further details see Hughes, "Prussian Generalcy," p. 141.

43. William I, *Militärische Schriften*, I: 53.

44. von Trotha, "Offizierberuf und Offizierlaufbahn," pp. 16–17.

45. Erich von Manstein, *Aus einem Soldatenleben 1887–1939* (Bonn: Athenäum Verlag, 1958), p. 13. The family referred to here is the Manstein, rather than the Lewinski, clan.

46. Paul von Hindenburg, *Aus meinem Leben* (Leipzig: Verlag von G. Hirzel, 1920), p. 3. Versen's comments were in his diary of 1860. See Count von Werthern, *General von Versen, ein militärisches Zeit und Lebensbild* (Berlin: E. S. Mittler & Son, 1898), p. 6. Bourgeois military families were no less successful in directing their sons into the officer corps. Erich Ludendorff recalled that his military career had been decided upon virtually while he was still in the cradle. General Eduard Leibert made similar comments. See Ludendorff, *militärischer Werdegang*, p. 4. Leibert received a title subsequent to his promotion to brigadier general. See von Leibert, *Leben*, p. 12. Count Paul von Schoenaich, *Mein Damaskus*, p. 18, also recalled that there was never any doubt that he and his brother would become officers.

47. Bernard von Schmitterlow, *Aus dem Leben des Generalfeldmarschalls Freiherr von der Goltz-Pasha* (Berlin: Verlag K. F. Koehler, 1926), p. 9.

48. Information on costs of education in the cadet corps may be found in two semiofficial handbooks, *Fircks Taschenkalender*, p. 162; and von der Boeck, *Das Heer*, pp. 250–60.

49. Friedrich von Schulte, "Adel im deutschen Offizier-und Beamtenstand," *Deutsche Revue* 21 (April–June 1896): 187.

50. About 49 percent of the generals attended the cadet corps. A much smaller percentage of the total officer corps did so.

51. The abitur was a certification that a student had successfully completed the course of study at a gymnasium and was eligible to attend a university.

52. von Schulte, "Adel," p. 187. By contrast, poor families could find relief in the much cheaper cadet corps. Eduard von Leibert and his brother, sons of a deceased officer, attended the cadet corps at Bensburg. Their impoverished mother had to pay only 90 marks a year for both sons. See von Liebert, *Leben*, p. 12. For similar reports see (anonymous), *Das alte Heer*, p. 1; and Franz von Lenski, *Aus den Leutnantsjahren eines alten Generalstabsoffiziers* (Berlin: Verlag Georg Bath, 1922), p. 8.

53. Schlieffen, *Briefe*, pp. 176, 231–32.

54. Hermann von Holleben, "Erinnerungen aus dem Leben des Generals der Infanterie," *Beihefte zur Militär-Wochenblatt* (1892): 5.

55. A few officers were older than 20 when commissioned. Most of these were of wealthy families and had attended a university for a year or two.

56. von Schulte, "Adel," pp. 186–87.

57. von Trotha, "Offizierberuf," p. 17, pointed to this factor in encouraging young men to joing the officer corps. Max von der Leyen's unpublished memoirs, BA/MA Nachlass von der Leyen, N 154/1, p. 14, make the same point.

58. After 1880 more than half the graduates of the gymnasia were more than 20 years old and more than one-fourth were over 21. See Bolton, *Secondary School System*.

59. Muncy, *Junker in Administration*, p. 92; Schulte, "Adel," p. 187.

60. BA/MA Nachlass von Below, N 87/37, p. 4.

61. On an officer's eligibility to attend court, see Wiegand Schmidt-Richberg, "Die Regierungszeit Wilhelms II," in *Handbuch zur deutschen Militärgeschichte*, V: 87. Van den Bergh, *Heer*, p. 20, makes the same point as does Franz von Lenski, *Lern-und Lehrjahre in Front und Generalstab* (Berlin: Bernard & Graefe, 1939), p. 249. See also Stolberg-Wernigerode, *unentschiedene Generation*, pp. 149–50.

62. G. von Gleich, *Die alte Armee und ihre Verirrungen*, 2nd ed. (Leipzig: K. F. Koehler, 1919), p. 42.

63. Breit, *Deutsche Generale*, pp. 9, 18.

64. See, for example, Vagts, *Militarism*, p. 223.

65. Prince Heinrich Schönburg-Waldenburg, *Erinnerungen aus kaiserliche Zeit* (Leipzig: K. F. Koehler, 1929), pp. 11, 48–49.

66. von Schoenaich, *Mein Damaskus*, p. 50.

67. von Gleich, *Alte Armee*, p. 53. Although Gleich reported the extravagant demands noted above, he served in a line infantry regiment and received only 30 marks a month from his family.

68. Hans von Krosigk, ed., *General-Feldmarschhall von Steinmetz. Aus den Familienpapieren dargestellt* (Berlin: E. S. Mittler & Son, 1900), p. 4; von Holleben, "Erinnerungen," p. 17.

69. Hermann von Chappuis, *Bei Hofe und im Felde, Lebenserinnerungen* (Frankfurt am Main: Carl Jügel's Verlag, 1902), p. 6. Carl von Clausewitz likewise was from a very poor family. See Paret, *Clausewitz and the State*, p. 74.

70. Eduard von Conrady, *Das Leben des Grafen August von Werder* (Berlin: E. S. Mittler & Son, 1889), p. 7.

71. Wilhelm von Schweinits, ed., *Denkwürdigkeiten des Botschafters General von Schweinitz*, 2 vols. (Berlin: Reimar Hobbing, 1927), I: 26.

72. von Werthern, *General von Versen*, p. 13. Interestingly, von Versen thought that a regular income of 69 marks a month would have been sufficient.

73. Otto von Hoffmann, *Lebenserinnerungen des königlich preussischen Generalleutnants Otto von Hoffmann* (Oldenburg: Schulzesche Hof-Buchhandlung und Hof-Buckdruckerei, 1907), p. 23. His first equipment was donated by a friend because none of his relatives were in a position to help him.

74. Although Moltke is sometimes cited as an officer without Zulage (for example, in a 1910 speech by Schlieffen, quoted in BA/MA Nachlass Scheibel, N 15/3), Kessel, *Moltke*, p. 29, indicates that his relatives gave some assistance. For Manteuffel's finances see Karl Heinrich Keck, *Das Leben des General-Feldmarschalls Edwin von Manteuffel* (Bielefeld: Velhagen & Klasing, 1890), p. 109, who reports that Manteuffel had to sell some of his diplomatic medals so that he could truthfully tell William I that he had no debts when he became chief of the Military Cabinet. Waldersee, *Denkwürdigkeiten*, I: 39, cites General von Voigts-Rhetz as a penniless officer who survived on very little. Von Stosch, *Denkwürdigkeiten*, pp. 11, 14, indicates that the general had a very small Zulage that he supplemented with his gambling earnings. Rosenburg, *Bureaucracy, Aristocracy, Autocracy*, p. 145, cites Roon as poverty stricken in his early years. Waldersee's own plight may be seen in his *Denkwürdigkeiten*, I: 7, and in his *militärischen Wirken*, I: 16.

75. Schlieffen, *Briefe*, p. 160.

76. Priesdorff, *Soldatisches Führertum*, no. 2780, contains citations from Lessel's unpublished memoirs, now lost, probably in the *Kriegsarchiv* fire.

77. von Hoffmann, *Lebenserinnerungen*, pp. 24, 116–17.

78. Julius von Verdy du Vernois, *Der Zug nach Bronzell (1850), Jugend Erinnerungen* (Berlin: E. S. Mittler & Son, 1905), p. 9.

79. Demeter, *Offizierkorps*, pp. 332–38, reprints the memorandum.

80. Ibid., pp. 332–33, for Manteuffel's comments.

81. Krieg, *Hermann von Tresckow*, p. 115.

82. See note 79, above.

83. BA/MA Nachlass von Mutius, N 195/1, pp. 53–54, 56.

84. von Schoenaich, *Mein Damaskus*, pp. 26–27; *Fircks Taschenkalender* (1909), p. 159.

85. BA/MA Nachlass Köstring, N 123/6, p. 16. The regiment was the Fifth Kürassier Regiment.

86. See note 84, above.

87. BA/MA Nachlass von der Leyen, N 154/1, p. 7.

88. BA/MA Nachlass von Stülpnagel, N 5/27, p. 39. This is reported in the memoirs of Joachim von Stülpnagel, a lieutenant in the First Foot Guards Regiment.

89. von Lenski, *Leutnantsjahren*, p. 22.

90. Ibid., p. 138. Hans von Beseler, BA/MA Nachlass von Beseler, N30/52, in describing his regiment (65th Infantry) in Cologne, termed the captains "very rich people" and noted that almost all the lieutenants had large private incomes.

91. Kurt von Bülow, *Pruessischer Militarismus zur Zeit Wilhelms II. Aus meiner Dienstzeit im Heer* (Schwiednitz: Hugo Reisse, 1930), p. 97.

92. van den Bergh, *Kriege*, p. 117.

93. Ludendorff, *Werdegang*, p. 13.

94. Manstein, *Soldatenleben*, p. 35.

95. BA/MA Nachlass Köstring, N 123/6, p. 16.

96. Demeter, *Offizierkorps*, pp. 339–40, prints these estimates, which seem somewhat high for ordinary infantry regiments.

97. Rabenau, *Land-und Seemacht*, p. 348; Krafft, *Dienst und Leben des jungen Infanterie-Offiziers, ein Lern-und Lesebuch* (Berlin: E. S. Mittler & Son, 1914), p. 271.

98. Krafft, *Dienst und Leben*, p. 271.

99. Most of the army's historians are silent on the fund for one reason or another; however, a considerable number of officers drew upon it during their early years in the army.

100. BA/MA Nachlass von der Leyen, N 154/1, p. 7.

101. von Lenski, *Lern-und Lehrjahre*, p. 268; G. (anonymous), *Offizierlaufbahn*, p. 113, also mentions the fund in the amount of 20 marks.

102. Priesdorff, *Soldatisches Führertum*, no. 2756. Heimburg's father was an *Oberamtmann*.

103. Mathilde von Gregory, *Dreissig Jahre preussische Soldatenfrau* (Munich: Rudolf M. Rohrer Verlag, ca 1931), p. 179.

104. *Das alte Heer*, p. 29.

Chapter 6

1. Except for the First *Garde Regiment zu Fuss* (First Foot Guards), the most elite infantry regiment, and the equal of all other regiments after the Garde du Corps.

2. von Trotha, "Offizierberuf," p. 12.

3. van den Bergh, *Heer*, pp. 152–53; Major M. von Schriebershofen, *Das deutsche Heer. Bilder aus Krieg und Frieden* (Berlin: Ullstein, 1913), pp. 15–32.

4. von Strombeck, *Fünfzig Jahre*, pp. 26–27, has an interesting example of friction between infantry and cavalry officers. On this point see also BA/MA Nachlass Chales de Beaulieu, N 187/1, p. 34; Litzmann, *Lebenserinnerungen*, I: 106, who comments on the hostility between the officers of the 49th Infantry Regiment and a dragoon regiment.

5. Schönburg-Waldenburg, *Erinnerungen*, p. 102, reports on the possibility of conflicts between the officers of these two elite units and the difficulties faced by the officer responsible for maintaining order.

6. Paul Klette, BA/MA Nachlass Klette, N 201/1, pp. 67–68, an infantry officer, admitted the better social position of the cavalry but complained that it was a worthless waste of money. Hans von Beseler, BA/MA Nachlass von Beseler, N 30/58, in a letter to Friedrich von Bernhardi, July 17, 1903, expressed his contempt for the cavalry. Beseler, formerly of the engineers, was then an infantry officer.

7. Schoenaich, *Mein Damaskus*, p. 54.

8. Hermann von Stein, *Erlebnisse und Betrachtungen aus der Zeit des Weltkrieges* (Leipzig: K. F. Koehler Verlag, 1919), p. 141.

9. Prince Krafft zu Hohenlohe-Ingelfingen became general of infantry in 1883, although he was an artillery officer of the purest sort. Max Edler von der

Planitz, who began his career in an artillery regiment, but commanded an infantry brigade while a brigadier general, became general inspector of artillery in 1894 and served in that capacity until 1902. As such, nevertheless, he was a general of infantry rather than general of artillery. The careers of these generals may be followed in Priesdorff, *Soldatisches Führertum*, nos. 2317, 2489, and 2683.

10. Gleich, *alte Armee*, p. 24.

11. Prince Krafft zu Hohenlohe-Ingelfingen, *Aus meinem Leben*, 4 vols. (Berlin: E. S. Mittler & Son, 1907), I: xiv–xv.

12. BA/MA Nachlass von Below, N 87/1, p. 396.

13. von Schoenaich, *Mein Damaskus*, p. 136, speaks of the officer's contempt for the train officers. Once an officer joined the supply officer corps, he was ineligible for further duty as a regular officer. See Rabenau, *Land-und Seemacht*, p. 25.

14. Count Friedrich von der Schulenberg, BA/MA Nachlass von der Schulenburg, N 58/1, pp. 16–17, comments on the manifold possibilities of meeting distinguished and highly placed persons. Max von Mutius, BA/MA Nachlass von Mutius, N 195/1, also comments on the benefits of making such acquaintances in the elite regiments.

15. Count Oskar von der Lancken-Wakenitz, *Meine dreissig Dienst-jahre 1888–1918* (Berlin: Verlag für Kulturpolitik, 1931), p. 22.

16. Vogt, *Heere*, p. 28.

17. For more complete information, see this author's "Non-Prussian Officers in the Prussian Army, 1867–1914," *Red River Valley Historical Journal*, 6, no. 2 (Winter 1981): 14–32.

18. Information based on data not presented in tables.

19. BA/MA Nachlass von Mutius, N 195/1, p. 54.

20. Kessel, *Moltke*, pp. 496–97.

21. Meier-Welcker, *Offiziere in Dokumenten*, pp. 162–65, reprints the report of the Military Reorganization Commission, September 25, 1807.

22. Ranier Wohlfeil, "Die Beförderungsgrundsätze," in *Untersuchungen zur Geschichte des Offizierkorps. Anciennität und Beförderung nach Leistung*, ed. Hans Meier-Welcker (Stuttgart: Deutsche Verlags-Anstalt, 1962), pp. 15–63, has the details.

23. van den Bergh, *Heer*, p. 113.

24. Meier-Welcker, *Offiziere in Dokumenten*, pp. 189–90.

25. Gleich, *alte Armee*, pp. 81–84; van den Bergh, *Heer*, p. 112; BA/MA Nachlass von der Schulenburg, N 58/1, p. 15.

26. Krosigk, *General-Feldmarschall von Steinmetz*, p. 172.

27. The complaints of a young officer on this point are preserved in BA/MA Nachlass von der Schulenburg, N 58/1, p. 15.

28. Messerschmidt, "preussische Armee," pp. 23–24.

29. Literally, the "major's corner." Captains who failed to gain promotion were forced to retire. Probably more officers received involuntary separations at this stage than at any other. Lenski, *Lern-und Lehrjahre*, p. 137, comments on this issue.

30. Messerschmidt, "preussische Armee," p. 25.

31. During Manteuffel's purge of old officers, a youthful appearance suddenly became more fashionable. A too-old countenance might jeopardize a career.

Lothar von Schweinitz, for one, was grateful to his commanding officer for secretly giving him a potion to darken his prematurely gray hair. See Schwienitz, *Denkwürdigkeiten*, I: 88.

32. Roon's reorganization of the Landwehr increased the standing army by 16 infantry, 16 cavalry, and three artillery regiments. The military conventions concluded between 1867 and 1873 added an additional infantry and three cavalry regiments. These increases were accompanied by corresponding increases in division and other staffs. The reorganization added a total of about 1,400 officers to the army.

33. Hans Black, "Die Grundzüge der Beförderungsordnungen," in Meier Welcker, *Anciennität und Beförderung*, pp. 129–36. Indicative of the years spent in grade was the new rule in 1867 that captains could not serve in that rank beyond the age of 54.

34. For contemporary accounts of the slow rates of advancement in the 1880s see BA/MA Nachlass von Beseler, N 30/52; Waldersee, *Denkwürdigkeiten*, I: 43; Waldersee, *Briefwechsel*, p. 103; Count Edgar von Matuschka, "Die Beförderung in der Praxis," in Meier-Welcker, *Anciennität und Beförderung*, p. 161. Many officers gave William II credit for the improvements after 1888. See BA/MA Nachlass von der Schulenburg, N 58/4; Nachlass Chales de Beaulieu, N 187/1, p. 56. Even in the last prewar years there were murmers of discontent over promotions. See BA/MA Nachlass von der Leyen, N 154/1, p. 16.

35. Prussian officers were eligible for pensions after ten years of service. A captain might expect to receive about 1,800 marks a year, depending on his years of service.

36. van den Bergh, *Heer*, p. 110; von der Boeck, *Heer*, pp. 133–34.

37. Rapid advancements were more difficult to obtain in the rank of captain and below.

38. They did, however, have better assignments and better connections. Their long-term prospects, therefore, were better although they received no guarantee of success.

39. Schmidt-Bückeburg, *Militärkabinett*, p. 165; Waldersee, *Denkwurdig-keiten*, II: 18, 20.

40. Schocnaich, *Mein Damaskus*, pp. 57, 62.

41. Verdy to Waldersee, March 19, 1889, in Waldersee, *Briefwechsel*, p. 244; Schlieffen, *Briefe*, p. 88.

42. Kitchen, *Officer Corps*, p. 24; Breit, *Generale*, p. 24.

43. On this point see BA/MA Nachlass Chales de Beaulieu, N 187/2, pp. 99–100. Each year a number of lieutenants were temporarily assigned to the General Staff. Those who measured up to its high standards became General Staff officers. Most, however, returned to line duty after one to three years. See Vogt, *Heer*, p. 109.

44. Ibid., p. 109.

45. Officers with only five or six years of duty with the General Staff out of 30 or more in their careers have been counted in the "limited" category. Eight officers had careers not applicable to Table 17. They were older non-Prussian officers whose rank at the time of entry into the Prussian army made a General Staff appointment impossible.

46. The figure for the decade 1893–1903 is 17.40 percent. Because of the large number of unknown generals (168 of 647) this column is suspect. Probably most of these 168 were not General Staff officers.

47. Alexander von Kluck, *Wanderjahre-Kriege-Gestalten* (Berlin: Verlag R. Eisenschmidt, 1929), p. 34.

48. Louis A. von Scharfenort, *Die königlich preussische Kriegsakademie* (Berlin: E. S. Mittler & Son, 1910), pp. 2–4, has the details.

49. Ibid., Chapter 1, passim. Paret, *Clausewitz*, pp. 187–204, discusses the original concept and the role of Clausewitz in it. He served as director of the school from 1819 to 1830 but had little to do with the program of instruction. On this point see also Kessel, *Moltke*, pp. 34–35.

50. Bernard Schwertfeger, *Die grossen Erzieher des Heeres* (Potsdam: Rütten & Loening, 1936), pp. 32, 47, emphasizes the role of General von Peucker. Paret, *Clausewitz*, makes the same point. As early as 1819 Clausewitz had insisted on abandoning the lecture approach.

51. E. von Conrady, *Das Leben des Grafen August von Werder* (Berlin: E. S. Mittler & Son, 1889), p. 11; Matuschka, "Beförderung," p. 196; Messerschmidt, "Preussische Armee," p. 76. See also Bernhardi, *Denkwürdigkeiten*, p. 212. Scharfenort, *Kriegsakademie*, pp. 191, 197, examines the changing official definition of the Academy's functions and its subordination to the chief of the General Staff.

52. Kitchen, *Officer Corps*, p. 24.

53. Gerhard Förster et al., *Der preussisch-deutsche Generalstab 1640–1945* (East Berlin: Dietz Verlag, 1966), pp. 57–58.

54. The large number of generals from the decade 1893–1903 who are classified as "unknown" may be a source of some distortion but cannot have altered the overall picture too greatly. The large proportion (40.35%) among the hold-over generals is a result of their being a select group, even among the generals.

55. On the content of the examination, see Vogt, *Heer*, p. 187. Countess von Wartensleben, ed., *Hermann Graf von Wartensleben-Carow. Ein Lebensbild 1826–1921* (Berlin: E. S. Mittler & Son, 1923), p. 12, is also useful. See also BA/MA Nachlass Chales de Beaulieu, N 187/1, p. 24; von Lenski, *Lern-und Lehrjahre*, p. 134, recalled that at least half of his class had gained admittance on their second attempt.

56. von Scharfenort, *Kriegsakademie*, p. 15; Schwertfeger, *Erzieher des Heeres*, pp. 19, 41.

57. This is especially noteworthy because the guards cavalry regiments stationed in Berlin offered opportunities for preparation for the entrance examinations to a much greater extent than did most of the artillery units scattered throughout the provinces. Probably a great many cavalry officers had no desire to take the War Academy and General Staff route to further their careers. There was no necessity for them to do so because successful careers in the cavalry had little to do with education, civilian or military. Those cavalry officers who planned to leave the army after a short career had no reason to exert themselves in the vigorous preparations required for examinations.

58. The engineer branch was an important exception to the rule.

59. Computations based on data not presented in tables.

60. The material for such a study may not exist. There is no list of War Academy students. Partial information might be gleaned from the various Ranglisten, regimental histories, and officer Stammlisten. The studies by von Scharfenort and Schwertfeger are not helpful on this point.

61. Many officers took the examinations very seriously and spent months in preparation. See Wilhelm Groener, *Lebenserinnerungen, Jugend, Generalstab, Weltkrieg*, ed. Baron Friedrich Hiller von Gaertringen (Göttingen: Vandenhoeck & Ruprecht, 1957), p. 46; Hartmann, *Lebenserinnerungen*, I: 132.

62. Count Bogdan von Hutten-Czapski, *Sechzig Jahre Politik und Gesellschaft*, 2 vols. (Berlin: E.S. Mittler & Son, 1936), I: 65, recalled that during the winter of 1881–82 his commander (Second Guard Dragoon Regiment) relieved him of all duties in order to ease his preparation for the examination. For other comments on the advantages of elite units, see BA/MA Nachlass von Mutius, N 195/1, p. 66; Nachlass von der Schulenburg, N 58/1, p. 16; Nachlass Keitel, N 54/2, p. 107.

63. On this point see von Lenski, *Leutnantsjahren*, pp. 132–33.

64. Breit, *Deutsche Generale*, p. 12. Although Breit is possibly correct in assuming that nobles were, in fact, significantly more numerous among the War Academy's students, he has made no effort to establish that. The evidence on the point is very meager. See von Lenski, *Leutnantsjahren*, p. 132. This author has found no evidence that there were serious allegations of tampering with the examinations.

65. Each written examination was graded by two officers and by a third if such was necessary to resolve differences. See BA/MA Nachlass von der Leyen, N 154/1, p. 55.

66. On the continuing preponderance of officers from elite units, see Matuschka, "Organisationsgeschichte," p. 197; Seeckt, *Leben*, p. 32; and (anonymous), *alte Heer*, p. 64. For comments on the disadvantages of isolated garrisons, see von Stein, *Erlebnisse*, p. 32; BA/MA Nachlass von der Leyen, N 154/1, p. 152; Nachlass von Mutius, N 195/1, p. 66; Nachlass von der Schulenburg, N 58/1, p. 16.

67. Information based on statistical findings not presented in tables. For more information see Hughes, "Prussian Generals," p. 183.

68. Demeter, *Offizierkorps*, pp. 13, 29.

69. Classified as "elite" are all cavalry and guards infantry regiments. The General Staff category includes generals who served with various types of regiments but whose service there was part of normal General Staff careers.

70. However greatly the stereotype of the guards officer has influenced the army's image over the years, generals from such regiments were hardly typical of the vast majority of their peers, especially after 1892.

71. Nowhere are the limitations of Briet's *Deutsche Generale*, based solely on published memoirs, more apparent than on this point. The men who set their lives on paper were not necessarily typical generals. Reliance on them alone can be highly misleading.

72. Hans von Beseler, for example, was disappointed when in 1893 he received an assignment to the War Ministry. See BA/MA Nachlass von Beseler, N 30/52. Waldersee, *Briefwechsel*, p. 244, and *Denkwürdigkeiten*, II: 18, 20–21, has interesting comments on the inferior position of the War Ministry and its officers.

Some General Staff officers, however, served in the War Ministry at some point in their careers.

73. Interestingly, von Flotow was of the best old-Prussian Uradel stock. His father had been a Prussian officer and his grandfather a Napoleonic civil servant in Westphalia. A younger brother was killed in 1871. Lehmann, by contrast, was the son of a director of an orphanage in Pomerania. Their careers may be followed in Kleist, *Generale*, and BA/MA Priesdorff Manuscripts, 1911, 44, respectively.

74. The Military Cabinet, as already indicated, was only too happy to channel capable noble officers into the most desirable types of careers.

75. For example, Kitchen, *Officer Corps*, pp. 23–25; Demeter, *Offizierkorps*, pp.30–31; Endres, *Social Structure*, pp. 18–19.

76. This is not to deny the importance of the army's image as a political factor. But the reality behind the facade was not that of the Garde du Corps or of the First Foot Guards Regiment.

77. The social composition of the General Staff will be examined in a subsequent chapter.

78. These are generals whose predominant type of service before promotion to brigadier general was with the General Staff. The noble-bourgeois relationship among the officers who served on the General Staff after promotion to brigadier general was vastly different. This question will be further explored in Chapter 6.

79. Von Strombeck, *Fünfzig Jahre*, p. 38. Roughly translated the saying is: "My yellow cavalrymen love the money, the Queslinburg ladies, the 'vons'." Yellow refers to the regiment's colors.

80. von der Osten-Sacken, *Preussens Heer*, III: 478.

81. Lange received a title in 1896, after promotion to brigadier general. His father had been a Prussian colonel and his grandfather a civil servant. His career may be followed in A. von Maltzahn, ed., *Stammliste des Ulanen-Regiments Kaiser Alexander II von Russland (1. brandenburgischen) Nr. 3* (Berlin: E. S. Mitler & Son, 1908). Paul Reichenau, a General Staff officer, was promoted to brigadier general of infantry in 1913 and met his end while in action in 1914. His career is recounted in BA/MA Priesdorff Manuscripts, 1913, 28.

82. Heinzel's career may be found in BA/MA Priesdorff Manuscripts, 1908, 71. His father had been a civil servant in Silesia.

83. The examples cited above refer to the following cases: Karl Ranisch, promoted to brigadier general in 1871, who married into the Uradel von Below family while still a captain. Hermann Delius, inspector of field telegraphs in 1909–10, married Marageretha von Krosigk, daughter of a landed officer from Prussian Saxony. His career may be found in BA/MA Priesdorff Manuscripts, 1909, 10. Friedrich Mejer, brigadier general of infantry, married into the von der Groeben family in 1876. He received a title in 1908, seven years after retirement. His career is in Otto Zimmer-Vorhaus, ed., *Offizier-Stammliste des Infanterie-Regiments von Lützow (1. Rheinishe) Nr. 25* (Berlin: Otto Beckmann Verlag, 1913).

84. In the Prusso-German diplomatic service during the same period, between 14 percent and 24 percent of the ministers were bachelors. See Lamar J. R. Cecil, *The German Diplomatic Service 1871–1914* (Princeton: Princeton University Press, 1976), p. 92.

85. Retired officers holding budgeted positions and therefore classified as *zur Disposition* also needed approval before marriage.

86 Prussia, Kriegsministerium, *Verordnung über das Heirathen der Militärpersonen des preussischen Heeres und der preussischen Landgendarmerie* (Berlin: E. S. Mittler & Son, 1902), pp. 9–10. See also Meier-Welcker, *Offiziere in Dokumenten*, p. 178.

87. Hans Pommer, *Zwanzig Jahre im Reichslände* (Frankfurt am Main: Neuer Frankfurter Verlag, 1914), pp. 112–13.

88. Prussia, Kriegsministerium, *Verordnung über das Heirathung*, pp. 8, 17.

89. Ibid., p. 8.

90. BA/MA Nachlass von Below, N 87/44, p. 595.

91. Groener, *Lebenserinnerungen*, p. 45.

92. It was commonly accepted that a wife might reasonably be expected to provide the necessary income. See Lieutenant Colonel (retired) Thilo von Trotha, "Offizierberuf und Offizierlaufbahn," *Jahrbücher für die deutsche Armee und Marine* (1910), I: 19. A specific example may be found in BA/MA Nachlass Keitel, N 54/2, pp. 173, 195.

93. It is possible that low-ranking officers, including those who reached the ranks of the generals, had more wives from marginally acceptable families. There is no information currently available for a judgment on this point.

94. Hutten-Czapski, *Sechzig Jahre*, I: 54, reports the case of General Baron von Zedlitz-Leipe, whose wife was the daughter of a Belgian diplomat. She brought him great wealth and an estate in Silesia.

95. Rhode's case is recorded in Count Richard von Pfeil, *Zwischen den Kriegen, Meine ersten Jahren im Ersten Garde-Regiment zu Fuss 1864 bis Anfang 1870* (Schweidnitz: Verlag von L. Heege, 1912), p. 117. Otto von Below, BA/MA Nachlass von Below, N 87/37, p. 84, does not mention the officer's name. The person in question may have been Maximilian von Wartenberg, who retired after serving as a brigadier general for one year.

96. In the Wartenberg case cited above, for example, the official reason was illness. See BA/MA Priesdorff Manuscripts, 1908, 53. There is good reason to believe that the lady, previously married to Wartenberg's first cousin, was the cause of his "illness." This interesting case may be traced in the Gotha Uradel volume for 1910, pp. 795–96, and in Joachim von Goertzke, ed., *Offizier Stammliste des königlich preussischen Kaiser Franz Garde-Grenadier Regiment Nr. 2 1814–1914* (Berlin: Verlag von Paul Parey, 1914). Other examples of officers forced to leave the army because of unacceptable wives may be found in Otto von Hoffmann, *Lebenserinnerungen des königlich preussischen Generalleutnants Otto von Hoffmann*, ed. Colonel von Hoffmann (Oldenburg & Leipzig: Schulzesche Hof-Buchhandlung und Hof-Buchdruckerei, 1907), p. 83; and Prince Krafft zu Hohenlohe-Ingelfingen, *Aus meinem Leben*, 4 vols. (Berlin: E. S. Mittler & Son, 1907), IV: 15.

97. Otto von Below, BA/MA Nachlass von Below, N 87/38, p. 181, has an example of a poor officer using his marriage to a wealthy Berlin Jewess to escape his debts. Other examples may be found in Lamar Cecil, "Jew and Junker in Imperial Berlin," *Leo Baeck Institute Yearbook* 20 (1975): 49; van den Bergh, *Heer*, p. 134; BA/MA Nachlass Keitel, N 54/2, pp. 75, 143; Breit, *Deutsche Generale*, p. 10.

98. One important exception occurred in cavalry regiments, which were sometimes commanded by senior majors, usually for a year or so before promotion to lieutenant colonel. Such officers normally remained in that position until after their promotion to colonel. Even while a major, however, a cavalry regimental commander received the extra pay associated with that position. This aroused bitter jealousy among some infantry officers. See Pommer, *Zwanzig Jahre*, p. 107.

99. Thilo Krieg, *Hermann von Tresckow, General der Infanterie und General Adjutant Kaiser Wilhelms I* (Berlin: E. S. Mittler & Son, 1911), p. 51; Strombeck, *Fünfzig Jahre*, p. 171; August Keim, *Erlebtes und Erstrebtes. Lebenserinnerungen* (Hanover: Ernst Letsch Verlag, 1925), p. 88.

100. Up to 1888 there were 72 cavalry regiments; after 1890, 73.

101. Figures based on the author's analysis of the Ranglisten for the years 1871–1914. The hold-over generals distort the picture slightly because they were regimental commanders before 1871.

102. Information taken from the Ranglisten. The guards infantry regiments were the core of the army. It is not surprising, therefore, that most of their commanders became generals. Nevertheless, the high percentage indicated above is impressive.

103. Forty-nine of the regiments were created after 1871. Otherwise the figure would be substantially higher because these regiments would have had more commanders.

104. The exact percentage cannot be obtained without a study of each colonel involved. Such information is not yet available.

105. Only the very few railway repair regiments offered such opportunities to engineer officers. Before 1890 only one such regiment existed.

106. See for example, Schoenaich, *Mein Damaskus*, p. 41.

107. Otto von Below, BA/MA Nachlass von Below, N 87/43 and N 87/44, p. 618. Other cases may be found in Nachlass Chales de Bealieu, N 187/1, p. 23; and Baron von Werthern, *General von Versen. Ein militärischer Zeit und Lebensbild* (Berlin: E. S. Mittler & Son, 1898), p. 11.

108. Otto von Below, BA/MA Nachlass von Below, N 87/44, p. 23–24, has an interesting example of this in regard to an appointment to the General Staff. See also Karl Litzmann, *Lebenserinnerungen*, 2 vols. (Berlin: Verlag R. Eisenschmidt, 1927), I: 61–63.

Chapter 7

1. Prince Frederick Karl, for example, also was only 26, but he had been a few weeks older at his promotion. Because he was older than Frederick William, and received his promotion in 1854, he held seniority throughout their careers until they became field marshals on the same day. On Frederick Karl, see Wolfgang Foerster, ed., *Prinz Friedrich Karl von Preussen, Denkwüridgkeiten aus seinem Leben*, 2 vols. (Berlin: Deutsche Verlags-Anstalt, 1910).

2. Crusius, whose career began in the fourth Field Artillery Regiment in 1870, spent most of his career in the trains. In January 1912 he became a brigadier general and train inspector. His father had been an Evangelical minister in Brandenburg. His 51 years between commissioning and promotion were also a record. His career may be followed in BA/MA Priesdorff Manuscripts, 1912, 94.

3. The following information is based on findings not presented in a table. Complete data may be found in the author's dissertation.

4. These figures exclude the three princes who were commissioned at ages 10, 12, and 15 and two nobles commissioned at age 29 as well as one bourgeois general commissioned at age 27. All these were special cases and can only add distortions, however slight, to be sure, to the figures.

5. Included are generals whose careers were primarily spent in General Staff service. Some were not in a General Staff position at the time of their promotions to brigadier general.

6. Kessel, *Moltke*, p. 232.

7. On Waldersee's role, see Schmidt-Bückeburg, *Militärkabinett*, p. 165; and Waldersee, *Denkwürdigkeiten*, III: 18, 20. Wiegand Schmidt-Richberg, "Die Regierungsseit Wilhelms II," *Handbuch zur deutschen Militärgeschichte*, V: 71, comments on the practice in the years just before World War I.

8. Information based on statistical findings not presented in tables. See Hughes, "Prussian Generalcy," p. 216, for further details.

9. Excluded from the 15.03 percent are the five noble brigadier generals who remained in that rank for nine years or longer. Their cases were quite extraordinary and need not be included in the discussion. Guido von Streit, for example, served as commandant of Spandau for nine years while a brigadier general. He had not commanded a regiment and was not suitable for command of a brigade or larger unit. He, however, had fairly good family connections. His father had been an officer in Saxe-Meiningen, and his first wife's father was a Prussian officer. An artilleryman by trade, he had not attended a cadet corps and had neither War Academy nor General Staff experience.

10. Complaints of this nature may be found in BA/MA Nachlass von Beseler, N 30/52; Waldersee, *Denkwürdigkeiten*, I: 43; Waldersee, *Briefwechsel*, p. 103.

11. On the problem in the lower ranks see Matuschka, "Beförderung in der Praxis," p. 161.

12. This officer was Friedrich Aldenkortt, from the Rhineland, son of a civil servant. He was, interestingly, a Catholic. He had attended the cadet corps and was a combat veteran of 1866 and 1870–71. He had no War Academy or General Staff experience. He served as commandant of Graudenz, normally a dead-end position, as indeed it was for him. His career may be followed in Paul Grossman, ed., *Offizier-Stammliste der 6, Rheinischen Infanterie-Regiments Nr. 68* (Coblenz: Kindt & Meinardus Nachf., 1902). Aldenkortt never received a patent as brigadier general but was instead listed as *characteriziert*. Like many of his fellow generals, he held only an honorary rank as brigadier general but was listed as such in the army lists.

13. This includes those men who were in that rank when the war began in August 1914.

14. The remaining few nobles have been excluded because they were not nobles in the sense that the others were. Their exclusion, moreover, preserves homogeneity in the data base.

15. Hausmann and Schubert were both inspectors of artillery, positions outside the normal command progression to a division and corps command. Officers in these technical posts frequently remained on active duty for long periods of time. It should be noted, however, that Schubert commanded the 39th division for several years. Their careers may be found in Priesdorff, *Soldatisches Führertum* nos. 2483

and 3297 respectively. The author is indebted to Herr Friedrich Euler of the Institut zur Erforschung historische Führungsschichten in Bensheim for information on Schubert.

16. The position will be discussed more fully later in this chapter.

17. Excluded from Table 28 are generals still on active duty in 1914 and those whose careers terminated abnormally for various reasons.

18. Commanding generals had direct access to the king and in theory had no superior officer other than the king himself. All, or nearly all, changes in the rank of general were made only after the express approval of the all-highest commander. Age was not necessarily a factor in the time spent in the army's very highest ranks and positions. Generals whose services were especially valued continued to serve on active duty long after their less fortunate peers had retired.

19. Most of the 117 bourgeois and 112 noble generals counted as having careers with a last position not relevant to Table 29 were still on active duty in August 1914. As in many tabulations in this study, they have been excluded because their future careers cannot be predicted in retrospect.

20. Only in wartime did army inspectors become army commanders. In peacetime they had no command powers over corps commanders. See Ludendorff, *Werdegang*, p. 38.

21. Alexander von Kluck, ennobled in 1909 while commander of the First Army Corps, is the person in question.

22. Two of the five, August Lentze and Karl Blume, received titles before promotion to general. Two others, Friedrich Scholtz and Otto Emmich, received titles after promotion to general. Only Louis Stoetzer failed to win a title. He was a General Staff officer and was a favorite of both Waldersee and Schlieffen. All five of these bourgeois generals were from solid old-Prussian backgrounds. Lentze and Emmich were sons of officers. Both had paternal grandfathers who were civil servants. Lentze married into a noble officer's family; Emmich's wife was the daughter of a civil servant. The other three fathers were a civil servant (Stoetzer), an Evangelical pastor and superintendent (Scholtz), and the director of a gymnasium and *Ritterakademie* in Potsdam (Blume).

23. Specifically, 341 of 406 division commanders were nobles, exclusive of a few still serving in August of 1914.

24. Twenty-four of the 59 bourgeois division commanders had acquired titles after their promotion to brigadier general (hence they are counted as bourgeois) but before they became lieutenant generals.

25. These posts are listed in the Ranglisten as *Kommandanturen*.

26. In some cases the fortresses were absolete relics of a bygone era. Others retained military value. They were usually a combination of military installation and garrison. Installation commander might be a more meaningful rendering of the term.

27. Strassburg and Metz, for example, had governors, not commandants.

28. Although the information is fragmentary, enough is known about these men to establish that they were hardly typical bourgeois officers. Hans Gronau, for example, governor of Thorn from 1908 through 1910, was from a family occupied in the bureaucracy and state church, from Brandenburg. He attended the War Academy and was a General Staff officer. Another of the six, Karl Waag, had an identical occupational background. He also married an officer's daughter. His career, however, was spent entirely in line infantry units. At least one of the

remaining four, Otto Leo, governor of Strassburg from 1894 through 1898, was the son of a Prussian officer.

29. Other than army inspectors, all positions so designated were purely supervisory positions not in the regular command structure. Inspectors of engineers, for example, would hardly become army commanders in wartime.

30. Like their engineer counterparts, artillery inspectors were just that and commanded no larger units, either in peace or war.

31. Generals in this category were active officers whose final military assignments were listed as a la suite the army. The many purely honorary generals, listed in the army as such, have been entirely excluded from this study. The two bourgeois officers in this category were special cases. Christian Streccius, an infantry officer, was placed in the category because of illness. He died shortly thereafter (1889) and had been a brigadier general for only 11 months at the time of his death. Karl Galster, an artillery officer, was likewise placed a la suite the army very briefly and retired after less than two years of service. He held the rank of brigadier general from January 1875 until November 1876.

32. The General Staff is the subject of the following chapter.

33. With the exception of the Guards-Cavalry Division, there were no peacetime cavalry divisions. Cavalry officers therefore frequently commanded infantry divisions.

34. Karl von Mudra (ennobled after promotion to brigadier general) was an engineer officer and commanded the 39th Infantry Division in 1908 and 1909. He was on active duty in 1914, holding the dual position of chief of engineers and pioneers and general inspector of fortresses. His background was that of a typical engineer officer. His father had been a construction contractor in Silesia. His grandfather worked as a cobbler. His wife, apparently of some wealth, was the daughter of a factory owner. I am indebted to Herr Friedrich Euler of the Institut zur Erforschung historischer Führungsschichten in Bensheim for information on this officer.

35. The corps commander was frequently referred to simply as the commanding general. On his position see Ritter, *Sword and Scepter*, I: 171; van den Bergh, *Heer*, p. 38; Meisner, *Kriegsminister*, pp. 12, 23, 81.

36. Busch, *Der Oberbefehl*, p. 23.

37. Meisner, *Kriegsminister*, pp. 12, 81.

38. Seeckt, *Aus meinem Leben*, p. 39, repeats the tribute to the two generals, Count Gottlieb von Haeseler and August von Lentze. A translation would be: "God save me from the frontier, Gottlieb Haeseler, August Lentze."

39. This incident is related in Keim, *Erlebtes und Erstrebtes*, pp. 30–31.

40. Ernst Buchfinck, *Feldmarschall Graf von Haeseler* (Berlin: E. S. Mittler & Son, 1929), concentrates on his military exploits in 1866 and 1870–71, thus missing the essence of Haeseler's career. Pertev Bey, *Unter Graf von Haeseler* (Berlin: E. S. Mittler & Son, 1904), is better. On his career see also Kleist, *Generale*, no. 1563; Lt. Gen. Marx, "Graf Haeseler als Erzieher. Erinnerungen und Betrachtungen an seinem 100. Geburtstag" *Wissen und Wehr* (1936): 10–31; and Ernst Buchfinck, "Feldmarshall Graf von Haeseler 19.1.1836–26.19.1919" *Wissen und Wehr*, (1936): 3–9.

41. Also in this case Herr Friedrich Euler provided information not otherwise available.

Chapter 8

1. On the clash in 1870, see Otto Pflanze, *Bismarck and the Development of Germany: The Period of Unification 1815–1871* (Princeton: Princeton University Press, 1963), pp. 462–68. The disagreement began as early as 1864 over Moltke's proposed campaign in Jutland. It continued throughout the wars of unification. See Craig, *Prussian Army*, pp. 180–219. Still of some use, though incorrect on some points, is Hans von Haeften, "Bismarck und Moltke," *Preussische Jahrbücher* 177 (July–September 1919): 85–105. Eberhard Kessel, "Bismarck und die Halbgötter," *Historische Zeitschrift* 171 (1956): 249–86, attempts to minimize the conflict. Hollyday, *Stosch*, pp. 82–89, is good on this point. An important supplement is Peter Rassow's preface to Paul Bronsart von Schellendorff, *Geheimes Kriegstagebuch 1870–1871* (Bonn: Athenäum Verlag, 1954), pp. 9–31.

2. Pflanze, *Bismarck*, p. 468; Ritter, *Sword and Scepter*, I: 187–260.

3. The tangled and acrimonious dispute permanently embittered relations between Bismarck and Moltke. On this point see Kessel, *Moltke*, p. 705. Waldersee's published papers contain a number of informative comments on Moltke's disdain for the chancellor. See his *Denkwürdigkeiten*, II: 44; and H. O. Meisner, ed., "Aus der Erinnerungen des General-Feldmarschalls Grafen Waldersee: Kaiser und Kaiserin Friedrich," *Deutsche Revue* 46 (July–September 1921): 3; and the same editor, "Aus den Erinnerungen des General-Feldmarschalls Grafen Waldersee: Über seine Tätigkeit als Generalquartiermeister und Chef des Generalstabs," *Deutsche Revue* 46 (June 1921): 213.

4. Craig, *Prussian Army*, pp. 217–341, has an extensive treatment of this and related problems. Ritter, *Sword and Scepter*, II, passim, treats the issue. Fischer, *Krieg der Illusionen*, argues that the General Staff was a main force pushing for war in 1914. Gerhard Förster et al, *Der preussisch-deutsche Generalstab 1640–1945* (East Berlin: Dietz Verlag, 1966), pp. 23–107, presents the East German view. Messerschmidt, *Militär und Politik*, is important. Also note the articles by Messerschmidt and Wilhelm Deist in *Das Kaiserliche Deutschland*, cited earlier.

5. They were, literally, General Staff generals. Included are all general officers, both in the Great General Staff in Berlin and in the Unit General Staff (*Truppengeneralstab*), who served on the General Staff while holding the rank of brigadier general or higher. General Staff officers who attained the rank of brigadier general but who did not serve on the General Staff in that rank are not included.

6. A list of their names would be a veritable who's who of the army. Included, in addition to the chiefs of the General Staff, are such luminaries as Friedrich von Bernhardi, Count Colmar von der Goltz, Count Paul von Schoenaich, Hans von Beseler, Paul von Hindenburg, Adolf von Deines, Count Walter von Lüttwitz, and Erich von Falkenhayn.

7. All these generals are included in the 2,443 and are included in all earlier tables where relevant.

8. Moltke II may also be differentiated from his uncle in that he was not a count. Count von Moltke's title devolved upon his direct descendants but not upon the entire family.

9. Friedrich von Bernhardi, ed., *Aus dem Leben Theodor von Bernhardis*, 7 vols. (Leipzig: Verlag von S. Hirzel, 1895), IV: 166. Rudolf Stadelmann, *Moltke*

und Der Staat (Krefeld: Scherpe-Verlag, 1950), p. 407. The best biography is Kessel, *Moltke*. Moltke's private papers are printed in his *Gesammelte Schriften und Denkwürdigkeiten*, 8 vols. (Berlin: E. S. Mittler & Son, 1891–93); and in Friedrich von Schmerfeld, ed., *General-Feldmarschall Graf von Moltke. Ausgewählte Werke*, 4 vols. (Berlin: Verlag Reimar Hobbing, 1925), which also has some of his military writings. Moltke's official papers are in Prussia, General Staff, ed., *Moltkes militärische Werke*, 17 vols. (Berlin: E. S. Mittler & Son, 1892–1912).

10. See, for example, the letter of Hans von Beseler to his brother, August 17, 1888, BA/MA Nachlass von Beseler, N 30/52, and the comments of Otto von Below, BA/MA Nachlass von Below, N 87/34, p. 287.

11. There is no scholarly biography of Waldersee. He figures prominently in the literature on the period; however, and much of his writing is available. See the previously cited *Briefwechsel, Denkwürdigkeiten,* and *Militärischen Wirken*. Kitchen, *Officer Corps*, pp. 64–95 has a chapter on Waldersee. Craig, *Prussian Army*, pp. 255–66, also discusses him at length. Eberhard Kessel, "Die Tätigkeit des Grafen Waldersee als Generalquartiermeister und Chef des Generalstabes der Armee," *Die Welt als Geschichte* 14 (1954): 181–211, is a useful contribution.

12. Although Waldersee did not leave the General Staff until 1891, his relationship with William II began to deteriorate in March 1888. On March 20 William publicly criticized some of Waldersee's military map exercises for young General Staff officers. Otto von Below, who was present, recorded that all in attendance knew then that Waldersee's days were numbered. See BA/MA Nachlass von Below, N 87/39, pp. 257–58. Waldersee, *Denkwürdigkeiten*, II: 119–121, has a diary entry of March 21, 1890, noting his deteriorating relations with the kaiser.

13. On this point see especially Craig, *Prussian Army*, pp. 266–73.

14. Schlieffen sometimes referred to William II as "Willy," in his letters to his family. See Schlieffen, *Briefe*, pp. 287, 300, 302. Schlieffen, probably because he knew he could not afford to anger the kaiser, allowed the emperor's desire for massed cavalry attacks and personal victory at the head of an army corps to deprive the annual maneuvers of much of their military value. Schlieffen's biographers usually rise to his defense on this subject. See Count Hugo von Freytag-Loringhoven, *General-Feldmarschall Graf von Schlieffen* (Leopzig: Historia Verlag Paul Schraepler, 1920), pp. 53–57. Some officers were critical of Schlieffen for allowing William such freedom of action. See BA/MA Nachlass Chales de Beaulieu, N 187/2, p. 97. Schlieffen's laconic comment that if the kaiser were going to lead then he would have to be the victor is recorded in Stein, *Erlebnisse*, p. 35.

15. Kitchen, *Officer Corps*, p. 32. See also Freytag-Loringhoven, *Schlieffen*, p. 37. Gleich, *alte Armee*, p. 77, makes a similar statement.

16. Ritter, *Sword and Scepter*, II: 106.

17. On his relations with Holstein, see Norman Rich, *Friedrich von Holstein: Politics and Diplomacy in the Era of Bismarck and William II*, 2 vols. (Cambridge: Cambridge University Press, 1965), II: 698; and Peter Rassow, "Schlieffen and Holstein," *Historische Zeitschrift* 173 (1954): 297–313. For Schlieffen's private criticism of statesmen and diplomats, see the letter of his son-in-law, Wilhelm von Hahnke, to Baron von Freytag-Loringhoven, May 5, 1929, BA/MA Nachlass von Hahnke, N 36/10, p. 8.

18. In addition to the sources cited above there is important biographical information in Helmuth Kittel, *Alfred Graf Schlieffen, Jugend und Glaube* (Berlin: Verlag des Evangelischen Bundes, 1939); in Hugo Rochs, *Schlieffen* (Berlin: Vossische Buchhandlung Verlag, 1926); and in Friedrich von Boetticher, *Schlieffen* (Göttingen: Musterschmidt Verlag, 1957). Of less value is Eugen Bircher and Walter Bode, *Schlieffen, Man und Idee* (Zurich: Scientia A.G., 1940). Schlieffen's works have been partly published as *General-Feldmarschall Graf Alfred von Schlieffen, Gesammelte Schriften*, 2 vols. (Berlin: E. S. Mittler & Son, 1913). His campaign plan has been most thoughtfully studied by Gerhard Ritter, *The Schlieffen Plan: Critique of a Myth*, trans. Andrew and Eva Wilson (London: Oswald Wolff, 1958 [1956]).

19. See the comments on the selection in Hutten-Czapski, *Sechzig Jahre*, I: 410. Prince Bernhard von Bülow, *Denkwürdigkeiten*, 4 vols. (Berlin: Verlag Ullstein, 1930), II: 183–84, is interesting on Haeseler's objections. Einem, *Erinnerungen*, pp. 148–50, has first-hand information on Moltke's appointment. Isabel V. Hull, *The Entourage of Kaiser Wilhelm II, 1888–1918* (London: Cambridge University Press, 1982), pp. 239–48, has an excellent discussion of Moltke.

20. BA/MA Nachlass von Hahnke, N 36/10, pp. 7–9; Nachlass Chales de Beaulieu, N 187/3, p. 157; Wilhelm Groener, *Wilhelm Groener, Lebenserinnerungen, Jugend, Generalstab, Weltkrieg*, Count Friedrich Hiller von Gaertringen, ed. (Göttingen: Vandenhoeck & Ruprecht, 1957), p. 91. Ludendorff, *Werdegang*, p. 89, is probably reliable on this point. The Bavarian military attache in Berlin reported widespread dissatisfaction in the army over the choice of Moltke. See Baron Ludwig von Gebsattels, "Politische Berichte Ludwigs Freiherr von Gebsattels," *Preussische Jahrbücher*, Karl Demeter, ed., 231 (January–June 1933): 30–32.

21. Helmuth von Moltke, *Erinnerungen, Briefe, Dokumente 1877–1916*, ed. Eliza von Moltke (Stuttgart: Kommende Tag Verlag, 1922), p. 304.

22. Einem, *Erinnerungen*, p. 149, comments on Moltke's unsuitable background, as does Boetticher, *Schlieffen*, p. 72.

23. The limited number of General Staff generals in some cases precludes the division of data into large numbers of categories. In many cases this is not necessary, however, because the General Staff generals were such a homogenous group.

24. The General Staff expanded considerably between 1871 and 1914. In 1871 the General Staff consisted of about 175 officers, including 40 on temporary assignment. By 1913 this number exceeded 330. See Osten-Sacken, *Preussens Heer*, III: 315, 492–93; Schlieffen, *Gesammelte Schriften*, I: xv–xvi; and Paul Bronsart von Schellendorff, *Der Dienst des Generalstabes*, 2 vols. (Berlin: E. S. Mittler & Son, 1875, 1876), for the earlier years.

25. The comparison, therefore, is between General Staff generals appointed between 1871 and 1890 and all generals promoted between 1871 and 1892. Both groups include those generals appointed or promoted before 1871 but still at their posts at the conclusion of the Franco-Prussian War.

26. They were nobles at the time of their appointment to the General Staff, not necessarily at the time of their promotion to the generalcy.

27. These figures were first assembled by Demeter, *Offizierkorps*, pp. 28–29. They have been repeated by Kitchen, *Officer Corps*, p. 24, and by Craig, *Prussian Army*, p. 235, and by many other authors.

28. See Chapter 2, pp. 00–00.

29. Schlieffen's family was doubtless an Uradel clan, although 1440 was their earliest verifiable title. His family, however, was youthful compared to the ancestors of the Moltke pair, whose titles (Danish and Mecklenburg) dated at least to 1220.

30. Lamar Cecil, "The Creation of Nobles in Prussia, 1871–1918" *American Historical Review* 75, no. 3 (February 1970): 757–95, has exhaustively studied the factors involved in the creation of these new titles.

31. The minor discrepancies between Professor Cecil's figures and those for generals in this study appear to be a result of differing definitions of the sample. His study includes some generals not so classified here.

32. Information based on findings not presented in tables.

33. Information based on statistical findings not presented in tables. See Hughes, "Prussian Generalcy," pp. 264–66.

34. Impoverished young officers had no alternative to finding wives with incomes sufficient to meet the army's requirements.

35. The small numbers make direct comparisons difficult.

36. During the decade 1893–1903, 24.53 percent of bourgeois generals whose titles postdated their promotions had noble wives; only 13.89 percent of those who remained bourgeois had married aristocrats.

37. As was the case with previous occupational tables, fathers who served in the army for only a short period of time have not been counted as officers. The vast majority of the officer/fathers served for at least 20 years and attained the rank of major or higher.

38. This may be at least partially attributed to the reluctance of young landed officers to accept the rigorous demands imposed by the War Academy and the General Staff.

39. This point is developed more fully in Chapter 4.

40. Einem, *Erinnerungen*, pp. 25–26.

41. As more information on the occupations becomes available, the percentage of landowners may decrease.

42. The proportion of purely agricultural fathers-in-law is also a variation from the earlier findings. Only about one father-in-law in five (19.52%) of the larger group of generals was a landowner without another occupation.

43. Count Moltke's appointments had married officers' daughters in only slightly fewer cases (28.57%) than had Schlieffen's. This difference is probably not very significant in view of the small number of women involved and the number of unknown cases.

44. Schlieffen's father had been a major when he retired to his estates. His grandfather, likewise an officer, retired as a colonel. He did not own land. Schlieffen's wife, his cousin, was an officer's daughter. Two of his brothers became Prussian generals. A third, Heinrich, died in action in 1870.

45. The proportion of wives from bureaucratic families was similar to the overall figures for all generals serving 1871–1914. During this period, 35.79 percent of the generals' wives' fathers were civil servants, of whom 7.88 percent owned

land. The percentage of such wives' fathers increased from the hold-over generals (33.57%) to the decade 1893–1903 (37.84%) but dropped to 32.63 percent during the final decade.

46. Franz von Oberhoffer, who served as a brigadier general and chief of the railway section first under Waldersee and then under Schlieffen, had the most exotic background. His father, not a noble, was a court singer in Baden. His mother was a noble and his wife, the daughter of a bourgeois civil servant. He attended the Baden Cadet Corps and joined the Prussian army in 1871 while a captain. His career may be traced in Priesdorff, *Soldatisches Führertum*, no. 3085. Count Hans von Hülsen-Haeseler, later chief of the Military Cabinet, was the son of an illustrious Berlin aristocrat and general-intendant of the royal theater, who might easily be counted among the civil servants. Count Georg von Rechenberg, also a section chief in the General Staff, was the son of a church official in Anhalt. His background was thoroughly aristocratic. His father was of Uradel stock; his grandfather, a civil servant. His father-in-law was an officer. Hermann von Stein, the later war minister, was a General Staff *Oberquartiermeister* under Moltke II. His father had been a pastor in Prussian Saxony. Moltke II's other maverick father was none other than Hermann von Kuhl, whose father was a distinguished academician.

47. Information not presented in tables. One searches in vain for the large number of rising middle-class families, that is, generals whose fathers or grandfathers were entrepreneurs, small businessmen, artisans, and so forth. Such families rarely produced General Staff generals, even in the technical positions.

48. Schlieffen's tenure as chief of the General Staff is best compared with this decade although there is a slight distortion because of the time difference.

49. Information based on findings not presented in tables.

50. Because of the limited number of generals involved in Table 36, a more detailed breakdown of their titles is not productive.

51. After 1800, of course, there were fewer German states able to grant titles than had been the case in earlier centuries. Many of the new noble families received titles for the service in the Prussian army or bureaucracy. Such families naturally had Prussian titles. Most of the foreign families stemmed from Austria or Bohemia. A few were of mixed Prussian and Polish origins. Many of these families, moreover, had a considerable tradition of Prussian military service by the time the generals were born. General Eduard von Mikusch-Buchberg, for example, held a Reichsadel title, but both his father and grandfather had been Prussian officers. General Emil von Conrady likewise had an Austrian title, dating to 1779, but his father had been a lieutenant colonel in the Prussian army. Maximilian Vogel von Falckenstein, general of infantry and chief of engineers and pioneers, held an Austrian title. His father and grandfather had been Prussian officers whereas his older brother served in the Austrian army. Ernst von der Burg, whose title was Bohemian in its 16th-century origins, also had forefathers in the Prussian army.

52. Many of Prussia's prominent military leaders in the late 18th and early 19th centuries, especially during the Napoleonic era, were of foreign origin.

53. Many foreign noble families in Prussian military and bureaucratic service lacked proof either of the dates of their titles or, in some cases, that their claims to nobility were genuine. In many such cases Prussia's kings granted Prussian titles to end any doubts or rumors about their loyal servants.

54. For example, the Freytag-Loringhoven and Osten-Sacken families, to name only two.

55. The small number (18) involved in the General Staff group precludes a further breakdown, but a few remarks may safely be made. Only one Hanoverian, no Bavarian nobles, and no Hessians were appointed to the General Staff in the rank of brigadier general or higher between 1871 and 1914. Anhalt was represented by two generals, as was Württemberg, while the Mecklenburgs contributed three. Obviously the General Staff's highest positions were reserved for Prussians and for nobles from states that had proven their loyalty to Prussia in the recent past.

56. See Table 8 for a complete list for all generals.

57. Moltke's appointments held Prussian titles in 58.16 percent of the cases. The corresponding percentage among all generals were hold-over generals, 57.50 percent; generals promoted 1871–81, 56.09 percent; and generals promoted 1882–92, 58.43 percent.

58. The younger Moltke's General Staff generals held Prussian titles in 65.00 percent of the cases. The corresponding figure for all generals promoted 1904–14 was 47.40 percent.

59. Evangelical is used here, as earlier, to signify the Prussian state church. The Lutheran minority was a small sect that refused to join the amalgamated state church.

60. Schliefen's appointments were 90.91 percent Evangelical. The corresponding figure for all generals promoted 1893–1903 was 83.69 percent.

61. Kittel, *Schlieffen*, p. 60.

62. Ibid., pp. 77–79, where the entire essay is printed.

63. On this point see the remarks by Eberhard Kessel in his introduction to Schlieffen, *Briefe*, p. 31.

64. It is characteristic of Schlieffen, however, that he had no patience for what he thought was incompetent preaching. He complained sarcastically in a letter to his wife (February 16, 1868) that he had just heard a sermon of less interest than a Cathlolic mass.

Chapter 9

1. W. S. Hamer, *The British Army: Civil–Military Relations, 1885–1905* (Oxford: Clarendon Press, 1970), pp. 14–17.

2. Wildman, *End of Russian Imperial Army*, pp.22–23, stresses the noble content of the czar's officer corps. Kenez, "Prerevolutionary Officer Corps," p. 131, establishes the numerous and recent peasant roots of many officers of all ranks.

3. Barge, "Generals of the Republic," pp. 7–11. Information on the Austro-Hungarian army is even less clear. See Rothenberg, *Army of Francis Joseph*, pp. 62, 151.

4. Kenez, "Prerevolutionary Officer Corps," p. 137.

5. Rothenberg, *Army of Francis Joseph*, pp. 118, 151.

6. The French promotion law, basically unchanged from 1832 until 1914, established a strict seniority principle as the basis for most promotions. Officers were usually guaranteed promotions at certain intervals. A fixed percentage of

officers, supposedly the best, advanced more rapidly. For further information see Ralston, *Army of the Republic*, p. 14.

7. French officers faced similar barriers. They had to obtain the permission of the war minister. Local police and the army investigated the women and their families, to determine wealth, reputation, and social status. The minimum dowry was 1,200 francs of income a year. See Barge, "Generals of the Republic," IV.

8. On the British, see Otley, "Social Affiliations of the British Army Elite," p. 90. Wildman, *End of Russian Army*, pp. 23–24, has figures for Russian generals in 1903. Barge, "Generals of the Republic," Table I-28, has information on French generals. His figures, however, include fathers who did not own land.

9. In this respect cavalry officers were similar to their counterparts in the British and Russian armies. See Harries-Jenkins, *Army in Victorian Society*, pp. 159–60, and Wildman, *End of Russian Army*, p. 9.

Bibliography

Manuscript Sources

The following collections of private papers are in the German Federal Republic's Bundesarchiv/Militärarchiv in Freiburg.

Below Nachlass. Contains unpublished papers of General Otto von Below, whose memoirs are an exceeding valuable source.

Beseler Nachlass. Private papers of Hans Hartwig von Beseler, also very valuable.

Chales de Beaulieu Nachlass. Papers of General Martin Chales de Beaulieu.

Friedrich Nachlass. Private papers of Colonel Karl Friedrichs.

Hahnke Nachlass. Papers of Wilhelm von Hahnke, Schlieffen's son-in-law.

Gossler Nachlass. Papers of War Minister General Heinrich von Gossler, General Konrad Ernst von Gossler, and Karl von Gossler, cofounder of the German National Peoples Party.

Keitel Nachlass. Primarily Wilhelm Keitel's papers after World War I.

Köstring Nachlass. Papers of Ernst Köstring, a reserve officer before 1914 and later military attaché in Moscow.

Lequis Nachlass. Papers of a low-ranking officer, later a general officer.

Leyen Nachlass. Contains the very significant papers of Ludwig von der Leyen.

Moltke Nachlass. Papers of Count Helmuth von Moltke.

Mutius Nachlass. Papers of Colonel Maximilian von Mutius.

Schiebel Nachlass. Papers of Erich Schiebel, a captain in 1914.

Schlieffen Nachlass. Papers of Count Alfred von Schlieffen and other members of his family. Packet N 43/99 contains some of his personal financial records.

Schulenburg Nachlass. Papers of Count Friedrich von der Schulenburg-Tressow, adjutant to William II and a lieutenant colonel in 1914.

Stülpnagel Nachlass. Contains fragments on several family members, primarily of Joachim von Stülpnagel.

193

Official and Semiofficial Military Sources

Anonymous. *Offizierstammliste des Ersten Garde-Regiments zu Fuss 1869–1913.* Berlin: E. S. Mittler & Son, 1913.

Berkun, Ludwig, and Walter Krüger, eds. *Stammliste des Infanterie Regiments von Alvensleben (6. brandenburgisches) Nr. 52.* Oldenburg: Druck und Verlag von Gerhard Stalling, 1910.

Bock, Baron Werner von, ed. *Stammliste des Offizierkorps des 2. Garde-Regiments zu Fuss 19.6.1813–15.5.1915.* Berlin: Verlag von R. Eisenschmidt, 1913.

Boeck, Friedrich Albert von der. *Deutschland: Das Heer.* 3rd ed. Berlin: Verlagsbuchhandlung Alfred Schall, 1903.

Bronsart von Schellendorff, Paul. *Der Dienst des Generalstabes.* 2 vols. Berlin: E. S. Mittler & Son, 1875, 1876.

Gall, Baron von, ed. *Fircks Taschenkalender für das Heer, mit Genehmigung des königliches Kriegsministerium.* Berlin: Verlag von A. Bath, 1909.

Grassman, Paul, ed. *Offizier-Stammliste des 6. rheinisches Infanterie Regiments Nr. 68.* Coblenz: Kindt & Meinardus Nachf., 1902.

Goertzke, Joachim von, ed. *Offizier-Stammliste des königlich preussischen Kaiser Franz Garde-Grenadier-Regiments Nr. 2 1814–1914.* Berlin: Verlag von Paul Parey, 1914.

Krafft, (?). *Dienst und Leben des jungen Infanterie-Offiziers, ein Lern-und Lesebuch.* Berlin: E. S. Mittler & Son, 1914.

Maltzahn, Baron A. von, ed. *Stammliste des Ulanen-Regiments Kaiser Alexander II von Russland (1. brandenburgischen) Nr. 3.* Berlin: E. S. Mittler & Son, 1908.

Prussia, Kriegsministerium. *Rangliste der königlich preussischen Armee und des XIII (königlich Württembergischen) Armeekorps.* 42 vols. Berlin: E. S. Mittler & Son, 1870/71–1914.

———. *Verordnung über das Heirathen der Militärpersonen des preussischen Heeres und der preussischen Landgendarmerie.* Berlin: E.S. Mittler & Son, 1902.

Rabenau, von. *Die deutsche Land-und Seemacht und die Berufspflichten des Offiziers.* 4th ed. Berlin: E. S. Mittler & Son, 1914.

Schreibershofen, M. von. *Das deutsche Heer. Bilder aus Krieg und Frieden.* Berlin: Ullstein, 1913.

Vogt, Hermann. *Das Buch vom deutschen Heer.* Bielefeld and Leipzig: Verlag von Velhagen & Klasing, 1886.

Zimmer-Vorhaus, Otto, ed. *Offizier-Stammliste des Infanterie-Regiments von Lützow (1. Rheinische) Nr. 25.* Berlin: Otto Beckmann Verlag, 1913.

Published Primary Sources

Anonymous. *Das alte Heer, von einem Stabsoffizier.* Charlottenburg: Verlag der Weltbühne, 1920.

———. *Das Ende der Offizierlaufbahn. Freimüthige Betrachtungen eines alten Offiziers über die Verabschiedungen.* Berlin: Militär Verlag R. Felix, 1902.

Bergh, Max van den. *Das deutsche Heer vor dem Weltkriege.* Berlin: Sanssouci Verlag, 1934.

Bernhardi, Friedrich von, ed. *Aus dem Leben Theodor von Bernhardis.* 7 vols. Leipzig: Verlag von S. Hirzel, 1895.

―――. *Denkwürdigkeiten aus meinem Leben.* Berlin: E. S. Mittler & Son, 1927.

Beseler, Hans Hartwig von. *Vom Soldatenberufe.* Berlin: E. S. Mittler & Son, 1912.

Bey, Pertev. *Unter Graf v. Haeseler.* Berlin: E. S. Mittler & Son, 1904.

Bismarck-Schönhausen, Prince Otto von. *Die gesammelten Werke.* 19 vols. Berlin: Verlag für Politik und Wirtschaft, 1924–32. Volumes six and nine cited herein.

Blau, Erich-Günter. *Die operative Verwendung der deutschen Kavallerie im Weltkrieg 1914–1918.* Vol I: Friedensvorbereitung. Munich: C. H. Beck'sche Verlagsbuchhandlung, 1934.

Blumenthal, Count Albrecht von. *Tagebücher des General-Feldmarschalls Graf von Blumenthal aus den Jahren 1866 und 1870/71,* edited by Count Albrecht von Blumenthal. Stuttgart and Berlin: J. G. Cott'asche Buchhandlung Nachfolger, 1902.

Brandt, Heinrich von. *Aus dem Leben des Generals der Infanterie z. D. Dr. Heinrich von Brandt,* edited by Heinrich von Brandt. 3 vols. Berlin: E. S. Mittler & Son, 1868.

Bronsart von Schellendorff, Paul. *Geheimes Kriegestagebuch 1870–1871,* edited by Peter Rassow. Bonn: Athenäum Verlag, 1954.

Budde, Hermann von. *Aufzeichnungen und Erinnerungsblätter.* Berlin: E. S. Mittler & Son, 1916.

Bülow, Prince Bernhard von. *Denkwürdigkeiten.* 4 vols. Berlin: Ullstein, 1930.

Bülow, Kurt von. *Pruessischer Militarismus zur Zeit Wilhelms II. Aus meiner Dienstzeit im Heer.* Schweidnitz: Hugo Reisse, 1930.

Chappuis, Hermann von. *Bei Hofe und im Felde. Lebenserinnerungen.* Frankfurt: Carl Jügels Verlag, 1902.

D'Abernon, Viscount Edgar Vincent. *An Ambassador of Peace. Lord D'Abernon's Diary.* 3 vols. London: Hadder & Stoughten, 1929.

Dissow, Joachim von. *Adel im Übergang.* Stuttgart: W. Kohlhammer Verlag, 1961.

Dungern, Baron Otto von. *Unter Kaiser und Kanzlern, Erinnerungen.* Coburg: Veste Verlag, 1953.

Einem, Karl von. *Erinnerungen eines Soldaten 1853–1933.* Leipzig: Verlag K. F. Koehler, 1933.

Fabur du Faur, Moritz von. *Macht und Ohnmacht, Erinnerungen eines alten Offiziers.* Stuttgart: Hans E. Günther Verlag, 1953.

Fransecky, Eduard von. *Denkwürdigkeiten des preussischen Generals der Infanterie Eduard von Fransecky,* edited by Walter von Bremen. Bielefeld and Leipzig: Velhagen & Klasing, 1901.

Freytag-Loringhoven, Baron Hugo von. *Menschen und Dinge wie ich sie in meinem Leben sah.* Berlin: E. S. Mittler & Son, 1923.

Friedrich III. *Kaiser Friedrich III. Tagebücher von 1848–1866,* edited by Heinrich Otto Meisner. Leipzig: Verlag von K. F. Koehler, 1929.

―――. *Kaiser Friedrich III. Das Kriegstagebuch von 1870/71.* Ed. Heinrich Otto Meisner. Berlin and Leipzig: Verlag von K. F. Koehler, 1926.

Friedrich Karl von Preussen. *Prinz Friedrich Karl von Preussen. Denkwürdigkeiten aus seinem Leben,* edited by Wolfgang Foerster. 2 vols. Stuttgart: Deutsche Verlags-Anstalt, 1910.

Gebsattels, Baron Ludwig von, "Politische Berichte Ludwigs Freiherr von Gebsattels," edited by Karl Demeter, *Pruessische Jahrbücher* 231 (January–June 1933): 24–39, 116–33.

Gleich, G. von. *Die alte Armee und ihre Verirrungen*. 2nd ed. Leipzig: Verlag von K. F. Koehler, 1919.

Goltz, Baron Colmar von der. *Denkwürdigkeiten*, edited by Wolfgang Foerster and Baron Friedrich von der Goltz. Berlin: E. S. Mittler & Son, 1929.

————. *The Nation in Arms*. Translated by Philip A. Ashworth. London: W. H. Allen, 1887.

Gregory, Baroness Mathilde von. *Dreissig Jahre preussische Soldatenfrau*. Munich: Rudolf M. Rohrer Verlag, ca 1931.

Groener, Wilhelm. *Wilhelm Groener. Lebenserinnerungen. Jugend, Generalstab, Weltkrieg*, edited by Baron Friedrich Hiller von Gaertringen. Göttingen: Vandenhoeck & Ruprecht, 1957.

Guderian, Heinz. *Erinnerungen eines Soldaten*. Heidelberg: Kurt Vowinckel, 1951.

Gündell, Erich von. *General Erich von Gündell aus seinen Tagebücher*, edited by Walther Obkircher. Hamburg: Hanseatische Verlagsanstalt, 1939.

Hartmann, Friedrich. *Erinnerungen eines deutschen Offiziers 1848 bis 1871*. 3rd ed. 2 vols. in 1. Wiesbaden: Verlag J. F. Bergmann, 1890.

Hartmann, Julius von. *Lebenserinnerungen, Briefe und Aufsätze*. 2 vols. Berlin: Verlag von Gebrüder Paetel, 1882.

Hassel, Ulrich von. *Erinnerungen aus meinem Leben 1848–1918*. Stuttgart: Belsersche Verlagsbuchhandlung, 1919.

Hindenburg, Herbert von. *Am Rande zweier Jahrhunderte. Momentbilder einem Diplomatenleben*. Berlin: Schlieffen Verlag, 1938.

Hindenburg, Paul von. *Aus meinem Leben*. Leipzig: Verlag von G. Hirzel, 1920.

Hoffmann, Otto von. *Lebenserinnerungen des königlich preussischen Generalleutnants Otto von Hoffman*, edited by Colonel von Hoffmann. Oldenburg and Leipzig: Schulzesche Hof-Buchhandlung und Hof-Buchdruckerei, 1907.

Hohenlohe-Ingelfingen, Prince Krafft zu. *Aus meinem Leben*. 4 vols. Berlin: E. S. Mittler & Son, 1907.

————. *Aus meinem Leben. Aufzeichnungen aus den Jahren 1848–1871*, edited by Lt. Col. W. von Bremen. Berlin: E. S. Mittler & Son, 1918.

Hohenlohe-Schillingsfüurst, Prince Chlodwig zu. *Denkwürdigkeiten des Fürsten Chlodwig zu Hohenlohe-Schillingsfürst*, edited by Friedrich Curtius. 2 vols. Stuttgart: Deutsche Verlags-Anstalt, 1907.

Holleben, Albert von. *Briefe aus den Kriegsjahren 1866 und 1870/71*, edited by Wilhelm von Holleben. Berlin: Verlag von Karl Siegismund, 1913.

Holleben, Hermann von. "Erinnerungen aus dem Leben des Generals der Infanterie," *Beihefte zur Militär-Wochenblatt, 1892*: 1–62.

Holleben, Wilhelm von. "Die wissenschaftliche Grundlage für den Offizier und die Reorganisation des Kadetten-Korps," *Jahrbücher für die deutsche Armee und Marine* (1902): 461–75.

Hutten-Czapski, Count Bogdan von. *Sechzig Jahre Politik und Gesellschaft*. 2 vols. Berlin: E. S. Mittler & Son, 1936.

Jagemann, Eugen von. *Fünfundsiebzig Jahre des Erlebens und Erfahrens (1849–1924)*. Heidelberg: Carl Winters Universitätsbuchhandlung, 1925.

Keim, August. *Erlebtes und Erstrebtes. Lebenserinnerungen.* Hanover: Ernst
    Letsch Verlag, 1925.
Kluck, Alexander von. *Wanderjahre-Krieg-Gestalten.* Berlin: Verlag R. Eisens-
    chmidt, 1929.
Kretschmann, Hans von. *Kriegsbriefe aus den Jahren 1870/71*, edited by Lily
    Braun, born von Kretschman. Berlin: Meyer & Jessen, 1911.
Lancken-Wakenitz, Baron Oscar von der. *Meine dreissig Dienstjahre 1888–1918.*
    Berlin: Verlag für Kulturpolitik, 1931.
Lenski, Franz von. *Aus den Leutnantsjahren eines alten Generalstabsoffiziers.*
    Berlin: Verlag Georg Bath, 1922.
_____. *Lern-und Lehrjahre in Front und Generalstab.* Berlin: Verlag Bernard &
    Graefe, 1939.
Liebert, Eduard von. *Aus einem bewegten Leben.* Munich: J. F. Lehmanns Verlag,
    1925.
Lignitz, Albrecht von. *Aus drei Kriegen.* Berlin: E. S. Mittler & Son, 1904.
Litzmann, Karl. *Lebenserinnerungen.* 2 vols. Berlin: Verlag R. Eisenschmidt,
    1927.
Loë, Baron Walther von. *Erinnerungen aus meinem Berufsleben.* Stuttgart:
    Deutsche Verlags-Anstalt, 1906.
Ludendorff, Erich. *Mein militärischer Werdegang. Blätter der Erinnerung an unser
    stolzes Heer.* Munich: Ludendorffs Verlag, 1933.
Lüders, Hermann, *Ein Soldatenleben in Krieg und Frieden.* Stuttgart and Leipzig:
    Deutsche Verlags-Anstalt, 1898.
Mackensen, August von. *Mackensen, Briefe und Aufzeichnungen*, edited by
    Wolfgang Foerster. Leipzig: Bibliographisches Institut, 1938.
Manstein, Erich von. *Aus einem Soldatenleben 1887–1939.* Bonn: Athenäum
    Verlag, 1958.
Meier-Welcker, Hans, ed. *Offiziere im Bild von Dokumenten aus drei Jahrhunder-
    ten.* Stuttgart: Deutsche Verlags-Anstalt, 1964.
Moltke, Count Helmuth von. *Essays, Speeches, and Memoirs of Count Helmuth
    von Moltke.* Translated by Charles Flint McClumpha, C. Barter, and Mary
    Herms. 2 vols. New York: Harper & Brothers, 1893.
_____. *Generalfeldmarschall Graf von Moltke. Ausgewählte Werke*, edited by
    Friedrich von Schmerfeld. 4 vols. Berlin: Reimar Hobbing, 1925.
_____. *Gesammelte Schriften und Denkwürdigkeiten des General-Feldmarschalls
    Grafen Helmuth von Moltke.* 8 vols. Berlin: E. S. Mittler & Son,
    1892–1918.
_____. *Moltkes Militärische Werke.* 17 vols. Berlin: E. S. Mittler & Son,
    1892–1912.
Moltke, Helmuth von. *Erinnerungen, Briefe, Dokumente 1877–1916*, edited by
    Eliza von Moltke. Stuttgart: Der Kommende Tag Verlag, 1922.
Natzmer, Oldwig von. *Unter den Hohenzollern. Denkwürdigkeiten aus dem Leben
    des Generals Oldwig von Natzmer*, edited by Gneomar Ernst von Natzmer.
    4 vols. Gotha: Friedrich Wilhelm Peethes, 1888.
Pfeil, Count Richard von. *Vor vierzig Jahre.* Schwiednitz: Verlag von L. Heege,
    1911.
_____. *Zwischen des Kriegen. Meine ersten Jahre im Ersten Garde-Regiment zu
    Fuss 1864 bis Anfang 1870.* Schwiednitz: Verlag von L. Heege, 1912.

Pommer, Hans. *Zwanzig Jahre im Reichslande.* Frankfurt am Main: Neuer Frankfurter Verlag, 1914.

Ranke, Leopold von. *Leopold von Ranke. Neue Briefe*, edited by Bernard Hoeft and Hans Herzfeld. Hamburg: Hoffmann and Campe Verlag, 1949.

Ritter, H. *Kritik des Weltkrieges. Das Erbe Moltkes und Schlieffens im grossen Kriege.* 2nd ed. Leipzig: Verlag von K. F. Koehler, 1921.

Roon, Count Albrecht von. *Denkwürdigkeiten aus dem Leben des General-Feldmarschalls Kriegsministers Grafen von Roon*, edited by Count Waldemar von Roon. 3 vols. Breslau: Verlag von Eduard Trewendt, 1897.

Schlieffen, Count Alfred von. *Generalfeldmarschall Graf Alfred von Schlieffen. Gesammelte Schriften.* 2 vols. Berlin: E. S. Mittler & Son, 1913.

————. *Graf Alfred Schlieffen, Briefe*, edited by Eberhard Kessel. Göttingen: Vandenhoeck & Ruprecht, 1958.

Schoenaich, Baron Paul von. *Mein Damaskus. Erlebnisse und Bekenntnisse.* Berlin-Hessenwinkel: Verlag der Neuen Gesellschaft, 1926.

Schönburg-Waldenburg, Prince Heinrich von. Erinnerungen aus kaiserliche Zeit. Leipzig: Verlag von K. F. Koehler, 1929.

Schweinitz, Hans Lothar. *Denkwürdigkeiten des Botschafters General von Schweinitz*, edited by Wilhelm von Schweinitz. 2 vols. Berlin: Reimar Hobbing, 1927.

————. *Briefwechsel*, edited by Wilhelm von Schweinitz. Berlin: Reimar Hobbing, 1928.

Seeckt, Hans von. *Aus meinem Leben 1866–1917*, edited by Friedrich von Rabenau. Leipzig: Hase & Koehler Verlag, 1941.

Stein, Hermann von. *Erlebnisse und Betrachtungen aus der Zeit des Weltkrieges.* Leipzig: K. F. Koehler Verlag, 1919.

Steinmetz, Karl Freidrich von. *General-Feldmarschall von Steinmetz. Aus den Familienpapieren dargestellt*, edited by Hans von Krosigk. Berlin: E. S. Mittler & Son, 1900.

Stosch, Albrecht von. *Denkwürdigkeiten des Generals und Admirals Albrecht von Stosch*, edited by Ulrich von Stosch. Stuttgart: Deutsche Verlags-Anstalt, 1904.

Strombeck, Baron Richard von. *Fünfzig Jahre aus meinem Leben.* Leipzig: Friedrich Wilhelm Grunow, 1894.

Templehoff, Henny von. *Mein Glück um Hause Ludendorff.* Berlin: Druck und Verlag August Scherl, 1919.

Tirpitz, Alfred von. *Erinnerungen.* Leipzig: K. F. Koehler, 1920.

Treutler, Karl Georg von. *Die graue Exzellenz. Zwischen Staatsräson und Vassalentreue. Aus den Papieren des kaiserlichen Gesandten Karl Georg von Treutler*, edited by Karl-Heinz Janssen. Frankfurt am Main: Verlag Ullstein, 1971.

Trotha, Thilo von. "Offizierberuf und Offizierlaufbahn," *Jahrbücher für die deutsche Armee und Marine* (1910): 1–33.

Verdy du Vernois, Julius von. *Der Zug nach Bronzell (1850). Jugend Erinnerungen.* Berlin: E. S. Mittler & Son, 1905.

Voigts-Rhetz, Konstans Bernhard von. *Briefe des Generals der Infanterie von Voigts-Rhetz aus den Kriegsjahren 1866 und 1870/71.* Berlin: E. S. Mittler & Son, 1906.

Wartensleben-Carow, Count Hermann von. *Hermann Graf von Wartensleben-Carow. Ein Lebensbild 1826–1921*, edited by Countess Elisabeth von Wartensleben. Berlin: E. S. Mittler & Son, 1923.

Waldersee, Count Alfred von. *Aus dem Briefwechsel des Generalfeldmarschall Alfred Grafen von Waldersee*, edited by H. O. Meisner. Berlin: Deutsche Verlags-Anstalt, 1928.

————. "Aus den Erinnerungen des Generalfeldmarschalls Grafen von Waldersee: Kaiser und Kaiserin Friedrich," edited by H. O. Meisner, *Deutsche Revue* 46 (July–September 1921): 1–9.

————. "Aus den Erinnerungen des Generalfeldmarschalls Grafen von Waldersee. Über seine Tätigkeit als Generalquartermeister und Chef des Generalstabes," *Deutsche Revue* 46 (June 1921): 208–24.

————. *Denkwürdigkeiten des General-Feldmarschalls Alfred Grafen von Waldersee*, edited by H. O. Meisner. 3 vols. Berlin and Stuttgart: Deutsche Verlags-Anstalt, 1925.

————. *General-Feldmarschall Alfred Graf von Waldersee in seinem militärischen Wirken*, edited by Hans Mohs. 2 vols. Berlin: Verlag R. Eisenschmidt, 1929.

Wilhelm I. *Briefe Kaiser Wilhelms des Ersten*, edited by Erich Brandenburg. Leipzig: Insel Verlag, 1911.

————. *Kaiser Wilhelms des Ersten. Briefe, Reden und Schriften*, edited by Ernst Werner. 2 vols. Berlin: E. S. Mittler & Son, 1906.

————. *Kaiser Wilhelms I. Briefe an Politiker und Staatsmänner*, edited by Johannes Schulte. 2 vols. Berlin and Leipzig: Verlag Walter de Gruyter, 1930–31.

————. *Militärisches Schriften weiland Kaiser Wilhelms des Grossen Majestät*, edited by Prussia, Kriegsministerium. 2 vols. Berlin: E. S. Mittler & Son, 1897.

————. *Wilhelms I. Briefe an seinen Vater König Friedrich Wilhelm III (1827–1839)*, edited by Paul Alfred Merbuch. Berlin: Verlag Karl Curtius, 1922.

Wilhelm II. *Kaiser Wilhelm II. Ereignisse und Gestalten aus den Jahren 1878–1918*. Leipzig and Berlin: Verlag K. F. Koehler, 1922.

Biographical and Genealogical Sources

Bettelheim, Anton, ed. *Biographisches Jahrbuch und deutscher Nekrolog*. 18 vols. Berlin: Verlag von George Reimer, 1896–1917.

Brachvogel, A. E., ed. *Die Männer der neuen deutschen Zeit. Eine Sammlung von Biographieen*. 4 vols. Hanover: Carl Rümpler, 1873.

Genealogisches Handbuch Bürgerlicher Familien: ein deutsches Geschlechterbuch, edited by Bernard Koerner et al. Görlitz: Druck and Verlag C. A. Starke, 1904–79.

Genealogisches Handbuch des Adels, edited by Hans Friedrich von Ehrenkrook and Paul von Heuck. 72 vols. Glücksburg: C. A. Starke Verlag, 1951–81.

Genealogisches Taschenbuch der Adeligen Häuser. 19 vols. Brunn: Druck und Verlag Friedrich Irrgang, 1870–94.

Genealogisches Taschenbuch des Uradels, edited by Baron Alexander von Dachenhausen. 2 vols. Brunn: Druck und Verlag von Friedrich Irrgang, 1891, 1893.

Gothaisches Genealogisches Taschenbücher der Fürstliche/Gräfliche/Freiherrliche/ Adelige Häuser. Gotha: Justus Perthes, 1764–1942.

Kleist, Bogislav von. *Die Generale der königlich preussischen Armee von 1840–1890.* 2nd ed. 3 vols. Leipzig: Zuckschwerde & Möschke, 1894–95.

Kneschke, Ernst Heinrich, ed. *Neues Allgemeine Deutsches Adels-Lexicon.* 9 vols. Leipzig: Friedrich Vogt, 1860–70.

Priesdorff, Kurt von, ed. *Soldatisches Führertum.* 10 vols. Hamburg: Hanseatische Verlagsanstalt, 1936–42.

Wer Ist's. 10 vols. Berlin and Leipzig: Verlag von H. A. Degener, 1905–35.

Zedlich-Neukirch, Baron L. von, ed. *Neues preussisches Adels Lexicon oder genealogische und diplomatische Nachrichten.* 6 vols. Leipzig: Gebrüder Reichenback, 1837.

Secondary Sources

Anderson, Eugene. *The social and Political Conflict in Prussia, 1858–1864.* New York: Octagon Books, 1976 [1953].

Angress, Werner T. "Prussia's Army and the Jewish Reserve Officer Controversy before World War I," *Leo Baeck Institute Year Book* 17 (1972): 19–42.

Bald, Detlef. *Zur Sozialen Herkunft des Offiziers.* Bonn: Sozialwissenschaftliches Institut der Bundeswehr, 1977.

Balfour, Michael. *The Kaiser and His Times.* New York: W. W. Norton, 1972 [1964].

Barge, Walter S. "The Generals of the Republic: The Corporate Personality of High Military Rank in France, 1889–1914." Ph.D. dissertation, University of North Carolina, 1982.

Berghahn, Volker R. *Der Tirpitz Plan, Genesis und Verfall einer innenpolitischen Krisenstrategie unter Wilhelms II.* Düsseldorf: Droste Verlag, 1971.

————. *Germany and the Approach of War in 1914.* New York: St. Martin's Press, 1973.

————. *Probleme der Reichsgründungszeit 1848–1879.* Cologne: Kiepenheuer & Witsch, 1968.

Bethcke, Ernst. *Politische Generale! Kreise und Krisen um Bismarck.* Berlin: Verlag Tradition, 1930.

Bircher, Eugen, and Walter Bode. *Schlieffen. Man und Idee.* Zurich: Scientia A.G., 1940.

Black, Hans, "Die Grundzüge der Beförderungsordnungen," *Untersuchungen zur Geschichte des Offizierkorps. Anciennität und Beförderung nach Leistung,* edited by Hans Meier-Welcker, pp. 65–151. Stuttgart: Deutsche Verlags-Anstalt, 1962.

Blanke, Richard. *Prussian Poland in the German Empire, 1871–1900.* New York: Columbia University Press, 1981.

Blume, Wilhelm von. *Kaiser Wilhelm der Grossen und Roon.* Berlin: B. Behrs Verlag, 1906.

Bobbe-Wernigerode, J. "Der Offizierersatz im deutschen Heere." *Jahrbücher für die deutsche Armee und Marine* (1912): 623–30.

————. "Offiziermangel und Offizierersatz im deutschen Reichsheere." *Jahrbücher für die deutsche Armee und Marine* (1911): 623–30.

Boetticher, Friedrich von. *Schlieffen.* Göttingen: Musterschmidt Verlag, 1957.

Bolton, Frederick E. *The Secondary Schools of Germany.* New York: D. Appleton, 1900.

Bramsted, Ernest K. *Aristocracy and the Middle Classes in Germany: Social Types in German Literature, 1830–1900.* Chicago: University of Chicago Press, 1964 [1937].

Briet, Gotthard. *Der Staats-und Gesellschaftsbild deutscher Generale beider Weltkriege im Spiegel ihrer Memoiren.* Boppard am Rhein: Harald Boldt Verlag, 1973.

Bronsart, Friedrich von. "Die alte Kaiser und sein Kriegsminister von Bronsart," *Historische Vierteljahresschrift* 31 (1937–39): 293–306.

Bry, Gerhard. *Wages in Germany, 1871–1945.* Princeton: Princeton University Press, 1960.

Buchfink, Ernst. *Feldmarschall Graf von Haeseler.* Berlin: E. S. Mittler & Son, 1929.

————. "Feldmarschall Graf Haeseler 19.1.1836–26.10.1919." *Wissen und Wehr* (1931): 3–9.

Busch, Eckart. *Der Oberbefehl, seine rechtliche Struktur in Preussen und Deutschland seit 1848.* Boppard am Rhein: Harald Boldt, 1967.

Bushnell, John. "The Tsarist Officer Corps, 1881–1914: Customs, Duties, Inefficiency." *American Historical Review* 86, no. 4 (October 1981): 753–81.

Bussmann, Walter. "Bismarck: Sein Helfer und seine Gegner." In *Reichsgründung 1870/71,* edited by Theordo Scheider and Ernst Deuerlein, pp. 119–47. Stuttgart: Seewald Verlag, 1970.

Cecil, Lamar J. R. "The Creation of Nobles in Prussia, 1871–1918." *American Historical Review* 75, no. 3 (February 1970): 757–95.

————. *The German Diplomatic Service, 1871–1914.* Princeton: Princeton University Press, 1977.

————. "Jew and Junker in Imperial Berlin." *Leo Baeck Institute Yearbook* 20 (1975): 47–58.

Cochenhausen, R. von, ed. *Von Scharnhorst zu Schlieffen 1806–1906.* Berlin: E. S. Mittler & Son, 1933.

Conrady, Eduard von. *Das Leben des Grafen August von Werder.* Berlin: E. S. Mittler & Son, 1889.

Craig, Gordon A. *Germany 1866–1945.* New York: Oxford University Press, 1978.

————. *The Politics of the Prussian Army 1640–1945.* New York: Oxford University Press, 1956.

Crousaz, Adolf von. *Das Offizierkorps der preussischen Armee.* Halle: Verlag Otto Hendel, 1876.

————. *Geschichte des königlich preussischen Kadetten-Corps.* Berlin: Verlag von Heinrich Schindler, 1857.

Czernin, Gebhard. *Das Leben des königlich preussischen Generals der Infanterie August von Goeben.* 2 vols. Berlin: E. S. Mittler & Son, 1895, 1897.

Diest, Wilhelm. "Die Armee in Staat und Gesellschaft 1890–1914." In *Das kaiserliche Deutschland. Politik und Gesellschaft 1870–1918,* edited by Michael Stürmer, pp. 312–39. Düsseldorf: Droste Verlag, 1970.

————. "Kaiser Wilhelm II in the Context of His Military and Naval Entourage." In *Kaiser Wilhelm II: New Interpretations*, edited by John C. G. Röhl and Nicolaus Sombart. Cambridge: Cambridge University Press, 1982, pp. 169–92.

————. *Militär und Innenpolitik im Weltkrieg 1914–1918*. 2 vols. Düsseldorf: Droste Verlag, 1970. Volume I used.

Demeter, Karl. *Das deutsche Offizierkorps in Gesellschaft und Staat 1650–1945*. 4th ed. Frankfurt am Main: Bernard & Graefe, 1965 [1930].

Deussen, Walter. *Ernstes und Heiteres aus dem Kadettenleben zur Gross-Lichterfelde*. Zentralkartei ehem. kgl. preussischer und sächischer Kadetten, 1967 [1921].

Dissow, Joachim von. *Adel im Übergang*. Stuttgart: W. Kohlhammer Verlag, 1961.

Endres, Franz Karl. *The Social Structure and Corresponding Ideologies of the German Officer's Corps before the World War*. Translated by S. Ellison. New York: Columbia University Press and the Works Progress Administration, 1937.

Engelberg, Ernst, ed. *Diplomatie und Kriegspolitik vor und nach der Reichsgründung*. Berlin: Akademie Verlag, 1971.

Engelberg, Ernst, and Horst Bartel, eds. *Die grosspreussisch-militaristische Reichsgründung 1871*. 2 vols. Berlin: Akademie Verlag, 1971.

Eley, Geoff. *Reshaping the German Right: Radical Nationalism and Political Change after Bismarck*. New Haven: Yale University Press, 1980.

Epstein, Klaus. *Matthias Erzberger and the Delimma of German Democracy*. Princeton: Princeton University Press, 1959.

Ergang, Robert. *The Potsdam Führer: Frederick William I, Father of Prussian Militarism*. New York: Columbia University Press, 1941.

Fischer, Fritz. *Krieg der Illusionen. Die deutsche Politik von 1911 bis 1914*. Düsseldorf: Droste Verlag, 1969.

Ford, Guy Stanton. *Stein and the Era of Reform in Prussia 1807–1815*. Princeton: Princeton University Press, 1922.

Förster, Gerhard, Heinz Helmert, Helmut Otto, and Helmut Schnitter. *Der preussisch-deutsche Generalstab 1640–1945, zu seiner politische Rolle in der Geschichte*. East Berlin: Dietz Verlag, 1966.

Foerster, Wolfgang, et al. *Generaloberst von Seeckt. Ein Erinnerungsbuch*. Berlin: E. S. Mittler & Son, 1937.

Fraley, Jonathan David. "Government by Procrastination: Chancellor Hohenlohe and Kaiser Wilhelm II, 1894–1900." *Central European History* 7, no. 2 (June 1974): 159–83.

Freytag-Loringhoven, Baron Hugo von. *General-Feldmarschall Graf von Schlieffen*. Leipzig: Historia Verlag Paul Schraepler, 1920.

Gablentz, Otto-Heinrich von der. "Das preussisch-deutsche Offizierkorps." In *Schicksalsfragen der Gegenwart*, III: 47–71, edited by Bundesministerium für Verteidigung, 7 vols. Tübingen: Max Niemeyer Verlag, 1958.

Garthhoff, Raymond L. "The Military In Russia, 1861–1965." In *Armed Forces and Society*, edited by Jacques van Doorn. The Hague: Mouton, 1968.

Gilbert, Felix, ed. *The Historical Essays of Otto Hintze*. New York: Oxford University Press, 1975.

Gillis, John R. *The Prussian Bureaucracy in Crisis 1840–1860: Origins of an Administrative Ethos*. Stanford: Stanford University Press, 1971.

Gollwitzer, Heinz. *Die Standesherren. Die politische und gesellschaftliche Stellung der Mediatisierten 1815–1918*. Stuttgart: Friedrich Vorwork Verlag, 1957.

Goodwin, Albert, ed. *The European Nobility in the Eighteenth Century*. London: Adam and Charles Black, 1953.

Görlitz, Walter. *Die Junker. Adel und Bauer im deutschen Osten*. Glücksburg: C. A. Starke Verlag, 1956.

————. *History of the German General Staff 1657–1945*. Translated by Brian Battershaw. New York: Praeger, 1957.

Gradmann, Wilhelm. *Die politischen Ideen Edwin von Manteuffels und ihre Auswirkungen in seiner Laufbahn*. Düsseldorf: Dissertations Verlag G. H. Nolte, 1932.

Haeften, Hans von. "Bismarck und Moltke." *Preussische Jahrbücher* 177 (July–September 1919): 82–105.

Hahn, Peter-Michael. *Struktur und Funktion des brandenburgischer Adels in 16. Jahrhundert*. Berlin: Colloquium Verlag, 1979.

Hamer, W. S. *The British Army: Civil-Military Relations, 1885–1905*. Oxford: Clarendon Press, 1970.

Hamerow, Theodore. *The Social Foundations of German Unification*. 2 vols. Princeton: Princeton University Press, 1969, 1972.

Harries-Jenkins, Gwynn. *The Army in Victorian Society*. London: Routledge and Kegan Paul, 1977.

Herwig, Holger. *The German Naval Officer Corps: A Social and Political History 1890–1918*. Oxford: Clarendon Press, 1973.

Herzfeld, Hans. *Die deutsche Rüstungspolitik vor dem Weltkrieg*. Bonn: Kurt Schroeder, 1923.

Höfele, Karl Heinrich, ed. *Geist und Gesellschaft der Bismarckzeit 1870–1890*. Göttingen: Musterschmidt Verlag, 1967.

Hoffmann, Hubert, ed. *Das deutscher Offizierkorps 1860–1960*. Boppard: Harald Bold & Verlag, 1980.

Höhn, Reinhard. *Die Armee als Erziehungsschule der Nation. Das Ende einer Idee*. Bad Harzburg: Verlag für Wissenschafter, Wirtschaft und Technik, 1963.

Hollyday, Frederic B. M. *Bismarck's Rival: A Political Biography of General and Admiral Albrecht von Stosch*. Durham: Duke University Press, 1960.

Hossbach, Friedrich. *Die Entwicklung des Oberbefehls über das Heer in Brandenburg Preussen und im deutschen Reich 1655–1945*. Würzburg: Holzner Verlag, 1957.

Hughes, Daniel J. "Non-Prussian Officers in the Prussian Army, 1867–1914." *Red River Valley Historical Journal* 6, no. 2 (Winter 1981): 14–32.

————. "Occupational Origins of Prussia's Generals, 1871–1914." *Central European History* 13, no. 1 (March 1980): 3–33.

————. "The Social Composition of the Prussian Generalcy, 1871–1914." Ph.D. dissertation, University of North Carolina, 1979.

Hull, Isabel V. *The Entourage of Kaiser Wilhelm II, 1888–1918*. London: Cambridge University Press, 1982.

Jany, Kurt. *Geschichte der königlich preussischen Armee*. 4 vols. Berlin: Verlag von Karl Siegismund, 1933.

Kaiser, Klaus-Dieter. "Die Eingliederung der ehemals selbständigen Norddeutschen Truppenkörper in die preussische Armee in den Jahren nach 1866." Ph.D. dissertation, Free University of Berlin, 1972.

Keck, Karl Heinrich. *Das Leben des General-Feldmarschalls Edwin von Manteuffel*. Bielefeld and Leipzig: Velhagen & Klasing, 1890.

Kenez, Peter. "A Profile of the Prerevolutionary Officer Corps." *California Slavic Studies* 7 (1973): 121–58.

Kessel, Eberhard. "Bismarck und die Halbgötter." *Historische Zeitschrift* 171 (1956): 249–86.

———. "Die Tätigkeit des Grafen Waldersee als Generalquartiermeister und Chef des Generalstabs der Armee," *Die Welt als Geschichte* 14 (1954): 181–211.

———. *Moltke*. Stuttgart: K. F. Koehler Verlag, 1957.

———. "Zu Boyens Entlassung." *Historische Zeitschrift* 175 (1953): 41–54.

Kitchen, Martin. *The German Officer Corps, 1890–1918*. Oxford: Clarendon Press, 1968.

———. *A Military History of Germany from the Eighteenth Century to the Present Day*. Bloomington: Indiana University Press, 1975.

Kittel, Helmuth. *Alfred Graf Schlieffen, Jugend und Glaube*. Berlin: Verlag des Evangelischen Bundes, 1939.

———. "Kriegsakademie und Generalstab. Ein Beispiel aus der deutschen Hochschulgeschichte." *Deutsche Theologie* (1936): 329–56.

Kolb, Eberhard. "Kriegführung und Politik 1870/71." In *Reichsgründung 1870/71*, edited by Theodor Scheider and Ernst Deuerlein, pp. 95–118. Stuttgart: Seewald Verlag, 1970.

Krieg, Thilo. *Hermann von Tresckow, General der Infanterie und General-Adjutant Kaiser Wilhelms I*. Berlin: E. S. Mittler & Son, 1911.

Kulczycki, John. *School Strikes in Prussian Poland, 1901–1907: The Struggle over Bilingual Education*. New York: Columbia University Press, 1981.

Lambsdorff, Count Gustav von. *Die Militärbevollmächtigten Kaiser Wilhelms II am Zarenhofe 1904–1914*. Berlin: Schlieffen Verlag, 1937.

Lütge, Friedrich. *Deutsche Sozial-und Wirtschaftsgeschichte*. Berlin: Springer Verlag, 1952.

Marcks, Erich. "Albrecht von Roon, seine Persönlichkeit und seine geschichtliche Stellung." *Deutsche Rundschau* 115 (April–June 1903): 202–29.

———. *Kaiser Wilhelm I*. 3rd ed. Leipzig: Verlag von Duncker and Humboldt, 1899.

Marschall von Bieberstein, Baron Fritz Adolf. *Verantwortlichkeit und Gegenzeichnung*. Berlin: Verlag von Franz Vahlen, 1911.

Martin, Günther. "Gruppenschicksal und Herkunftschicksal. Zur Sozialgeschichte der preussischen Generalität 1812–1918." Ph.D. dissertation, Saarbrücken, 1970.

Marx, Lt. Gen. "Graf Haeseler als Erzieher. Erinnerungen und Betrachtungen." *Wissen und Wehr* (1931): 10–31.

Matuschka, Count Edgar von. "Die Beförderung in der Praxis." *Untersuchung zur Geschichte des Offizierkorps. Anciennität und Beförderungnach Leistung*, edited by Hans Meier-Welcker, pp. 153–76. Stuttgart: Deutsche Verlags-Anstalt, 1962.

———. "Organisationsgeschichte des Heeres 1890–1918." *Handbuch zur Deutschen Militärgeschichte 1648–1939*, edited by Hans Meier-Welcker and Wolfgang von Groote, V: 157–282. 5 vols. Frankfurt am Main: Bernard & Graefe, 1962–76.

Meinecke, Friedrich. "Boyen und Roon. Zwei preussische Kriegsministers." *Historische Zeitschrift* 77 (1896): 207–33.

———. *Das Leben des Generalfeldmarschall Hermann von Boyen.* 2 vols. Stuttgart: J. G. Cotta'sche Buchhandlung Nachfolger, 1899.

Meisner, Heinrich Otto. *Der Kriegsminister.* Berlin: Hermann Reinshagen Verlag, 1940.

———. "Militärkabinett, Kriegsminister und Reichskanzler zur Zeit Wilhelms I." *Forschungen zur brandenburgpreussischen Geschichte* 50 (1938): 86–106.

Messerschmidt, Manfred. "Die Armee in Staat und Gesellschaft—Die Bismarckzeit." In *Das kaiserlich Deutschland, Politik und Gesellschaft 1870–1918,* edited by Michael Stürmer, pp. 89–119. Düsseldorf: Droste Verlag, 1970.

———. "Die politische Geschichte der preussisch-deutschen Armee." In *Handbuch zur deutschen Militärgeschichte,* edited by Friedrich Forstmeister and Hans Meier-Welcker, IV, part 1: 218–86. Munich: Bernard & Graefe, 1962–76.

———. "Die preussische Armee." In *Handbuch zur deutschen Militärgeschichte 1648–1939,* edited by Friedrich Forstmeister and Hans Meier-Welcker, IV, part 2: 10–225. Munich: Bernard & Graefe, 1962–76.

———. *Militär und Politik in der Bismarckzeit und im wilhelminishchen Deutschland.* Darmstadt: Wissenschaftliche Buchgesellschaft, 1975.

———. "Preussens Militär in seinem gesellschaftlichen Umfeld." In *Preussen im Rückblick,* edited by Hans-Jurgen Puhle and Hans-Ulrich Wehler. Göttingen: Vandenhoeck & Ruprecht, 1980, pp. 43–88.

Messerschmidt, Manfred and Ursula von Gersdorff, eds. *Offiziere im Bild von Dokumenten aus drei Jahrhunderten.* Stuttgart: Deutsche Verlags-Anstalt, 1964.

Morris, Warren B. Jr. *The Road to Olmütz: The Career of Joseph Maria von Radowitz.* New York: The Revisionist Press, 1976.

Morsey, Rudolf. *Die oberste Reichsverwaltung unter Bismarck 1867–1890.* Münster: Aschendorffsche Verlagsbuchhandlung, 1957.

Muncy, Lysbeth Walker. *The Junker in the Prussian Administration under William II, 1888–1914.* Providence, Brown University Press, 1944.

———. "The Prussian Landräte in the Last Years of the Monarchy: A Case Study of Pomerania and the Rhineland in 1890–1918." *Central European History* 6, no. 4 (December 1973): 299–338.

Nichols, J. Alden. *Germany after Bismarck: The Caprivi Era, 1890–1894.* New York: W. W. Norton, 1958.

Niemann, Alfred. *Kaiser und Heer. Das Wesen der Kommandogewalt und ihre Ausbildung durch Kaiser Wilhelm II.* Berlin: Verlag für Kulturpolitik, 1929.

Obermann, Emil. *Soldaten, Burger, Militaristen. Militär und Demokratie in Deutschland.* Stuttgart: J. G. Cotta'sche Buchhandlung Nachfolger, n.d. (1955?).

Oertzen, Friedrich Wilhelm von. *Junker. Preussischer Adel im Jahrhundert des Liberalismus.* Oldenburg and Berlin: Gerhard Stalling Verlags-Buchhandlung, 1939.

Osten-Sacken und von Rhein, Baron Ottomar von der. *Preussens Heer von seinen Angängen bis zur Gegenwart.* 3 vols. Berlin: E. S. Mittler & Son, 1914.

Otley, C. B. "Militarism and the Social Affiliations of the British Army Elite." In

Armed Forces and Society: Sociological Essays, edited by Jacques van Doorn. The Hague: Mouton, 1968.

Otto, Helmut. *Schlieffen und der Generalstab. Der preussisch-deutsche Generalstab unter der Leitung des Generals von Schlieffen 1891–1905*. Berlin (East): Deutsche Akademie der Wissenschaften, 1966.

Papke, Gerhard. "Offizierkorps und Anciennität." In *Untersuchung zur Geschichte des Offizierkorps. Anciennität und Beförderung nach Leistung*, edited by Hans Meier-Welcker, pp. 177–206. Stuttgart: Deutsche Verlags-Anstalt, 1962.

Paret, Peter. *Clausewitz and the State*. Oxford: Clarendon Press, 1976.

―――. *Yorck and the Era of Prussian Reform, 1807–1815*. Princeton: Princeton University Press, 1966.

Peck, Abraham J. *Radicals and Reactionaries: The Crisis of Conservatism in Wilhelmine Germany*. Washington, D.C.: University Press of America, 1978.

Pflanze, Otto. *Bismarck and the Development of Germany: The Period of Unification 1815–1871*. Princeton: Princeton University Press, 1963.

Porch, Douglas. *The March to the Marne: The French Army, 1871–1914*. New York and London: Cambridge University Press, 1981.

Preradovich, Nikolaus von. *Die Führungsschichten in Österreich und Preussen (1804–1918)*. Wiesbaden: Franz Steiner Verlag, 1955.

Priebatsch, Felix. *Geschichte des preussischen Offizierkorps*. Breslau: Priebatische Verlagsbuchhandlung, 1919.

Puhle, Hans-Jürgen. *Agrarische Interessenpolitik und preussischer Konservatismus in wilhelminischen Reich (1893–1914)*. Hanover: Verlag für Literatur und Zeitgeschehen, 1966.

Puhle, Hans-Jürgen and Hans-Ulrich Wehler, eds. *Preussen im Rückblick*. Göttingen: Vandenhoeck & Ruprecht, 1980.

Rassow, Peter. "Schlieffen und Holstein." *Historische Zeitschrift* 173 (1954): 297–313.

Reif, Hans. *Westfälischer Adel, 1770–1860: Vom Herrschaftsstand zur regionelen Elite*. Göttingen: Vandenhoeck & Ruprecht, 1979.

Rich, Norman. *Friedrich von Holstein*. 2 vols. Cambridge: Cambridge University Press, 1965.

Ritter, Gerhard. *The Schlieffen Plan: Critique of a Myth*. Translated by Andrew and Eva Wilson. London: Oswald Wolff, 1958 [1956].

―――. *The Sword and the Scepter: The Problem of Militarism in Germany*. Translated by Heinz Norden. 4 vols. Coral Gables: University of Miami Press, 1964–73.

Rochs, Hugo. *Schlieffen*. Berlin: Vossische Buchhandlung Verlag, 1926.

Röhl, John C. G. *Germany without Bismarck: The Crisis of Government in the Second Reich, 1890–1900*. Berkeley and Los Angeles: University of California Press, 1967.

Röhl, John C. G., and Nicolaus Sombart, eds. *Kaiser Wilhelm II: New Interpretations*. Cambridge and New York: Cambridge University Press, 1982.

Rosenberg, Arthur. *Imperial Germany: The Birth of the German Republic*. Translated by Ian F. D. Morrow. Boston: Beacon Press, 1970 [1931].

Rosenberg, Hans. *Bureaucracy, Aristocracy, and Autocracy: The Prussian Experience 1660–1815.* Boston: Beacon Press, 1966 [1958].

————. "Die Pseudodemokratisierung der Rittergutsbesitzerklasse." In *Moderne Deutsche Sozialgeschichte,* edited by Hans-Ulrich Wehler, pp. 287–308. Berlin: Gesamtherstellung Kleins Druck und Verlangsanstalt, 1968.

————. *Grosse Depression und Bismarckzeit, Wirtschaftablauf, Gesellschaft und Politik in Mitteleuropa.* Berlin: Walter de Gruyter, 1967.

Rosinski, Herbert. *The German Army.* Washington, D.C.: The Infantry Journal, 1944.

Rothenberg, Gunther E. *The Army of Francis Joseph.* West Lafayette, Indiana: Purdue University Press, 1976.

Rüdt von Collenberg, Freiherr Ludwig. *Die deutsche Armee von 1871 bis 1914.* Berlin: E. S. Mittler & Son, 1922.

————. "Die staatsrechtliche Stellung des preussischen Kriegsministers von 1867 bis 1914." *Wissen und Wehr* 8 (1957): 293–312.

Rumschöttel, Hermann. *Das bayerische Offizierkorps 1866–1914.* Berlin: Duncker & Humboldt, 1973.

Sauer, Wolfgang. "Das Problem des deutschen Nationalstaates." In *Probleme der Reichsgründungszeit 1848–1879,* edited by Helmut Böhme, pp. 448–80. Köln: Kiepenheuer & Witsch, 1968.

Scharfenort, Louis von. *Bilder aus der Geschichte des Kadetten Korps.* Berlin: E. S. Mittler & Son, 1889.

————. *Die königlich preussische Kriegsakademie.* Berlin: E. S. Mittler & Son, 1910.

————. *Die Pagen am brandenburg-preussischen Hofe 1415–1895.* Berlin: E. S. Mittler & Son, 1895.

Scheider, Theodor, and Ernst Deuerlein, eds. *Reichsgründung 1870/71.* Stuttgart: Seewald Verlag, 1970.

Schissler, Hanna. "Die Junker. Zur Sozialgeschichte und historischer Bedeutung der agrarischen Elite in Preussen." In *Preussen im Rückblick,* edited by Hans-Ulrich Wehler and Hans-Jürgen Puhle, pp. 89–123. Göttingen: Vandenhoeck & Ruprecht, 1980.

Schlözer, Leopold von. *Generalfeldmarschall Freiherr von Loë.* Stuttgart: Deutsche Verlags-Anstalt, 1914.

Schmidt-Bückeburg, Rudolf. *Das Militärkabinett der preussischen Könige und deutscher Kaiser. Seine geschichtliche Entwicklung und staatsrechtliche Stellung 1787–1918.* Berlin: E. S. Mittler & Son, 1932.

Schmidt-Richberg, Wiegand. *Die Generalstäbe in Deutschland 1871–1945. Aufgaben in der Armee und Stellung im Staate.* Stuttgart: Deutsche Verlags Anstalt, 1962.

————. "Die Regierungszeit Wilhelms II." In *Handbuch zur deutschen Militärgeschichte 1648–1939,* edited by Hans Meier-Welcker and Wolfgang von Groote, V: 3–155, 1962–76.

Schmitterlow, Bernhard von. *Aus dem Leben des Generalfeldmarschalls Freiherr von der Goltz-Pasha.* Berlin: Verlag K. F. Koehler, 1926.

Schröder, Wolfgang. "Junkertum und preussisch-deutsches Reich. Zur politischen Konzeption des Junkertums und zu ihrer Wiederspiegelung in der Kreuz-Zeitung 1871–1873." In *Die grosspreussisch-militärische Reichsgrün-*

dung 1871, edited by Horst Bartel and Ernst Engelberg, II: 170–234, 2 vols. East Berlin: Akademie Verlag, 1971.

Schulte, Friedrich von. "Adel im deutschen Offizier-und Beamtenstand." *Deutsche Revue* 21 (April–June, 1896): 181–92.

Schwertfeger, Bernhard. *Die grossen Erzieher des deutschen Heeres. Aus der Geschichte der Kriegsakademie.* Potsdam: Rütten & Loening, 1936.

Shanahan, William O. *Prussian Military Reforms, 1786–1813.* New York: AMS Press, 1966 [1944].

Simon, Walter M. *The Failure of the Prussian Reform Movement, 1807–1819.* Ithaca: Cornell University Press, 1955.

Sombart, Werner. *Die deutsche Volkswirtschaft im neuenzehnten Jahrhundert.* 3rd ed. Berlin: Georg Bondi, 1913.

Spiers, Edward M. *The Army and Society.* London and New York: Longman, 1980.

Stadelmann, Rudolf. *Moltke und der Staat.* Krefeld: Scherpe Verlag, 1940.

Stehlin, Stewart A. *Bismarck and the Guelph Problem: A Study in Particularist Opposition to National Unity.* The Hague: Martinus Nijhoff, 1973.

Stern, Fritz. *Gold and Iron: Bismarck, Bleichröder, and the Building of the German Empire.* New York: Alfred A. Knopf, 1977.

Stolberg-Wernigerode, Count Otto zu. *Die unentschiedene Generation. Deutschlands konservative Führungsschichten am Vorabend des Ersten Weltkrieges.* Munich and Vienna: R. Oldenbourg, 1968.

Stürmer, Michael, ed. *Das kaiserliche Deutschland. Politik und Gesellschaft 1870–1918.* Düsseldorf: Droste Verlag, 1970.

Tipton, Frank B., Jr. *Regional Variations in the Economic Development of Germany during the Nineteenth Century.* Middletown, Connecticut: Wesleyan University Press, 1976.

Trumpener, Ulrich von. "Junkers and Others: The Rise of Commoners in the Prussian Army, 1871–1914." *Canadian Journal of History* 14 (April 1979): 29–47.

Tuchman, Barbara. *The Proud Tower.* New York: The Macmillan Company, 1966.

Vagts, Alfred. *A History of Militarism, Civilian and Military.* Rev. ed. New York: The Free Press, 1959 [1937].

Van Doorn, Jacques, ed. *Armed Forces and Society: Sociological Essays.* The Hague: Mouton, 1968.

Vetter, Klaus. *Kurmärkischer Adel und preussische Reformen.* Weimar: Herman Böhlaus Nachfolger, 1979.

Wehler, Hans-Ulrich. *Krisenherde des Kaiserreichs 1871–1918.* Göttingen: Vandenhoeck & Ruprecht, 1970.

———., ed. *Moderne deutsche Sozialgeschichte.* Berlin: Gesamtherstellung Kleins Druck und Verlagsanstalt, 1968.

Werthern, Baron von. *General von Versen. Ein militärisches Zeit und Lebensbild.* Berlin: E. S. Mittler & Son, 1898.

Wheeler-Bennett, John. "Men of Tragic Destiny: Ludendorff and Groener." In *Essays Presented to Sir Lewis Namier*, edited by Richard Pares and A. J. P. Taylor, pp. 506–41. London: Macmillan, 1956.

Wildman, Allan K. *The End of the Russian Imperial Army: The Old Army and the Soldiers' Revolt (March–April 1917).* Princeton: Princeton University Press, 1980.

Wilhelm, Rolf. *Das Verhältnis der süddeutschen Staaten zum Norddeutschen Bund 1867–1870.* Husum: Matthiesen Verlag, 1978.

Wilke, Ekkehard-Teja. *Political Decadence in Imperial Germany: Personnel-Political Aspects of the German Government Crisis, 1894–1897.* Urbana: University of Illinois Press, 1976.

Witte, Hermann. *Die Reorganisation des preussischen Heeres durch Wilhelm I.* Halle am Saal: Verlag von Max Niemeyer, 1910.

Wohlfeil, Ranier. "Die Beförderungsgrundsätze." In *Untersuchungen zur Geschichte des Offizierkorps. Anciennität und Beförderung nach Leistung,* edited by Hans Meier-Welcker, pp. 15–63. Stuttgart: Deutsche Verlags-Anstalt, 1962.

Zechlin, Egmont. *Bismarck und die Grundlegung der deutschen Grossmacht.* Stuttgart: J. G. Cotta'sche Buchhandlung, 1960.

Zernin, Gebhard. *Das Leben des königlich preussischen Generals der Infanterie August von Goeben.* 2 vols. Berlin: E. S. Mittler & Son, 1895, 1987.

Ziekursch, Johannes. *Politische Geschichte des neuen deutschen Kaiserreiches.* 3 vols. Frankfurt am Main: Frankfurter Societäts Druckerei GMBH, 1927.

Index